A

Dream

SETS SAIL

PART I

The Awesome Adventures of Amazing Grace

A

Dream

SETS SAIL

Part I

The Awesome Adventures of Amazing Grace

Kay Koudele

Mill City Press, Inc.
212 3rd Avenue North, Suite 290
Minneapolis, MN 55401
612.455.2294
www.millcitypublishing.com

ISBN - 978-1-936107-33-9
ISBN - 1-936107-33-3
LCCN - 2009911202

Cover Design by Kristeen Wegner
Typeset by Peggy LeTrent

Printed in the United States of America

To: Emi, Marley, Elli,

Lauren, Ema and Ella

Dare to dream.

And then make it happen.

Grandma and Grandpa Koudele

TABLE OF CONTENTS

One
Creating A Dream

"Oh my gosh! Look at the dock," yelled a friend nearby. My husband, Fred, and I stopped our excited chatter with friends who had just arrived at our "Bon Voyage Party" on this beautiful summer Sunday afternoon. Looking up from our sailboat, *Amazing Grace,* we immediately saw the reason for his concern. The six foot wide dock, with boats on either side, was leaning at a precarious angle due to all the partygoers who were gathered in front of our boat.

"We'd better balance things a bit before we all end up in the water," Fred laughed. And so we did, even though no one seemed particularly perturbed that we were in any danger. It was just that kind of day—one so filled with excitement, joy, anticipation, disbelief, and celebration, that a little thing like a sinking dock was no big deal!

It was a day that concluded a 17-year dream: a dream to go *cruising!* Now, cruising can mean different things to different people. To us, it meant that the following day we would untie our dock lines and head out on a voyage to unknown places for an unknown length of time. The dream was to become a reality.

"It could be six months, or it could be six years," Fred was often fond of saying about the upcoming journey. "We'll just keep going until we're ready to come home."

Our plan was to sail from Portland, Oregon, down the Columbia River to the Pacific Ocean, and then south along the U.S. coastline into Mexico and likely Central America. At that point, there was the possibility of heading west, crossing the Pacific over to the South Seas, or choosing to go south and through the Panama Canal—perhaps over to Europe by crossing the Atlantic. It was a loose plan, somewhat like the idea of flipping a coin when we arrived in each place and deciding from there which way to continue. That was the adventure of it all.

How did the dream begin? It's difficult to describe. Certainly it was a beginning, of sorts, when we bought our first sailboat about 17 years earlier and were quickly hooked. A few years later we decided that our family had outgrown the little 20-foot Santana, and we purchased a roomier, 25-foot Catalina. Later, when some friends took off for the cruising life with their two sons, we shared in their excited and careful anticipation. We also devoured their letters while they were underway and found our own dream beginning to take shape. Could we do what Elsa and Imants were doing? Could we leave our home (and family) and take off for distant waters?

We began more extensive preparations for such a possibility. There was an endless list of equipment that would be necessary to obtain. We also studied books and articles about the cruising life, including problems others had faced and their suggestions for this "blue water" adventure. We took as many classes as we could to acquire the knowledge needed for safety and maintenance of a boat. It was a fun time, and the dream remained "out there" in a general sort of way but had not yet crystallized.

One of the classes I planned to take was Celestial Navigation. It was rather complex and required a good deal of study if we planned to use that technique as a backup to our electronic navigational instruments. While modern equipment was wonderful, there was always the possibility that something would malfunction, thus we would need to depend on ourselves to ensure that we got to our destination. It was just being ready for Murphy's Law: If things could go wrong, they would.

"Do you think we will ever *really* do it?" I asked one evening when Fred and I were discussing the intricacies of celestial navigation and this cruising dream.

Fred looked thoughtful for a moment. "It doesn't really matter, does it? We're having a great time planning it, and even if we never go cruising, we've had a lot of fun in the process."

What a good way to look at it! That practical perspective, common sense, and wisdom of my husband of almost 30 years was something I would come to appreciate even more in the future that lay before us.

It certainly helped that both Fred and I shared the dream. We knew many other boating couples that were not so fortunate. Often the idea of cruising, or even just boating itself, was almost an obsession for one partner and something that was feared or disliked by the other. This incompatibility would lead to a good deal of tension and unhappiness for both. For cruising, it also seemed that couples that had been together for a long period of time were the ones who fared the best. Short-term relationships often seemed to come apart under the pressures of sailing and were sometimes referred to as "water-soluble romances."

It truly took a "team" to make cruising work. Fred and I were grateful that we both had similar expectations about this opportunity—complete with its joys and challenges. Not that we always agreed on the way to approach ideas and goals, but we complemented each other. I would sometimes work to get him excited about something; being enthusiastic came quite naturally to me. On the other hand, his input would often calm or ground me, or help me to be more realistic in working things through. Through the years, we had come to depend on this balancing act, and each of us appreciated the other for how it helped us both.

Then came a major opportunity. Our friends, Elsa and Imants, who had been cruising for almost a year on *Bolero*, were now in Hawaii. Knowing that we were considering the idea of the cruising life, they invited Fred and me to fly there and sail the boat home with Imants while Elsa and their sons flew back to the mainland. This would be an official "blue water" crossing, and one way of determining whether this cruising life was for us.

"Cross the *Pacific!* We are actually going to cross the Pacific Ocean in a sailboat!" I squealed.

"Well, half the Pacific," my husband added. But such a minor detail was not going to diminish my excitement as I jumped up and down in delight. "It's a great opportunity," he added, obviously excited as well. "But remember, this trip from Hawaii to Oregon in a small boat is often cold, wet, and rough."

"Then it will be a terrific way to determine whether we are up to the challenge and really want to go cruising ourselves," I replied.

And so it was. With that mindset, mixed with twinges of apprehension, we packed our bags and flew to Hawaii. It was on that voyage of 28 days from Honolulu, Hawaii, to Portland, Oregon, that we sealed the deal on the cruising dream for ourselves. Never mind that we both had problems with seasickness, even before leaving Hawaiian waters. Never mind that we endured three different major storms, often requiring us to remain in our bunks or lie on the floor with almost everything soaked in salt water. Never mind that my body was riddled with bruises from bumping into things as the boat heaved back and forth in the waves. There were also many joys and delights. Who would have thought that learning to bake a reasonably edible loaf of bread while riding a buckin' bronco would have created such pride? Who would have thought that it was possible to commune with birds that circled the boat hundreds of miles from land when there was nothing but water to be seen? Who would have thought that the simplicity of life on that trip would create a spiritual high unlike anything we had experienced on land? Probably, if you had asked us the night we stepped ashore after those 28 days whether we would attempt to go cruising on our own, we might have hesitated a bit. After a good night's sleep, though, and the relish of being on "terra firma," we knew our response would be affirmative. Our grand "make it or break it" experience confirmed the dream: *Let's go cruising!*

So we soon began the process of looking for *THE* boat. We wanted one that just the two of us could sail, as well as one that had a comfy interior for living. We had met other cruisers who said they were tired of being cold and wet when traveling in a sailboat, so we were interested in an inside steering station. Fred was also considering the safety factor of a steel boat, and we both wanted a sleek rather than boxy design. Our trip across the Pacific with Imants made us aware of the desire to have the head (bathroom) close to the companionway (cabin entrance). Those bruises on my body attested to the fact that, in wild seas, it was difficult to make your way to the bow of the boat, where most designers placed the head. I also wanted a functional galley that was not closed off from the main salon. We continued to develop our "wish list."

Each year, for a number of years, we had anxiously awaited the

Seattle Boat Show and circled the dates on the calendar. It was a weekend that always thrilled, and we savored the idea of seeing the new boats and equipment like children who anticipate the coming of Christmas. So the year after our sailing trip from Hawaii, we went to the Boat Show and ended up putting money down on *two* boats! Each had unique features and we needed more time to decide which boat was for us. A few months later, we canceled the orders on both of those boats when we found in a magazine what was, for us, the "perfect" boat—a Southerly, about 37 feet long. It was designed by the same person who had designed one of the boats we had seen and liked at the Seattle Boat Show. It had an inside steering station, an aft cabin, and a center cockpit. We thoroughly examined pictures and design blueprints.

"Look at that swing keel!" Fred exclaimed. "Having that would really take away a lot of the anxiety of running aground. You'd simply pump up the keel and sail off. It draws six feet eight inches, but it can be lifted to only two feet six inches. I've seen smaller boats with this feature, but I've never found it in a boat this size."

"And it's really engineered well. Did you read this article about the building of that keel?" I responded. "It's so heavy—it's almost like having a steel hull. With the keel up, the boat can just sit upright on the mud. How cool that would be when there are huge tidal changes, like in England."

There was more that excited us. The large windows of the pilot-house made it light and open inside, and the galley was easily accessible to the salon as well as the cockpit. Even the head was just inside the companionway! One drawback was that it was built in England and we couldn't find any in the U.S. We diligently researched the designer, the boatyard that built it, and all the specifications. Our excitement grew as we just *knew* that this was the boat for us! Friends thought we were crazy to buy a boat that we had neither seen nor sailed. How could we justify that? We simply said, "It's an affair of the heart!" Thankfully, we had some English friends who helped in the ordering and building process. In June of 1987, we flew with our kids to Northshore Yacht Yards in Itchenor, England, to undergo sea trials and take possession of our brand new Southerly 115 sailboat.

"Oh! It's beautiful," was all I could say upon first seeing the boat.

"Wow!" said Fred. We stood for a moment, filled with a sense of awe and gratitude. We knew, right then, that the name we had carefully chosen for this wonderful gift was perfect, and *Amazing Grace* became an official member of our family. In our minds, it was only because of the amazing grace of God that we were able to have this strong and beautiful boat, as well as the opportunity to go cruising. In addition, the movement of a boat under sail *is* truly graceful. It was all simply *amazing!* After sailing in the waters of southern England for about a month, we had our boat shipped back to our home port of Portland, Oregon, where we began the lengthy process of outfitting it for extended blue water cruising.

We had purchased our boat about five years before Fred could take early retirement, at age 55, and I could sell my office and psychotherapy practice and retire as well. Those years were filled with so many projects and preparations that it often made my head spin.

"Haven't you got that boat ready *yet*?" was the comment heard from so many during that period. It was difficult for others to really understand the great deal of time and effort needed to make a vessel blue water ready. When undertaking a passage and something breaks, boaters need to be able to make their own repairs. This means having backups for all the important systems. There would be no Coast Guard in foreign countries to come to the rescue, so there was much to do to make the boat as safe as possible in the event of emergencies. And, of course, it takes lots of money. For five years, every holiday or special occasion was celebrated by the purchase of a gift—something new for the boat.

"Happy Mother's Day!" Fred said with great enthusiasm.

"Oh my! It's just what I always wanted," I replied with a wink. "A portable wringer for washing clothes!" It was the old-fashioned type that we could attach to the steering pedestal in the cockpit.

One Christmas we purchased a water-maker as our gift to each other. And so it went. Fred was focused on the mechanics of our boat, including the installation of equipment and rigging. My job was primarily preparing for the aspects of living aboard—making this boat our home. I was also in charge of navigation. Despite this arbitrary division of duties, we both felt it was important that we each knew how to sail the

6

boat alone, should one of us become incapacitated during a voyage. That meant, for example, my learning the basics about diesel engines and Fred becoming comfortable with navigation. There was *so* much to learn. During one of the annual trips to the Seattle Boat Show, exhausted after a number of hours of viewing and talking about equipment, we went out to our car in the parking lot to take a break. We sipped a glass of wine while we discussed the equipment we were going to buy. I tended to worry about the costs that often seemed staggering.

"You know, if we spend all this money on the wind vane and survival raft, we really have to make a commitment to actually *go* cruising," I said.

"Good grief!" he quickly replied. "You think that after buying an oceangoing vessel, we aren't *committed*? Not to worry—we're going!" A big warm hug accompanied his reassuring reply.

Back at our home dock, the projects continued. Fred officially retired in June of 1992. Our plan was to leave in August of that year. I sold my office and practice, we found renters for our large five-bedroom house, and we moved onto a 37-foot boat. Now that was a major lifestyle change! It had been many years since we had shared the same bathroom. A major disagreement soon developed over how to hang the toilet paper. In hindsight, we laughed about it and realized it was not an issue about toilet paper but rather a symbol of having lost a sense of individual control in our lives after retiring from our professional careers. In our jobs, we had each experienced a good deal of control—both in what we did and how we did it. We also received a good deal of positive "strokes" and feedback from those we worked with that was rewarding and provided a sense of fulfillment. Suddenly, that was all gone.

It was also difficult on the boat to find privacy; many of our actions were closely dependent on or affected by each other. Fred would come along and close a porthole, not realizing I had just opened it.

"Hey, I just opened that! It's hot in here," I said somewhat testily.

"Oh. I thought we might take in some water from the wakes of the passing boats," replied Fred.

Although adjusting to our small living space was eased by having spent a good deal of time on the boat during the past five years, finding room for all the things we were bringing aboard was another matter.

Then, after putting them someplace, finding them later was truly a challenge. Many other aspects of living in a confined space affected us in mental, emotional, relational, and even spiritual ways. While there was an awareness of these factors, it was very much overshadowed, in those initial months, by the great excitement and anticipation of our cruising adventure as well as our "honeymoon" time. We spent two months living on the boat at our home dock as we made our final preparations. We had done all we could do to get ready, both for the boat and for ourselves. But we could never be completely ready for all the unknown experiences that lay ahead. It was a fine line between being adequately prepared and reaching the end of the "To Do" list.

AT LAST, WE'RE READY TO GO AND CELEBRATE WITH FRIENDS.

Finally, the day of our dock party arrived. We had invited different groups of people to come see the boat, share some refreshments, and say good-bye. For those unfamiliar with boating, it was a perfect day to convey the lure of living on the water and the fantasy of "sailing off into the sunset." Many of those who came to the party had not seen our boat before, and they were fascinated with hearing about all the features and systems. And, of course, we loved showing them. Fred and I wore our new *Amazing Grace* logo T-shirts that were a gift from Elsa and Imants. While Fred's mom lived in Nebraska and could not be with us, we loved having my mom and her husband, as well as two of our three adult children, with us for the party. Our children were the joy of our lives, and we were so proud of each of them. They were all "out of the nest" and doing well.

Our oldest daughter, Page, had just turned 27, was attending medical school and living in the Portland area with her husband, Steve. She would be receiving our mail, paying our bills, and handling any "loose ends" for us. We felt the least concern for her, as she had her own family unit now, and her time and energy were directed toward school and husband. This day, she and Steve helped host our friends, fill drinks, and set up our informal supper on the dock.

Dawn, our second daughter, was 24 and living in Tempe, Arizona. She was working and attending Arizona State University, so she was not able to be at the dock party. She had one more term to complete and was to graduate in mid-December. That presented a dilemma for us. One of our hopes in cruising was to fly our children to meet us in different ports so they could experience some of the different countries and cultures. Some time before, we had suggested to the kids that we would fly them to Mexico for a vacation and we could all spend Christmas together. Then we learned the date of Dawn's graduation.

"You'll have to choose," we had said to her some time ago on the phone. "If we come to your graduation, we won't have enough time to get to Cabo San Lucas for Christmas. We could all get together for Christmas in San Diego. Or, if you prefer, we could go on, miss the graduation ceremonies, and fly you all to Cabo for Christmas there."

"That's a no-brainer," she quickly replied. "Christmas in Cabo! That's far better than your coming to my graduation." Little did we realize, then, that we would question that decision for ourselves many times in the years to come.

Our son, Lance, was 22 and living and working in Tacoma, Washington, where he had just graduated from Pacific Lutheran University. After earning his degree, he decided to attend bartending school so he could go to a ski resort to work evenings and ski days. He would be leaving for Vail, Colorado, in the fall. Living his dream was so similar to what his parents were currently doing that we could not protest. The difference was that we had gone on the "pay now, play later" plan, while he was doing just the opposite. He had come to Portland for the party, helped Page and Steve with the food and drinks, and enthusiastically examined all the boating "toys." He was certainly more interested in sailing than the girls were, and we started hoping that he might join us in cruising for a while when ski season was over.

Family and close friends lingered after the others had gone. The sun had set in a blaze of color that filled the western sky, stars began to appear, and the gentle evening breeze seemed to nudge us all toward a time of parting. The excitement had lessened and, in its place, there was a bittersweet sadness. Saying goodbye to Mom and our children was incredibly difficult. Both my mom and Fred's were in their eighties, and the thought of losing them while we were away was truly painful. To their credit, although neither of them was really happy with our taking off on this adventure, they were both supportive and encouraged us to follow our dream. We prayed that the grace that would sustain us would envelop all of our loved ones as well.

After tearful goodbyes, Fred and I sat in the cockpit, watching the lights reflecting on the water, feeling the quiet of night surrounding us, and wondering about this incredible journey that lay before us. We felt alone after the crush of people all day, yet our excitement and anticipation of setting sail in the morning had us still too wound up to sleep. Getting up, I went into the cabin.

"Where are you going?" Fred asked.

"I want to get something," I replied. A minute later, I returned with a card I had brought aboard—the card Fred had given me the previous Christmas. Opening it, I began to read his inscription:

Kay,

My gift to you this 1991 Christmas is simply a promise for 1992.

I promise to take you to faraway places, to meet new people, to have exciting adventures.

I promise to love you, care for you, to share you with the world we will meet.

I promise to protect you, to give you space, to let you be you.

I promise to return you safely, when it is time, to our family whom you love so much.

"Yeah," was all he could say. Tears welled up in both of us. Surely the wonderful dock party and events of the day were the beginning of that promise. What an awesome adventure—and we hadn't even left the dock! We were now living the dream. We headed for the cabin and bed, knowing that this night we would dream on.

Two
Untying The Dock Lines

"This is it, sleepyhead. This is the day we untie those dock lines!" Fred said. He rolled over in bed and rubbed my head. "Let's get to it, mate."

Calling me "mate" was a playful jab designed to get a rise out of me, as we had many pseudo-serious discussions about who was the captain and who was the mate on this boat. Since we both had learned to sail at the same time, neither of us had more basic knowledge or skill than the other. Since we had both names on the boat's title, neither of us had more in the investment. Finally, I solved the dilemma one day when I acknowledged that, yes, he could be the captain, but I would be the *admiral*! After all, boating is all about compromise.

The day was perfect—the sun and light breeze, the smell of a beautiful summer morning. The light dancing on the river held such promise. Still not fully awake, I stumbled out of our aft cabin as Fred was preparing the coffee. Sipping our first cup, we recalled the wonderful events of the previous day and anticipated what lay ahead of us this day. *Untying the dock lines!* Those four special words held such great meaning for us. As we had worked toward our dream over the last five years, that little phrase became the symbol of our actually going cruising. Normally, the lines for a boat in a marina are "cast off" rather than untied, as they remained tied to the dock, ready to be used again when the boat returned. To untie our lines meant, to us, that we would not be returning to this particular place. We would be taking the lines with us, and tying them to new docks in new places. We would not be *returning.* At least, not for some time. That thought had us almost giddy with excitement.

We had hardly finished our coffee when we were surprised to see our son-in-law, Steve, walking toward our boat. As he climbed aboard we learned the reason for his coming.

"Dawn called from Arizona last night and was she ever upset! She didn't get to say goodbye, and she doesn't know how to contact you, or when she will see you. She really was having a hard time," he shared. "But the good thing was that Page had been crying all the way home, and when she talked with Dawn, it took the focus off her own feelings as she tried to help her sister. I really think it was a good thing for both of them!"

It was the first occasion during our journey that the kids would lean on each other when they had problems rather than relying on us. It definitely would not be the last. This turning to help each other was just what we had hoped would happen. Page, as the oldest daughter, would likely be the pivot person in their support system, and she was wonderful at staying calm and thinking things through. We continually reminded ourselves that they would be OK. Communication with us, however, was a problem for them. Cell phones were not available at that time for general use. Even email was not something available to most people. We could contact the family when we got to land and could use a phone, but it was not possible for them to phone us. That created considerable anxiety for all the family. We had established a way for them to contact us using the ham radio people in the event of an emergency, but it would only be for urgent matters.

Knowing Dawn was now at work, we promised we would call her from St. Helen's, a town downriver where we planned to stop for the night. We again said goodbye to Steve as he went on to work. The "Mother's Guilt Trip" descended on me like a shroud as I thought about Dawn. Fred gently reassured us both that she was an adult now, and that we would be seeing her soon as we traveled south along the coast. But it took several minutes for the guilt to lift and for me to remember that she was a truly capable and bright young woman who would be okay. *Wouldn't she?*

I finished washing the breakfast dishes and soon had the cabin cleaned up. Fred had jumped down onto the dock.

"Hey, let's go *cruising!*" he yelled.

As Fred leaned down to untie the lines, we grinned at each other and giggled like little kids ready to do some mischief. Just then our friends, Dave and Sally, came walking down the dock. We belonged to the same yacht club and they, too, were preparing to go cruising but were still a few weeks away from being ready to leave. We all hoped to connect somewhere down the coast. Their boat was tied just a few slips from ours, and we had all spent many an hour working on readiness projects, occasionally sharing tools, tips, and "happy hours" at the end of long work days.

"Why don't you get aboard, and we'll throw you the lines," they offered. "We'll be right on your tail, we hope."

In short time the lines were untied and taken aboard, and we were motoring into the river—our amazing adventure was underway. We laughed and shouted, yelling "Yahoo!" over and over, waved the hats that we had bought to use in the tropical sun, and pinched ourselves in order to believe that the time had actually arrived. Finally, our dream set sail!

"Fair winds and following seas," yelled Dave and Sally. We gave a final wave and slipped into the main channel of the Columbia River toward rivers and oceans beyond. With a prayer of thanksgiving in our hearts, we had begun what would become a four-year journey of travel, challenges, joys, and sorrows—the awesome adventures of *Amazing Grace!*

Three

Cruisin' Down The River

As we headed down the familiar channel of the Columbia River, we enjoyed the excitement of the moment while we continued to stow away all our gear and provisions. There were also new "toys" to learn how to use, like the marvelous new Global Positioning System (GPS). Despite the many things to do, we decided not to attempt much that first day. We had lots of time. Other than our desire to get to the San Francisco area in the next few weeks, the itinerary was ours to choose. The trip to the ocean was about 85 miles down river, and we planned to do it over several days. The last few days before our departure had been an emotional as well as physical roller coaster, and we motored along rather than attempting to sail, as the winds were light and, as usual, "on the nose."

"I wonder if we'll have to wait long at the railroad bridge," I said to Fred.

"I can see a train on the span right now," he replied. "It may take awhile."

While we could easily get under the large interstate bridge connecting Portland, Oregon, to Vancouver, Washington, the adjacent railroad bridge had to be opened to allow sailboats to pass. Sometimes this meant waiting for many minutes, but we were fortunate that day, and very soon we heard the familiar horn blasts signaling the opening. We motored through, waving to the bridge tender high up on a span. Because this area of the river has a significant current that sometimes runs between two and three knots, Fred was always careful to not be too close to the bridge while we waited for an opening. If our motor died, we could be pushed against the spans. His tendency towards caution and his ability to anticipate were attributes that I would come to appreciate more and more in the situations to come. I was often more impulsive and risk-taking in decisions, sometimes feeling frustrated with his conservative or cautious way of preparing for action. I learned quickly that, especially when sailing in unknown waters, his approach to sailing was definitely the better, safer one.

We were in an area of the river that was very familiar, as we had spent many days sailing in the waters close to Portland. It was not a difficult stretch, but one that always required us to be watchful for freighters and commercial river traffic. As on previous days, we passed several large ships coming into the ports to unload, or making their way to the ocean and beyond. We wanted to be well out of the main channel at those times, for the wakes from those huge ships moving swiftly up and down the river were significant and often caused us to roll or bounce a good deal.

We soon spotted the smoke stacks of St. Helens. We planned to tie up to the city dock, because there was no fee for spending the night there, and "free" is definitely good for the cruising budget. After finding a place and securing the boat, we walked into town and used a public phone to call Dawn. We spent many minutes reassuring her, as well as ourselves, and finalized our earlier plan to meet her in San Francisco. She would fly in and spend several days with us on the boat before classes started for fall term. Walking back to the boat in the summer twilight, we breathed a sigh of relief.

"One family hurdle down. Wonder what the next one will be," I mused. Fred just laughed and reached for my hand.

Our leisurely pace down river continued. We anchored behind islands, where the wake of ocean freighters couldn't reach us, and spent quiet nights in calm water. It was peaceful and contemplative. The weather continued to be gorgeous, and we wondered why we wanted to leave this beautiful part of the Northwest. Still, the dream called us onward.

Sitting in the cockpit one warm, sunny morning, I turned to look at Fred. "We are just incredibly blucky," I said. Seeing the quizzical look on his face, I added, "You know—blessed and lucky. Blucky!"

He grinned and agreed, "Yeah, we're truly blucky."

We had often felt the presence of God in this dream we shared, and we were acutely aware of the many blessings we had experienced throughout the years—all threads in the weaving of this marvelous tapestry that we were now experiencing. We also felt there was something expected of us in return, some way to express our gratitude and faith. We weren't exactly sure how that would unfold, but we looked for ideas and wanted to be open to possibilities. Choosing the name of our boat had been one of those occasions. We always enjoyed the chance to respond when someone asked us why we had chosen the name, *Amazing Grace*. We laughed, too, when we remembered the time in England when a man from the boat yard was painting the name on the stern of our boat. A couple from India was docked beside us, and they watched the painting process along with us.

"Tell me about this 'Grace.' It is something you say before eating, yes?" the Indian man had said.

We hadn't thought about that interpretation, but hey—that worked too! I think a table grace is a way of giving thanks, and asking blessings on a gift of food so that it could help us to show God's love to the world. Right? That's just what we had hoped for this boat!

A SPECIAL NAME FOR A SPECIAL BOAT.

We made our way into the marina at Cathlamet, a small logging and fishing community with a friendly business area and good restaurants. We chuckled as we walked into town, remembering our visit there several years previously. It was our first landfall after sailing back from Hawaii, and we had been making our way upriver to Portland. At that time, when walking on land after 28 days at sea, we could not stop laughing—not only with the joy of being back in Oregon, but also for the experience of trying to regain our "land legs" after so long on the rollicking ocean.

"Remember how we tried to walk up this road?" I said.

"I'll never forget it. As hard as we tried to walk a straight line, we just couldn't do it. We zigzagged all over the place!"

We continued to work our way down river the following day. The weather had turned cloudy, as it so often did closer to the coast. The wind was stronger, too, and we put on jackets as the temperature dropped. With the push of the wind, river, and tidal current, we were making good time towards Astoria. Navigational aids that marked the deepwater channel, either on the shore or floating buoys, were sometimes up to a mile apart. When it was foggy and we couldn't see between markers, we needed to keep a careful watch on the ship's compass heading, as well as our location on the charts. While that day there was no fog and the travel was leisurely, we still needed to be constantly aware and mindful of our course and position, particularly when freighters continued to pass us.

Although Astoria is still 14 miles from the river's mouth and its entrance into the Pacific Ocean, it is often the port from which boaters leave for fishing or cruising destinations. As we approached the marina entrance, the wind had picked up to well over 20 knots, and when we turned to lower the sails, the boat heeled over at a sharp angle. Waves slapped noisily all around the boat and sprayed us in the cockpit. The sails flapped violently as Fred pulled heavily on the line to bring in the jib, or headsail, while I tried to hold the bow of the boat into the wind using the motor. These conditions were physically strenuous for both of us. When Fred went forward to the mast to help pull down the mainsail, it was difficult to hear him due to the noise of the wind, waves, and slapping sails. I was anxious and felt the lump in my throat, or was it my stomach? The work at hand did not afford time to reflect on that, however. I just knew that the job needed to get done and tried to focus on that instead. We had done this many times before in similar conditions, but still the immediacy of the situation and the knowledge that things that go wrong in these conditions can be frightening had my heart rate jumping. Even after both sails were down and tied off, and we attempted to motor into the marina entrance, controlling the boat was tricky with that much wind and sea chop.

"I sure hope it calms down when we get inside the breakwater," I yelled to Fred.

Alas, although the water was calmer, the wind continued to be a challenge; we finally managed to maneuver into a slip and tie up. Even a simple thing like docking a boat on the river could be a challenge at times.

"Ahhhh. The joys of boating!" I laughed. The curious thing was that, after we were tied up and feeling snug, the challenges we had just faced created a mild euphoria—rather like completing a long race. It felt good.

Astoria is a delightful town with a wealth of history, architecture, arts, marine supplies, shopping, and wonderful seafood restaurants. We ate most of our meals aboard because eating out definitely added to the cruising costs, but we decided that this was the time for a splurge.

The following day we contacted the flight surgeon at the Warrenton Coast Guard Station. About a year before, I had made a cassette tape for avoiding seasickness by the use of self-hypnosis. Making the tape had started as a project to help a friend who suffered terribly each time she went on the ocean but who wanted to continue boating. She had tried everything she could find, with no relief. I suggested she try self-hypnosis. Since she couldn't find a product for that, I made a tape for her. Members of our local yacht club had tested the tape, and many had encouraged me to produce and market it as a drug-free option for boaters.

"Why are you calling the tape *SeaWellness*?" Fred had asked one day. "There is no such word."

"It's important in any kind of self-hypnosis to present things in a positive rather than negative way," I said. "Being sick is something negative, so I stress feelings of health and wellness, plus ways to maintain those feelings. You should try the tape, too."

And he did. We both used the tape in our preparation for blue water passages, and found it helpful. We knew we would be using it on this trip as well. As a part of the testing of the tape, I had contacted both Navy and Coast Guard people to see if they would consider using it. The Coast Guard flight surgeon at Warrenton was one of the more encouraging folks to respond. He had been testing it, found it effective for himself, and had invited us to tour the facilities there when we were in the area. As the time approached for us to go cruising, we became less interested in marketing the tape, but we very much wanted to see the Coast Guard Station and learn more about their rescue efforts. We arranged to meet him the next day, and we motored a few miles to the tiny town of Warrenton, Oregon.

After an informative tour of the facilities, we looked in the helicopters used in rescues and talked to the young men and women who were involved in those dramatic events. They were the ones who jumped into the water to help disabled boaters, often in terrifying conditions.

"Boy, I sure have a lot of respect for what those kids are doing," Fred said afterwards.

"Me too," I agreed. "But I sure hope we'll never have an occasion to have an 'up close and personal' encounter with any of them!"

"This sounds good," Fred announced, after we had listened for the tenth time to the weather forecast for the following day on the VHF radio. "I think it's a *go!*"

Our VHF radio allowed us to get weather information while in the United States, as well as contact other boats and, of course, call for help in the case of an emergency. It only had a range of about 20-25 miles, although sometimes on the ocean it could transmit a little further. It was also a source of amusement, as we could switch from the hailing channel to listen to boaters talk to each other on other channels.

"I always feel a little naughty when we listen to other people on the radio," I laughed long ago. "It's like 'eavesdropping.'"

"Just remember—almost everybody does it," Fred had said. "Nothing said on the radio is private."

We also knew that, once we left the country, we would not be able to use the VHF to hail the Coast Guard in times of trouble, but we hoped that we could depend on some other boater who was nearby to provide assistance.

It's no secret that the Columbia River Bar and the Oregon coastline command respect from even the most seasoned mariners. This particular bar crossing is one of the most treacherous in the world due to the many shoals in the area, which create angry waves when combined with the considerable current of the river. It has been called "The Graveyard of the Pacific" for good reason. There have been over 200 ships and 2000 other vessels shipwrecked in these waters, and pleasure craft, fishing boats, and even commercial ships continue to call the Coast Guard for assistance when conditions are rough. During winter storms, waves often reach 20 to 30 feet at the bar. It is not a crossing people take lightly. Finding the right tide is vital, because attempting to cross on an ebb (outgoing) tide can create very hazardous conditions. The ideal time is at slack tide, just before the current of the tide begins to turn in the opposite direction. It is also extremely important to know the weather forecast. On some occasions the bar is closed to all vessels. So when we heard, and reheard, favorable conditions predicted for the following day, our excitement grew.

We had crossed the bar into the Pacific on a sailboat several times before when we traveled north to Washington or Canada for vacations.

"This time it will be different, though," Fred had told his staff when he announced his retirement. "This time we are taking *Grace* out in the ocean, and instead of taking a right to Canada, we are 'hanging a left'—turning south and continuing on!"

So with much delight, mingled with small periods of apprehension, we jumped into the process of preparing the boat for travel on the ocean. Everything needed to be stowed. Anything that wasn't pinned down or put away would find itself on the cabin floor in the motion of the boat on the waves. We also studied the charts and put them where they would be readily available for the different places we intended to go on this particular passage. Food had to be either prepared or easy to get to for simple yet nutritious meals. This usually meant filling the thermos with boiling water to use for single cups of soup, coffee, or cocoa. Cream of Chicken soup was our first choice for calming the "queasies." Just the thought of a cup of warm soup made us feel better when conditions were rough and the stomach was complaining.

While I was working at the chart table, Fred asked, "Have you plotted a route on the GPS?"

"I have one to take us into Newport, since that is where we want to go, plus a back-up route to Port Orford," I replied. "Hopefully we won't need more than that, but I can enter more if necessary."

Our new GPS was amazing. With it, we could enter all the latitude and longitude coordinates of specific sites on our charts, and then connect them to create a route to reach our destination. I had spent many hours plotting all the points and putting them into routes for our trip south along the west coast of the U.S. Since we never knew in advance exactly what the weather, water, and wind conditions would be as we approached a port, we always prepared an alternate port of entry. Our plan was to "harbor hop" our way down the coast, with short passages of one to two days when possible.

"You know," I said, "some folks have decided that the Oregon coast is just too dangerous or difficult, and they are planning to go several hundred miles off shore and not come into a harbor until they get to the San Francisco area."

"I know," Fred replied. "Lots of Canadians do that. You can't run into rocks or go aground out in the ocean."

We had learned from our sail home from Hawaii that we preferred short hops to long passages, and thus looked forward to entering a number of ports on our way south—if conditions allowed it.

Having things easily accessible was important, particularly when the motion was rough. Even though it was early August, we knew that it could feel cold on the ocean, particularly at night. I got out our cold weather gear and put it where we could reach it easily. Fred was checking fluid levels in the diesel engine and making sure all was well with that system.

"You take good care of that engine," I said to him. "I sure wouldn't want to be without it in tight spots."

"You know what they say," he added. "You take care of the boat, and it will take care of you."

We had planned to go to Newport for our first ocean hop. We had made this leg of the trip with our friends when they left to go cruising and knew it would take about 24 hours. We checked the tide tables for the following day and found that the slack times occurred at three in the morning and three in the afternoon. Since we wanted to both leave and arrive in the daylight, we decided to cross the bar in the afternoon, leaving Warrenton about two. The plan was made. After dinner we listened to the "*SeaWellness*" tape again, preparing ourselves for that "ocean motion." It wasn't long before it was time for bed, but sleep would not come easily that night, and we tossed and turned in our berth. We were too excited to be on our way.

Four

Sailing For That Golden Gate

The next day dragged along as we waited for the right time to leave Warrenton. Finally, at two o'clock, we entered the small channel that led to the mouth of the Columbia River.

"Man! This feels *so* good to be really on our way south, going to new places," Fred said.

"Roger that, Skipper," I replied in my best "old salt" voice, and we laughed, knowing the concession I had made to acknowledge him as captain.

The wind was light, coming from a good direction, and there were occasional periods of sun in a sky heavy with clouds. The joy in our hearts could not be contained. Truly our "cup overfloweth." With prayers of thanksgiving, we entered the mighty Columbia.

That notorious Columbia River Bar that caused such apprehension was relatively quiet as we motored out under mainsail alone with the afternoon slack tide. The bar would not show its fearsome self that day, for which we were very grateful, and we took this as a positive omen for the journey ahead.

Soon we were in a place where we felt comfortable to raise the head sail and turn off the engine. What a wonderful sound—the sound of quiet. The only noise was that of *Grace* slipping through the water.

"Ahhhh! This is what it's all about," I yelled. "No growling engine."

It was cloudy, but the wind was fine, coming from the northwest as it usually does in the summer, and we relished the opportunity to do what a sailboat does best—sail.

We rather quickly settled into a routine, created a general plan for watches, and felt very content as we moved further out to sea. We wanted to be far enough from shore that we didn't have to worry about commercial crab pots. Tricky to see in the daytime, they were impossible to spot at night. Each trap on the ocean bottom had a long line tying it to a small float on the water's surface. Catching one of those lines in your propeller really ruined your day! It had happened to friends of ours, and it wasn't pretty. They had to jump into the water and cut the line with a knife. Needless to say, we didn't want to take a dip in the ocean on this part of the trip.

Soon we could no longer see the shore, and we turned south. San Francisco here we come! That evening there was no glorious sunset, due to the clouds, and I felt some disappointment. Ocean sunsets are the best. Before it became dark, we prepared for the night, which was seldom my favorite time in an ocean passage. I was aware that I was feeling a little apprehensive, as it was the beginning of a passage. Generally, nighttime on the ocean created a number of emotions for me, depending on the sea conditions, weather, and wind. On soft gentle nights full of moonlight and stars, it was a time of peace, contentment, and contemplation—and a sense of communion with the universe. Other times, when blackness enveloped us, and the boat was tossing roughly in the seas, hammered by cold rain and wind, it was frightening.

That first night I felt a mixture of emotions. The excitement of our first day at sea had eased, and a part of me felt alone, small, and vulnerable. There were no other boats or lights in sight. But the wind was behind us and we were making good progress, which felt very satisfying. Occasionally a huge Pacific swell would raise the stern of the boat up many feet into the air, causing the bow to point down at a sharp angle.

"Sometimes I think we will slide right on down into—and under—the water," I said, "but each time, *Grace* simply rises slowly up with the wave and then glides down the wave's back side."

"Yeah," Fred responded. "It sometimes feels like we are surfing."

We were enjoying the accompanying sound of the waves swishing by, but we also remembered that in such situations it was easy to lose control of the boat and be swept sideways—definitely not a good thing. Riding those big ocean swells, we continued to rise up high and then plunge down into troughs. Up and down, on and on.

We had decided earlier that evening to put a reef in the mainsail, which decreased its size and power. The wind was strong, and we really didn't want to have to reef in the dark if the wind increased. Shortening the mainsail at sunset was an example of those precautionary things Fred liked to do. This routine would become something we did each night when we were underway, and I was grateful many times to have that smaller sail in place. In hindsight, I realized that this was a mark of real wisdom on Fred's part, and that he was putting into action his promise to keep us safe on our journey.

"Do you want to take the first watch, or should I?" Fred asked.

"I really don't care. I know you aren't going to sleep much anyway. What works best for you?" I had known from earlier passages that Fred often just dozed when on a passage, and was quickly up and inquiring if he heard anything suspicious or unusual. I wished he could sleep more soundly so he would get enough rest, and rely on me to wake him if need be. I laughed to myself as I recognized that that's the way it goes—I worried about him, and he worried about me.

Normally boaters establish a watch system when on an overnight or extended passage. This could often mean four hours on duty for one person while the other one slept, and then an exchange. Such a system rotated around the clock, so that at least one person was always alert and in charge of the vessel. Our system of watches was a little less rigid. If one of us was on watch and feeling good, and the other one was sleeping, we often would extend the watch beyond the four hours. Conversely, if something required us both being awake, or if neither of us could sleep, the watch was sometimes shortened. It worked for us to be flexible.

There were a number of things that I needed to attend to when it was my turn on watch. I didn't take the responsibility lightly and, if conditions were rough, sometimes had to give myself a little "pep talk" because I dreaded getting out of bed and taking over. I had to make sure that the boat was heading in the right direction by monitoring the charts and GPS and seeing that the steering equipment was taking us where we wanted to go.

We had installed two self-steering devices, which meant that one of us did not need to constantly be at the wheel. One of these was an autopilot that ran on electricity and steered the boat according to a compass heading. It could be pushed off course by ocean currents, though, and I would need to make corrections to keep us on course. Fortunately, this could be done at the inside steering station. The other device was a wind-vane, which steered the boat via wind pressure on a paddle attached to the stern of the boat. We had rarely used the vane in the river due to the constant changes of wind direction. In the ocean it worked well, although it took a good deal of "tweaking" to set it correctly at first. I had to adjust the vane if the wind direction changed and altered the boat's heading. Since it was located off the stern, it meant going out to the rear of the cockpit, away from the comfort of the cabin when the weather and conditions were bad. I was often glad that we used the autopilot a good deal.

I also needed to plot our position on a chart each hour, so that if all the marvelous equipment were to fail we still had an idea of where we were and could make our way to our destination using the speed of the boat and the time sailed, along with compass directions and bearings. Although we could not use compass bearings in the ocean, as we came closer to land and had visual contact with a marker on shore, like a signal light, we could use the compass readings of that marker to plot our position. Navigation tasks were easy for me, and I enjoyed working with the charts and GPS system.

Making sure the sails were trimmed (set according to wind direction) was another important task. Sometimes this could be done simply by pulling them in tighter or letting them out, but occasionally a sail needed to be changed or taken down altogether. This meant waking Fred and both of us being on deck. Usually this was done when the wind was increasing and sea conditions were getting rougher. It was a tense time, and I was always glad when the job was done.

We had established early on that whenever one of us was in the cockpit at night we would be harnessed in. A harness was worn over (or attached) to our life jackets. It had a six-foot tether that could be buckled onto a cleat bolted to the deck, or onto a specific cable that ran the length of the boat, thus allowing us to move towards the bow. The harness and tether would not necessarily prevent us from being thrown overboard, but it would keep us attached to the boat so that we could be brought back aboard more easily. Also, Fred would use a harness if he went forward on the deck at night. (Neither of us would go forward—at any time—without the other being in the cockpit.)

While I became used to the routine of using a life vest and harness, it always made me anxious to think about falling overboard. In those huge Pacific swells, it was nearly impossible to see anyone down in the water, even a few feet away. Shoot! That wasn't anxiety—that was outright fear!

"How do you like our new life vests?" Fred called from the cockpit.

"They sure are more comfortable than the old ones," I responded. "And a lot less bulky." Our vests also had whistles and strobe lights attached. When one of us took over the night watch, we would put on our vest and attach the harness to the boat *before* leaving the cabin. These were our own rules, not used by everyone, but we felt that such precautionary measures were "the ounce of prevention that was worth the pound of cure." Looking into the steep swells, I needed no encouragement to follow these rules.

Perhaps one of the most important tasks I had when on watch was looking out for approaching freighters or other ocean-going vessels. We'd heard many a tale about small boats colliding with large freighters, and the small boats were always the losers! In certain areas of the sea, shipping lanes have been established for commercial vessel traffic. Whenever we were close to shipping lanes, we were keenly alert for traffic, sometimes altering our course to let the big ships go by.

"Do you think that expensive radar deflector we bought really works and they can see us?" I asked one night.

"I don't know, but we can't depend on them seeing us. There may not be anybody watching the radar on the bridge of those big ships," Fred replied.

Because they traveled at great speed, large vessels could be out of sight over the horizon and then on top of us within 15 to 20 minutes. This meant that when I was on watch I must look over the entire surrounding ocean at least every 15 minutes for the lights of freighters coming our way. In the nighttime, we could tell the direction they were heading by observing their navigational lights and then adjust our boat accordingly. Sometimes at night we would see the lights of fishing vessels, and they, too, needed to be avoided.

I used another special "toy" we had installed on *Grace*: radar. We used the term "toy" affectionately to describe some of the gear we had aboard, for not all boats had this equipment. We were especially grateful for our radar at night or in the fog. It not only helped identify land masses and track the course of other ships, but it also helped warn of approaching storms. It took some time and effort, however, to be able to interpret the green-lighted shapes or "blips" on the radar screen and to use that knowledge appropriately.

A disadvantage of the radar and some of the other navigational devices was that they required electricity, which was in limited supply on a sailboat. Our batteries were good, but we used them carefully. Refrigeration, radios, and lights were constant draws on the battery. Our engine could recharge the batteries, but when we were under sail that option was not available to us. Because of this ongoing problem, we had installed four solar panels before we left which were able to generate electricity to recharge our batteries. Of course, the solar panels could not produce energy from the sun at night, and this was when we were using most of the navigational equipment. Since the radar took a considerable amount of electricity, we left it on "Standby" position until we wanted to look at the screen. If we turned the radar off, it took several minutes for it to be ready to transmit. By using the standby mode, we conserved electricity but were able to get information quickly.

Late that first night, Fred was lying on the settee, trying to sleep. Our "sea berth" for sleeping while underway was in the main cabin to enable the off-watch person to be readily available if needed. I had made "Lee Cloths" that hooked to the cabin wall and would enable the person sleeping to remain on the settee when the boat pitched and rolled. It felt a little like being in a hammock or cradle when we pulled up the cloths, and it was rather comforting. It also made getting out of bed a bit tricky. We slept in our clothes, just removing our shoes. Cabin lights were low and red at night, so they would not interfere with our night vision. In order to sleep, I had learned to tune out the noise of the VHF radio, for we occasionally heard someone hailing another boat—usually fishermen. I don't think Fred was ever able to disregard the radio traffic, so he slept little or awakened often. Consequently, I kept the volume as low as possible when I was on watch.

"How's it goin'?" Fred asked from the settee.

"We have a freighter coming towards us, about 15 miles off the starboard bow. I'm watching it. Go back to sleep," I ordered.

I was perched on our inside steering seat by the chart table where all the navigational equipment was placed. I could see through our large pilothouse windows all of the ocean ahead and to both sides of us. By turning my head I could also see, through the open cabin door, most of the area behind us. We knew that watching astern was just as important as looking ahead. I occasionally would buckle up the harness and head into the cockpit to check the sails and have another good look around. We so loved this inside steering station! On the ocean at night, when it was cold or wet, we enjoyed being able to spend much of the watch inside. On the other hand, on warm, calm nights it was also a delight to sit in the cockpit, watching the stars and imaginary shapes the waves often formed. It afforded wonderful time for contemplation and prayer.

I went into the cockpit soon after talking with Fred. The lights of the freighter were getting closer. Returning to the cabin, I tracked its course on radar. It was about 10 miles away by now, and I began to think we would pass it closer than I would like. Even if it was a half mile away, at the speed it was going, that was too close. I needed to make a decision. My mouth felt dry and my pulse began to race. I reached for the VHF radio microphone.

"Calling the northbound freighter at 45 degrees north, 125 west," I said into the radio as quietly as I could, hoping Fred would not hear me. "This is the southbound sailing vessel, *Amazing Grace*. Do you see us?"

Instantly, Fred was at my side. We waited a minute and I again tried to hail the ship. No response. Fred had been checking the ship's course on the radar and its distance to us.

"I don't like this. Let's change course," he said, and we harnessed up and went quickly into the cockpit to change the direction of the wind-vane and sails. Soon the freighter passed us at a distance of a mile, and we returned to our original course. Looking at its lights as it passed, it seemed much closer—too close! We both breathed a sigh of relief. All this action was surely one way *not* to feel sleepy on a night watch, but it was one I'd just as soon do without.

When I awoke from a nap the following morning, I was surprised to see fog. The wind had also strengthened, but it continued to come from behind us, which made for a pleasant sail. We were making excellent time over the water. By noon the wind was so strong that we decided to take down the mainsail and sail with the jib alone. We figured that we would approach the Newport harbor earlier than expected. That was no problem, but the fog had become dense, and that was indeed worrisome. We could not see anything, even though we were close to shore. We turned east, where the GPS told us the harbor would be, trusting in its accuracy but oh so anxious to see land. As we made our turn, the wind suddenly hit us on the beam, the knot meter jumped significantly, and we rolled way over with the impact. We realized, too late, that we had underestimated the strength of the wind when we were running with it behind us. It was a beginner's mistake. How could we have done that? And that blasted fog. We could hardly see the bow of the boat!

"This is terrible," I yelled to Fred, who was hand-steering the boat at the helm in the cockpit. One foot was braced against the back of the side seat as he tried to remain standing with the boat heeled over so far.

"Just keep your eyes on that radar!" he yelled back through the sounds of the wind and waves.

Grace continued on like she was a race horse heading for the finish line, the starboard railing appearing way too close to the water. We approached the rock jetties—I could see them on the radar and yelled directions to Fred. There was neither time nor space in the narrow entrance to try to reduce the sail, so we flew onward. I glued my eyes to that radar screen as I held on to keep myself on the inside steering seat. The boat continued to be heeled over, and we went "screaming" along with just the jib.

"Hold on," yelled Fred. "I can see the jetties now! We're inside them. The fog is lifting. This wind will die down when we get into the harbor—I hope!"

Just as we were sailing through the two rock entrance jetties, I smelled smoke and, frantically looking back at Fred, saw smoke coming up from the cockpit floor.

"Fire! We're on fire," I yelled. Fred looked down at the smoke, but there was nothing he could do in that moment except hold on to the wheel while the boat flew into the harbor and under its huge bridge. The wind had not died down in the outer harbor, and it was not until we finally came into the bay and turned the boat that we were able to furl the jib. As soon as we rounded the boat into the wind, it righted itself. With the boat now level, there was no more smoke. We later realized that we were heeled over so far coming into the harbor and through the jetties that the engine water intake valve was no longer underwater and was unable to pump water to cool the engine. It had overheated, and thus the smoke. *What next?*

I had been petrified. Shaking after such a dramatic and frightening entrance, we pulled over to a small dock and tied up.

"Wow! This cruising life is all it's cracked up to be—and more!" Fred laughed later. We also laughed as we imagined people high up on the bridge watching our entrance to the harbor, likely thinking we were having lots of *fun* sailing in like that. Little did they know. It had been sheer white-knuckled terror, and it sure wasn't laughable at the time. Obviously, parts of this dream of ours were more like a nightmare!

Later we anchored in the bay and did some crabbing off the bow of the boat. The Dungeness crabs were good eating, and Fred had learned how to clean them before cooking them so we wouldn't get as much "fishy" smell in the cabin of the boat. Those Crab Louies were wonderful, and we relaxed and settled back into the cruising attitude of enjoying the moment while we explored the area. We visited the Newport Aquarium where we continued to learn more about the sea and this environment that was now our home. Gaining this kind of knowledge was one of the goals of our journey. We also wanted to learn as much as we could about the cultures and people we visited.

"Look over here," said Fred. "I didn't know that jellyfish were called 'Jellies.' It says they're not a fish at all. We'll likely be swimming with some further south."

"Those long tendrils can really sting when they touch skin. I'm glad we brought Lycra suits for snorkeling," I added.

Back at the boat, we researched some of the sea life we had seen at the aquarium. We had brought books about the fish and birds of different places. After a couple of days, we pulled anchor and left the harbor about seven in the evening for an overnight sail to Port Orford.

Again we were reminded why the Oregon coast has such an infamous reputation. Those huge Pacific swells made it difficult for the wind-vane to control the boat when the wind was strong and directly behind us. As we plunged down into the trough of a wave, the vane would groan and the boat would begin to turn sideways. Frightening! Aware of the danger of broaching, we would quickly grab the wheel and straighten our course, but it was difficult to do with the vane attached. We switched to using the autopilot and went to the inside steering station where we could more easily make corrections. This meant using the smaller inside wheel for steering when setting a course. It was physically difficult for me to turn the wheel when the seas were so large and the wind was strong. That northwest wind and northwest current were really giving us a ride! Unfortunately, we continued to be swept off course by the swells, and it would often take the efforts of both of us to reconnect the autopilot. The connection point was near the floor by the inside steering seat.

"I'll hand-steer us back onto course, and when I'm there, you reconnect the autopilot," Fred suggested after we had struggled trying to do this alone.

This worked pretty well, but since the autopilot was being thrown off course every few minutes, we knew that we would not be sleeping that night. One of us sat on the helm seat ready to steer us back onto course, while the other lay on the floor to be immediately available to reset the autopilot. It was too windy and cold outside to hand-steer from the cockpit wheel, and we were glad for the chance to be in the cabin. But it was, indeed, a long night.

Keeping about 10 miles offshore meant that when we turned to come into the harbor it was often another two hours before we reached land. As we turned east for Port Orford the next afternoon, the huge swells were again hitting us on the beam, making a most uncomfortable ride. This wasn't fun! I could hardly wait to pull into the little bay and find a protected place to anchor. The wind continued to increase, and it howled in the rigging. Sometimes it was so loud and eerie-sounding that it reminded me of a haunted house. My nerves were tight, my body was tired, and I was losing patience when we finally got the anchor down.

"Boy, am I ever glad to be tucked away inside," I sighed. "But the forecast sure isn't sounding good."

"The chop on the water inside the harbor here isn't very inviting either. Why don't we just stay onboard rather than trying to go ashore in the dinghy," Fred suggested.

Sounded good to me. I'd had enough of bouncing around and being sprayed by saltwater.

The following day, after listening to the forecast of continued storms and high seas, we decided to practice patience and stay put until we heard a more favorable weather report. Unlike our life in "the other world," where go, go and push, push seemed the norm, we knew that sometimes staying when we wanted to be going was the prudent thing to do. It was also the reason why a cardinal rule amongst cruisers is *not* to plan ahead for a time and place to meet someone. Too often doing so meant taking chances with unfavorable conditions in order to keep the appointment.

"I think I'll make some cookies," I said, and soon the smell of fresh chocolate chip cookies filled the cabin. The smell was comforting and it made us feel like we were home. Indeed, *Grace* was now our home. The wind continued to roar, making its mournful sounds about the boat, and we were very glad to be where we were, "Snug as a bug . . . ."

When the adverse weather subsided after a day and a half, we moved on down the coast. We had still not encountered rain, for which we were thankful. Having lots of wet gear aboard a sailboat, and trying to dry it out, is not much fun. The seas were "lumpy" after the storm of the last few days, and we bounced our way across the imaginary California border and into a marina at Crescent City, California.

Staying in marinas certainly added a strain to the cruising budget, and we often opted to anchor out. But oh, how nice to tie up to a dock occasionally and be able to come and go at leisure, without having to get into a dinghy to go ashore.

I'M READY TO FIND A LAUNDROMAT AND GROCERY STORE.

"Hey, let's go for a run and get a little land exercise," I suggested.

"Sounds good. It'll be nice to get off the boat and look around. I think I saw another cruising boat on the other side of the marina. Let's check them out," Fred replied.

We did just that and met Heidi and Harvey on *Ossuna*. They were from Canada and had planned to stay offshore until they reached the Bay area, but they had experienced huge electrical problems and had lost the use of all their navigational equipment except their VHF radio. They had sailed for several days using the Dead Reckoning system, but even that involved a lot of guesswork. They thought they were much further south and had radioed the Coast Guard for assistance in entering a harbor since they were not sure where they were. Then their radio also malfunctioned. Luckily, the Coast Guard had heard their call and sent out a helicopter to drop them a radio. The winds and waves it created, however, were astonishing. Finally, they were able to follow a Coast Guard boat into the harbor and make the electrical repairs to their boat. What a story! When they heard we were coastal hopping and, so far, it had worked well for us, they asked if they could join us as we worked our way down to San Francisco.

A short time later, another Canadian boat limped into the harbor.

KAY KOUDELE

They, too, had been far offshore when they encountered the storm of the last few days and then had to ride it out. The conditions they described were horrific.

"Look at our American courtesy flag," they said, and pointed to a tattered flag remnant that dangled limply from their spreaders. The red and white stripes were each torn into strips, and then each of the strips was knotted several times—all from the impact of those severe winds.

"Coastal hopping sounds mighty good to us now, too," they said. "We'd like to do that as well, but we don't have radar for entering harbors if there's fog. Since *you* have radar, perhaps we could follow you."

We were gathering quite a little entourage. It was great fun to sit, share a beer, and swap stories with other folks who were "out there" doing the same thing as us. We were all sharing the dream—along with its nightmare segments.

We continued south along the California coast. Sometimes we could see the other two boats some distance away, and other times not. We occasionally would call or be called on the radio to ask a location or share something interesting that we had seen on the water. It was nice to have company.

"Do you think it will be rough going around Cape Mendocino?" I asked Fred one evening at anchor as we listened to weather reports and planned the following day's passage. This particular cape had a nasty reputation among mariners. With the northwest wind and current, capes that jutted out into the ocean created obstacles that funneled the winds so they increased in velocity as one attempted to round the cape. Cape Mendocino was a significant projection of land, thus earning the notoriety.

"It sounds pretty good. Maybe if we get going really early in the day, we can sneak around before the winds build," he suggested. That became the game plan.

But one does not sneak around this cape undetected. The Sea Gods were there and waiting for us. And, true to form, we had a wild ride. Although the seas were fairly flat as the day began, the closer we came to the cape, the larger the waves grew. These weren't the large rolling swells we had experienced coming down the coast. They were close together and choppy, and they came from every which way. The wind increased as it hit the headlands, and in my imagination it became a mythical being, angry about being deflected around that cape. It flung its anger at us!

The current, too, was blocked by the jutting land, and created swirling waves. We gritted our teeth and rode it out, hanging on while we were thrown about, slowly inching our way forward. Finally we were around and ready for an anchorage. Such voyages may be the reason they call the harbor just south of the cape, Shelter Cove. As we thankfully slid into the quieter waters of the harbor, we thought of the many mariners, from times of old as well as today, that have relished the opportunity to be safely around the dreaded cape and anchored in the protection of Shelter Cove. Ahhhh. This cruising is work! And the sweet satisfaction of another challenge faced and conquered filled us with contentment and joy. All those prayers of friends and family at home were really helping.

One of the most charming harbors we have ever entered was the lovely little fishing community of Fort Bragg, on the Noyo River.

"Wow! Look at this," I exclaimed.

We passed through the entrance, made a sharp turn to our right, and were flabbergasted. The beautiful scenery that unfolded before us was something out of a storybook. The water of the river was immediately calm. Bushes and plants overhung the banks. Trees along the riverbank were draped with moss, and well-kept, colorful little houses with fragrant flower gardens lined the shore. It was everything you might expect in a coastal fishing community. The river wound its way a short distance to the fishing boats and docks, and, tying up, we set out to explore this little paradise. Talking with the busy fishermen was always fascinating. They also recommended some good seafood restaurants, and even gave me a beautiful sea urchin shell. We hated to leave Fort Bragg, but that Golden Gate beckoned us onward.

Our last "hop" before the one that would take us into the harbor of San Francisco brought us to Drake's Bay. As we motored into the bay in the late afternoon sunshine and dropped the "hook," we found a most undesirable welcoming committee: *flies!* There were thousands of them—or so it seemed. They covered the boat and us as well. We ducked for the cabin and put up the screens. Here we were, on a lovely summer evening in a quiet bay waiting for sunset, and we couldn't get out in the cockpit to enjoy it. I finally found the flyswatter and headed out for battle. It was a mighty fight. Sometimes I got two or three with one swat! I finally tired of the constant assault and returned to the cabin to prepare dinner and plan our course for the long-awaited entrance to San Francisco Bay. Our vision of sailing under the Golden Gate, that beautiful bridge, was somewhat of a benchmark for us; it symbolized our passing from the "rookie" stage of cruising into "the real stuff."

We were also more than a little nervous as we planned our approach.

"These are some of the busiest shipping lanes in the world," Fred reminded me. "I sure hope we don't have fog."

"Me too. I also hope we've timed the tides correctly so we don't have any strong current against us. I've heard of boats that couldn't make any headway against that strong out-going tide."

Looking through the screen on our companionway, we enjoyed a beautiful sunset and set about to ready things for the next day's sail.

"Oh no! Wouldn't you know it? Look at that fog," I said when I awoke the next morning.

Fred rolled over to look out the aft cabin porthole and said, "Thank goodness for our radar."

The traditional San Francisco Bay "pea soup" was upon us this day. (Some cruisers not so affectionately call August "Fogust" in this area.) But we were determined to go. Was this the right decision? *San Francisco Shipping Lanes!* Just thinking those words escalated my anxiety level. I felt the now familiar dry feeling in my mouth as I looked into the thick and gloomy fog. It felt like a shroud, and it was so disorienting. I could see nothing that gave me any clue as to where I was or where I wanted to go. This wasn't the way I pictured sailing under the Golden Gate. Why couldn't it be easy? And then I remembered Fred saying, *"If it was easy, everybody would do it!"* I didn't feel like breakfast; my stomach was tied up in knots. But I got something ready for Fred. Our Canadian friends had called on the radio and said they would line up behind us as we left Drake's Bay. We motored out into the looming fog and positioned ourselves just outside the shipping lanes where we thought we would be the safest.

Things were tense as we motored with only the mainsail up. We wanted to be ready to get out of the path of any ships that came too close. Several hours went by. At one point we got a call on the radio from one of the Canadian boats following us.

"Quack, quack," they said. "We look like little ducklings following their mother." A good laugh helped ease the tension.

Our radar showed a huge green obstacle all the way across the screen as we approached the bridge. It looked like we would run into a brick wall. We knew, however, that the image was the bridge. When we were about a mile away, we were delighted to see the fog beginning to lift and patches of sun appear. Soon we were in blazing sunshine and clear skies, with the glorious Golden Gate Bridge a short distance ahead of us.

"Yahoo!" I yelled, and ran into the cabin. I returned with a bottle of champagne I had been chilling in the refrigerator. As we slid under that famous span, we uncorked the champagne and toasted our good fortune. We took pictures of ourselves and laughed and yelled to our friends on the two Canadian boats who were alongside us now that the fog was gone. The delight of the moment burst around us like the bubbles in our champagne. Such a celebration! You'd think we had sailed around the world.

We were to spend almost a month in the San Francisco Bay area, and what a month it was. Docking near Fisherman's Wharf, we found that we could easily walk into the downtown area of San Francisco, so sightseeing was easy. We often went for a run in Union Square just as people in their business suits, carrying briefcases and looking tense, were headed to work. Oh yes, the "other world." The one we had *left*. It made us almost giddy with joy to know that those days were behind us.

One beautiful autumn morning we were part of thousands running across the Oakland Bay Bridge while it was closed to vehicles. What an exhilarating experience! Although it had been chilly in the early morning air, it soon warmed as we ran uphill towards the middle of the huge span over the bay. The sun shone brightly on the skyline of downtown San Francisco and beckoned us onward. At the top the wind blew gently, cooling our now heated bodies, and we could see the ocean stretching into the horizon beyond the bay. Our legs began to burn as we headed down into the streets of San Francisco, and with heaving chests we approached the finish line. Even though Fred beat me by a good deal, I was thrilled to have taken part in this memorable event.

We had talked with Dawn, and she was to fly into the San Francisco airport the next day to spend a few days with us. We sailed our boat to the southern part of the bay to a marina near the airport. Looking at a map, we decided we could get some exercise by running to the airport, changing clothes once we got there. Little did we know that our plan would involve climbing over a chain-link fence, walking the railroad tracks, jumping aside as the trains whizzed by, and crossing a deserted industrial area. It had looked so easy on the map. But we arrived at the airport and tried to clean our sweaty faces, change our clothes, and be ready to greet Dawn.

"Hey Sweetheart!" we cried when we saw her. After hearing about her trip, we walked her outside. "We jogged over here from the marina. It's about six miles away. Think you're up to running back?" we said, with mischief in our eyes and absolutely no intention of doing that.

With brief hesitation and a look that said, "*What will they think of next?*" she agreed to give it a try. We could only laugh as we hailed a taxi, knowing that our kids were a little stumped about what to expect from their parents now. It felt good to keep them guessing.

While Dawn would just as soon sit on the boat at the dock as go sailing, we had heard that the famous Blue Angels would be performing over the bay, so the three of us decided to sit in the middle of the bay in our boat. What a show we saw! We were so close to the planes that we could actually see the faces of the pilots as they looped their planes upside down, looking like they would fly right into our mast. It was impossible to talk to each other over the roar of the jets. We could only scream with delight at this amazing demonstration of skill and daring.

The day before Dawn was to leave, I awoke her, saying, "How about goin' shoppin'?"

She was up out of her berth before I could add, "a little later." Shopping in San Francisco—but *of course*! For Dawn was the original "shop 'til you drop" kid. There were several factory outlets we wanted to see, but most were not in the area or easily available by bus, so we walked several miles to as many stores as we could manage.

"Think how nice it will be when I come to see you in San Diego," she said. "Having my car there will really be great. Think of the shopping we can do then!"

Indeed, I was thinking of shopping, but it was primarily marine stores I had in mind. Being without a car while traveling by boat can be a real drawback when in large ports or cities. Getting from place to place by bus is not always convenient, and our cruising budget did not allow for taxis. Dawn firmly reminded us of that inconvenience late one night when we were walking through a rough neighborhood on the way back to the marina. The buildings were vacant or in disrepair, and the streets deserted. The tension in the three of us was palpable.

"I can't believe we are walking here. This is *dangerous!*" she said. There was both anxiety and irritation in her voice. "You guys should have taken a taxi!"

"You're probably right," Fred responded, looking around him. "I think it's only a little further to the marina. Let's walk out here."

And so the three of us walked quickly down the middle of the empty street, keeping a watchful eye all around. We were all glad to see the marina parking lot. That night I fell asleep thinking about mariners of days long past, being shanghaied and loaded on ships bound for faraway ports.

Much of the time we were in the bay area, we moored at different yacht clubs. The yacht club we belonged to at home had reciprocal privileges with other clubs up and down the coast. We enjoyed taking Dawn to some of the bigger, fancier places, although we preferred the smaller, more informal clubs. All were gracious and friendly to us, and allowed us to stay a couple of nights with no fee. This was *perfect* for the cruising budget. One of the clubs was close to the Golden Gate Bridge, so we all ran across the bridge one morning. That was a real "high," in both a physical and emotional sense.

Saying goodbye to Dawn wasn't so difficult, since we would be seeing her in San Diego for Thanksgiving. She would drive over from Tempe for school break and then had only a couple of weeks more before graduation. She was really looking forward to joining us in Cabo.

"I'm so glad Page and Mom are coming to your graduation," I told her before she left. "But I sure wish we had decided to delay our departure for Mexico so that we could be there too."

"It will work out great," she replied. "The day after graduation, Grandma will fly home, and Page and I will fly to Cabo to meet Steve there." A fine plan, but *we* wouldn't be there for her big day! Again, the "Mother's Guilt Trip" did a number on me.

One fine day we were out on the bay so Fred could try out the new additional fuel system he had installed before we left, but had not yet used. We were motoring along when the engine suddenly died.

"Was it supposed to do that?" I timidly asked.

"No. We'd better put up the sails. You can steer us to Treasure Island, and I'll try to get the engine going again." He was frustrated and grumpy.

So we did just that. But we encountered one of the most unusual circumstances for afternoons in San Francisco Bay: The wind died. There was *always* wind in this bay! Fred had been working for more than an hour without success while we drifted aimlessly. He continued to crawl around in the engine compartment while I sat nervously up on the deck. Keeping watch on our position through the GPS, I discovered that we were entering the shipping lanes. This was definitely not good. We threw out an anchor, and luckily it held. Fred continued to work, sweat, and cuss. Finally a light breeze came up, and we decided to try to sail back into the same marina we had left earlier that day. It was the only one in the area we knew the entrance to, so I called the marina on the radio.

"We are a 37-foot sailboat and have no engine power. Do you think we can sail into a slip in your marina?" I asked.

"No problem," he said quickly. "Just come on in, and we'll be waiting to help you get into a slip." It sounded okay, so we pulled up the sails and anchor and started in.

Ha! Now a little day-sailor might have been able to sail into that marina, but we found that, as soon as we turned into the harbor, the wind was on our nose. We would have to tack (sail back and forth) to get to where the docks were. A boat our size takes a considerable amount of room to make those turns. Once we had changed our direction with the wheel, we needed the wind to fill the sails again to get us going in the opposite direction. I looked frantically about but could see no one prepared to help us. After scrambling to get some headway with the sails, we found that we could make the first dock, which fortunately was empty. The sign on it said "Sea Scouts," but we were taking it. We made a hard landing, and I jumped off to take the dock lines and tie up while Fred dropped the sails.

"What were they thinking?" I said angrily. "I still don't see anyone available to help!"

"Well, at least we made it," he said calmly. At that particular moment I didn't want to be calm, I wanted to lash out with my anger. I soon found myself settling down anyway, and realized that continuing to be upset wouldn't help or solve a thing. Once again, Fred's temperament had helped me be in a better place. The "balancing act" of our relationship paid off. I may have been the one who received the most benefit, but, after all, he'd have missed a terrific 10K run over the bay bridge if I hadn't got him going!

Fred spent a considerable part of the next day working to get the diesel engine going. Much to his credit, I finally heard it roar to life, but we still called a mechanic to come look at it the following day. That was a good thing, because he taught Fred some techniques to bleed the engine quickly, and we bought a small device that helped the process. It seemed that, once again, we learned the most through a difficult situation; God allowed us struggles, but not more than we could handle. Surely, "'Tis Grace that brought us safe thus far, and Grace will see us home."

One evening we arranged to go to Chinatown for dinner with the two Canadian couples who accompanied us down the coast. We all felt we shared a special bond, and we were ready for a night on the town. We had a recommendation for a good restaurant and were about to enter when we saw other cruising friends coming out.

"This is a terrific place to eat," they all said. "It's the real San Francisco Chinatown experience."

We could hardly wait! We entered a small restaurant that was packed with diners.

"Follow me," said the waiter. "You must go upstairs."

To our amazement, he led us through the kitchen (that looked like a three ring circus), up a narrow winding stairway, and into a brightly lit room packed with people sitting at tables covered in oilcloth. We sat down quickly, along with one of the couples, but the other couple just stood there looking very upset.

"We can't eat here," they said. "People walking through where food is prepared, and oilcloth on the tables? No way."

We couldn't believe what we were hearing. Feeling very disappointed, we reluctantly got up and left with them, as we had all agreed to eat together. How sad, we thought, that this couple felt they had to maintain their familiar standards and judged a place negatively when it was, in fact, simply "different." Obviously, we had dissimilar expectations of situations and people that we would encounter. Fred and I were willing to come upon new experiences and lifestyles that were unlike our own. Apparently not everyone felt the same. It was not the last time we were to see this judgmental or rigid dynamic, and each time we did we wondered, *why do these people travel? Why don't they just stay home, where things are the same?* Several weeks later, we learned that this couple, indeed, had returned home to Canada.

After many enjoyable days, we knew it was time to be heading south. The night before we were to leave the bay, we called Lance. We were delighted to hear that he still was thinking of joining us for a few months after ski season, since he would not be able to come with the others to Cabo for Christmas (a busy time at a ski resort). But I surely did not like the idea of spending Christmas without the whole family together. How we would miss him!

Five
Seeking The Southern California Sun

"What a fabulous feeling it is to be able to just take off and go wherever we want whenever we wish," I said to Fred. We were sailing underneath the Golden Gate Bridge and entering the mighty Pacific once more. "Here it is the second of October, and the only place we really need to be is San Diego for Thanksgiving. That's a lot of leeway."

"Right. When you think of all the timetables and schedules of our working lives, this feels like some incredible sense of freedom," Fred replied. He adjusted the autopilot to guide us along the fringes of the shipping lanes.

"Freedom, yes. But also the call of adventure! It's one part anxiety to leave what we know and one part excitement to discover something new. Here we are, finally feeling comfortable in this area, and yet we leave to tackle someplace new, knowing that there is discomfort in approaching the unknown. Maybe we are just adrenalin junkies," I laughed.

After spending almost a month in the Bay, it was beginning to get colder, and we wanted some sun. We made a stop at Santa Cruz, enjoyed the seaside resort atmosphere of the boardwalk and carnival areas, and continued to sail south. When we turned into the harbor of Monterrey and looked for some dock space in the crowded marina, we heard a lot of barking sounds.

"Holy Cow! Look at that. Can you believe it?" I said.

There, on a portion of the dock in the marina, were at least seven or eight huge sea lions, some barking and others snoozing, pretty much taking over the space. We remembered seeing sea lions swimming in the ocean as though they were dancing a graceful ballet. Here on land they seemed slow, awkward, and formidable.

"I wouldn't want to get too close to those big guys," Fred replied. "They look like they could do some serious damage."

We found a slip and made arrangements to meet friends of ours, Pete and Sharon, who lived in the area. We would see them the following evening, after touring the huge, nationally recognized aquarium where they often served as volunteers. Fred and I were amazed at the many exhibits and explanations of sea life at the impressive aquarium. Now that the sea was our home, everything took on new importance.

That evening our friends picked us up and suggested we go to one of their favorite places for a glass of wine. As we sat out on the patio overlooking the beach and ocean, absorbing the last rays of the setting sun while a gentle breeze fanned our faces, we heard the faint sounds of a bagpiper far out on the dunes. As he slowly walked closer, the haunting, melodic sound of the bagpipe increased. Just as the sun slowly descended on the horizon in a spectacular display of light and color, we heard something that gave us "goose-bumps."

"Oh, listen," exclaimed Fred. "He's playing 'Amazing Grace!' *Listen!*"

"It *is!*" I said, with tears coming to my eyes. Turning to our friends, we saw the twinkle in their eyes and their knowing smiles, and we realized that this was the reason they had brought us here. What a gift. Friends who shared our faith, the incredible sunset, this *amazing* life opportunity we were having, and of course, *Grace*!

When we were ready to leave Monterrey to continue south, Pete wanted to sail with us. We arranged for Sharon to pick him up at our next planned anchorage, which was adjacent to the Pebble Beach golf course and near their home. It would only take a few hours to get there, so we left in the early afternoon. Pete was excited and anxious to learn all about the boat. As we left the harbor, we saw two people in the water next to a small, capsized sailboat.

"Do you think they are okay?" I asked Pete and Fred.

"It's a little day-sailor," Fred responded. "They probably know how to right it, but let's make sure."

We had not yet raised our sails, so we motored towards them and were glad to see that they both wore life jackets.

"Do you need some help?" Fred yelled to the man and woman in the water.

"*Yes!*" the woman quickly responded. "I want to go over *there!*" And she pointed towards the shore.

"Hold on while we lower our swim ladder so you can climb aboard," Fred responded.

While the woman laboriously climbed the ladder off our stern, her husband worked to right the small boat, but it was still partially submerged. Meanwhile, we were bringing towels, blankets, and hot coffee to the shaken woman, who was cold, tired, and angry. It was their first time sailing the boat, and she had not wanted to go so far out into the harbor. You could tell it would be a tense time at their house that night! Finally, the husband abandoned his attempts to right the boat. We threw him a towline that he connected to his boat, and he climbed aboard ours.

We could only move slowly through the water due to towing the submerged vessel, but finally we were able to get to a dock. The couple was extremely grateful for our assistance and thanked us profusely as they climbed ashore, wishing us well on our travels. Pete, of course, was absolutely thrilled with this unexpected experience and loved being involved in a real *rescue*. It was more than he had bargained for!

"Chalk one up for being saved by *Amazing Grace*," Fred laughed, and we pulled away. "But I'm a little concerned about getting around the corner to our anchorage now, since we are so late in leaving. I don't want to have to anchor in the dark. I think it will be all right, but let's hope we don't run into any more problems."

We left the harbor and turned south around the point.

"Oh *no,*" I cried. "Look at that fog bank! Just what we *don't* need."

Pete was really getting his money's worth this day. Hugging the coastline was a thick layer of fog—just where we wanted to go. We quickly turned on our radar and entered into the dense, restricting veil. We could see little past the bow, and our apprehension was almost palpable. To warn nearby ships of our presence, we got out our brass bell. Pete's job was to ring the bell every minute or so. It was a tense ride. While we wanted to get to our anchorage quickly, we slowed our approach due to the limited visibility.

Indeed, it was almost dark by the time we pulled into the little bay and searched for a place to anchor. We could see Sharon waiting on shore, likely worried that we were so late in arriving. When we tried to "set" the anchor by backing down with the engine, we found that it would not hold. Pulling up the anchor so it cleared the water, we tried again and again with the same results. This wasn't good. Fred finally pulled the anchor all the way in, and discovered it was covered with seaweed so it could not grab hold in the sand beneath. Darkness descended, and we wondered where and how we were going to be able to get the anchor down. Fred went inside to one of the lockers and pulled out a different type of anchor, hooked it up, and we tried once again. Hooray—it held! Thank goodness for those "back-up" systems. (And the thoroughness of Fred's preparations.)

We quickly put together our dinghy, which was a folding boat we stored on our foredeck. It was rather unique for a dinghy, and took a few minutes to set it up, but we liked it because, when stored, it lay flat and did not obstruct our vision from our inside steering station. Fred rowed Pete ashore while I prepared something for dinner. It had been an exciting day and we were all tired. Pete was ecstatic about his sailing adventure, and was ready to sign on as crew. He surely had gotten a taste of the unexpected, which by now seemed to be a "normal" part of cruising!

We continued our way south along the central California coastline. The promise of warmth and sunshine beckoned us onward. As we prepared our approach to Morro Bay, my anxiety began to rise.

"Goodness, the pilot book and cruising notes really make this entrance sound scary," I said. "Apparently the approach is broadside to the ocean swell, and there is a real risk of being hit and rolled by a wave. Doesn't sound good to me."

We proceeded carefully between the buoys marking the harbor. The ocean swells appeared calm, and we were just beginning to feel more relaxed when the VHF radio blared out, *"Amazing Grace. Amazing Grace.* Look out! Look out! You're about to be broached!"

We frantically looked all about us. *Where?* Where was the wave that was about to hit us? Nowhere could we see a threatening wave, and so, after a few moments of hesitation, we proceeded forward, now definitely on edge. When we finally made it into harbor and looked back at the sea, we thought we discovered the problem. When looking seaward, it is very difficult to have accurate depth perception. The boat that had called us was another cruising vessel we had met, and from their perspective the waves farther out to sea were right on top of us—thus the reason for their panic. The warning wasn't really needed this time, but it was nice to know that others were looking out for us—although it certainly didn't add to our comfort that day!

We were now meeting quite a few fellow cruisers, and it was amazing how quickly relationships developed. The word "fraternity" comes to mind. Such a collective became a sense of "family." Sharing the same experiences (as well as the immediacy that was frequently a factor) helped foster a feeling of intimacy that took much longer to develop in the "other world." Cruisers come from all walks of life, and very often we did not know what type of work they had done until we had known them for weeks or even months. At home, a person's occupation was usually discovered shortly after learning his or her name. Here, it didn't seem relevant. More interesting was, "where have you come from, and how was it?" Last names never entered the vocabulary, either. People were known by their first names, and the name of their boat. We were "Fred and Kay on *Amazing Grace.*"

As we made our way southward, one of the joys was quiet mornings at sea, which fostered times of contemplation. Even at night, while on watch, we often had the opportunity to reflect and muse.

"I think I'm becoming a philosopher," Fred announced one morning. "I've thought of just about everything that's possible to consider!"

A great joy for me was time to sit in the cockpit, play my guitar, and sing. Sometimes it was at anchor and sometimes at sea. One day, as I was singing, a large whale began circling the boat. I was thrilled and, thinking my music may have attracted it, began to sing louder, hoping to arouse the attention of Fred, who was down in the cabin.

"Get out here, Fred," I sang gaily. "There's a whale swimming with us!" I crooned. I don't think it will become a hit song, but it did the job in getting Fred to come out to see what I was singing about. We watched the large creature for several minutes before it sprayed the air with water and dove into the deep.

Besides watching sea lions dance their ballet, we never tired of seeing pelicans diving into the water from significant heights. The sound of the splash they made as they hit the water was so forceful that we were sure they died on impact. But up they came, often swallowing a fish, so I guess it worked for them. Sea otters were also fun to watch. So far, we had not seen dolphins or porpoises, but we were certainly looking forward to that. We often commented that we were "in school" because we were learning so many new things. We had learned about the areas we visited, about nature, about Grace (both the boat and the concept), and about ourselves. All good stuff!

Point Conception, sometimes known as the "Cape Horn of the Pacific," was the last of the major capes to pass on our way to southern California. We knew that, once around the cape, the going would get easier. We found that the farther we traveled, the more we came to have some idea of what to expect, and those anticipations helped prepare us. The idea of entering truly "southern" California waters was an enticement that also helped us to get by this big land mass.

Winds and seas were as expected—big and intimidating, but manageable. Our confidence level was growing. We were coming to trust *Grace* and her ability to handle these seas and winds, so we mostly just had to hold on and go along for the ride. It was a good feeling.

Shortly after rounding the Point and heading eastward toward Santa Barbara, we saw strange lights in the sea late at night. There were many of them in very strange patterns, unlike anything we had ever seen. From a distance, it appeared like some type of futuristic towers or buildings, or some sort of land mass. We knew that the eyes could play tricks on a person at sea. We'd read of folks having hallucinations, especially at night when on long passages. Some said it was sensory deprivation. We'd experienced a little of it when crossing the Pacific from Hawaii. But this was no hallucination—we were both seeing it!

"What in the world *is* that?" I exclaimed. "It looks like some kind of spaceship, and it's huge!"

"Hand me the binoculars," Fred replied. We could not tell the distance to the lights, which appeared stationary.

Meanwhile, I was searching the charts for some indication of a land mass off the coast in this vicinity. There were no islands, no rocks—nothing charted to explain these forbidding lights. As we continued to sail, our anxiety decreased and we became more curious than concerned. An hour or two later, after a good deal of speculation, we approached close enough to finally identify our "spaceships." They were *oil-drilling rigs!* We laughed at ourselves. It's amazing what the imagination can do to a person alone at sea in the dark! Passing at a safe distance, we gazed at the monstrous structures that were many stories high and oddly shaped. We wondered about the people who worked and lived aboard these huge rigs. There were quite a number of them, separated by many miles, and each lit up like a Christmas tree.

Coming into Santa Barbara, we felt the thrill of at last being in southern California. Palm trees and lovely Spanish style buildings could be seen from the marina entrance. We also felt the excitement of seeing Meaghan, whose mother and I had been best friends since high school. Maybe we could do some laundry at her home.

We found a slip in a marina and gasped at the cost. Southern California prices were a significant hit on the cruising budget. We knew that in many places we would be able to stay for free in yacht clubs due to those reciprocal privileges with our home club, but in Santa Barbara we stayed at a public marina because it was close to Meaghan's.

The air felt warm and the sun shone brightly as we left to find a phone.

"Oh boy. I could get used to this weather," I cried. "I think we can put away the long pants and winter jackets for good." Until then, it was often cold when at sea and we bundled up with warm jackets, hats, and gloves, especially for night watches. Most of our dream had been about warm, sunny climes, so we felt we had finally "arrived."

Ports were abundant in this area, and we often had just a day's sail to our next destination. We frequently encountered other cruising boats, for we were all moving in the same direction about the same time. The goal for most of us was to leave the U.S. for Mexico just after Thanksgiving, which would allow us to avoid the Mexican waters during hurricane season. Most boat insurers required that boats avoid certain areas during the hurricane season. We had purchased insurance—although many other cruisers had not, because it was so expensive. It was one of those precautionary things we obtained (along with many thousands of dollars' worth of emergency equipment) that we hoped we would never have to use.

"Hey, Kay. So where are the good Happy Hour places?" It was getting to be a familiar request amongst the cruisers. My "Scotch" blood always had me looking for good deals. So, when entering a port, I quickly sought out the places close by that offered free food during Happy Hour. I soon gained quite a reputation—and felt pressure to deliver the goods! For only the cost of a beer or two, the accompanying free food often sufficed for dinner. It was not only fun to share with other cruisers, but cost efficient as well. Combine a good Happy Hour with free food and free moorage at a yacht club, and I was in budget utopia! Hey—this cruising life was great.

A favorite stop as we cruised the southern California coastline was Oxnard, where we made contact with another good friend from high school and her family.

"John will come pick you up at the marina about four," my friend Linda said. "And yes, of course you can bring your laundry."

I hadn't even had to ask. What friends! Again, we savored being in a *house,* and sitting and eating without the movement of the water— although it did seem strange. It even seemed strange riding in a car. As in visiting with other friends, we enjoyed exchanging stories of our lives and realized, again, that each of us has an adventure to live and everyone's experience is certainly as interesting as ours, full of joys, challenges, opportunities, and lessons. Much of life's adventure for John and Linda came from giving of themselves through their church. It was an inspiration to hear and see. We were delighted they would pick us up the following Sunday to attend services with them. Often there was no church available when we were at anchor or without land transportation, so we had developed a greater appreciation of the gift of worship. It felt very different from when we were at home, where we often took those experiences for granted. Sometimes, at home, going to worship had even felt like a "should" rather than a "want."

Entering the Los Angeles area, we were faced with myriads of harbors, yacht clubs, and marinas. What a busy place. We "hopped" around, exploring several of the yacht clubs.

"Hey, look," Fred said excitedly. "There's *Ossuna!* I think I see an open slip. Let's stop there."

What fun to find our friends from Canada.

"Come over and have dinner with us," they yelled as we motored by. "We can celebrate your birthday."

Amazing! They had remembered that my birthday was the next day. How nice. It would be a "family" celebration after all—our cruising family.

The Los Angeles area was fascinating, but we soon longed for the quiet of a peaceful anchorage, fewer people, and less hustle and bustle. We wanted to visit the Catalina Islands before sailing on to San Diego. At that time of year, though, there was the possibility of Santa Ana winds; they would rocket down the mountainsides, shooting out from the mainland over the islands with terrific force. It was definitely not wise to be at anchor there during those times, nor at sea. But the weather was stable, so we decided to risk it.

Shortly before leaving for the islands, we talked to our son on the phone.

"We're going to Santa Catalina," I said.

"Where's that?" Lance replied.

"Just off the coast near Los Angeles. You know—like the song: 'Twenty-six miles across the sea, Santa Catalina is a-waitin' for me,'" I sang.

"Never heard it before," he said.

What? Never heard the song! Ouch—that really made us feel old.

Our sail to the islands was pleasant, and we anchored in the harbor of Avalon, by the big casino pictured in so many Hollywood movies. The water was crystal clear and sparkling. We could see the sand bottom even at a 20-foot depth. It was beautiful. Soon, one of the marina staff boarded *Grace* and put dye tablets into the head (toilet). This was the regular procedure for protecting the harbor. Anyone who discharged their head or holding tank into the water could be spotted by the subsequent dye mark around the boat and heavily fined. A boat even patrolled the harbor at night with lights, checking the water for dye. It was a system that worked, and the marine life was flourishing. Would that all our waters would be so clean, safe, and beautiful!

We spent several days around the islands, hiking, watching the grazing herd of buffalo, and chatting with other cruisers. Then we heard the dreaded news: Santa Ana winds were predicted for the following few days. We quickly motored behind one of the smaller islands to find a protected area in which to anchor.

"You were right when you insisted on making the anchor line all chain when outfitting the boat," I said to Fred. "It sure is comforting at a time like this."

"What's that you say?" He grinned. He just wanted me to say again that he had been right!

Sure enough, just as predicted, the winds showed up in a fury. They howled their mournful cry as they flew through the rigging of the boat. We had stripped the deck of any gear; everything not nailed down would be blown overboard. Fortunately we were in a good location and rode out the high winds in relative calm. We were close to shore, so that the waves created by the wind didn't have a chance to build up, and the boat swung around with the bow pointing into the wind. That was considerably more comfortable than being slammed up against a dock. We spent the time reading on the boat, as the water was too rough to dinghy to shore, and we felt snug and safe, rather enjoying the "time off." Later, when returning to the mainland, we aimed for San Diego, our last port before leaving the U.S.

After an uneventful passage, we were excited to enter Mission Bay in San Diego. There we saw boats of every shape and size—big ones, little ones, fancy ones, old dilapidated ones, and everything in between. And there were so *many* of them!

"Look! There's the big Coronado Shores resort," I said. "It's just like in the pictures. I'm sure our cruising budget won't allow staying there. Let's look for a yacht club on the list and see if we can find a free place to stay."

But after trying several yacht clubs in the bay, we found they were all full.

"Darn! Looks like we will need to stay in a marina," I lamented.

"I heard from another boat that there is a police dock that doesn't cost much. Let's check it out," suggested Fred.

Sure enough, there was a simple dock with very few amenities, but a number of cruising boats were there, and there was room for one more. We were in luck, although it was a long walk around the harbor to the shops and restaurants. Well, we needed the exercise. We found a few boaters whom we had met before, and we met lots of new ones—everyone anxious to make final preparations before leaving for Mexico (or, for a few, Hawaii and the other South Pacific islands). It was hard to get much done on our own boat because it was so easy to get to talking with others, and there was a wealth of useful information available.

One way to get some of this information was through the "Morning Net" on VHF radio. At a specific time each day, boaters would listen to a particular radio channel and call in with their boat name. It was rather like a conference call on the phone. After "checking in," people shared information or asked questions and others provided answers. It was extremely helpful, and a great way to connect with the other cruising boats. Topics included just about anything—where to get certain boat parts; how to get the static off the ham radio; where to reproduce charts; how to get to the nearest liquor store, bakery, or ice cream place; how to bleed an engine; what the weather forecasts were; inquiries as to who could fix something; and, of course, the best places for Happy Hours!

"Ahoy, *Amazing Grace*." Dawn was here! We jumped up from the cabin and ran outside to greet her. She had driven over from Arizona State University for Thanksgiving break, and we were so glad to see her. We were also excited to see her *car*, and knew that we'd now have transportation to marine stores to find those few remaining pieces of gear we wanted before leaving the States.

"How about going to the San Diego Yacht Club for Thanksgiving dinner tomorrow?" Fred asked Dawn that night.

"Wow. Do you think the cruising budget can handle that?" was her reply. We had these kids trained pretty well!

"Sure. It's a special splurge for a special day," replied Fred, with a twinkle in his eye. "In the morning, Kay and I are going to a woman's baptism on another cruising boat. We feel privileged to be invited. Then we'll go for dinner."

The next morning, sunshine filled the skies; the warmth of it *and* the holiday had us all in a festive mood. Fred and I, along with six others, went over to the cruising boat of a retired Episcopal priest. In a quiet, simple ceremony in the cockpit of the boat, he baptized a young woman who was going cruising to Mexico. We felt touched by God's presence as we shared Communion with one another after the baptism. It was special beyond words, and we felt truly blessed by this sharing of faith and community.

Afterwards, we did indeed go to the beautiful San Diego Yacht Club—so different from our home club, Sauvie Island. We had no fancy clubhouse but met instead in a school cafeteria. That seemed light years away from this! The three of us soaked up the elegant ambience and enjoyed a wonderful dinner in the lovely dining room of this special place.

"So that's the America's Cup! It really is beautiful," I exclaimed. The display case featuring the famous yacht-racing cup was prominently placed in the club's entrance. "Only the winning team gets to display this. We sure enjoyed watching the races on TV." A racing boat is very different from a cruising boat, but we had real appreciation for the sailors' skills and the remarkable construction of those huge sailboats.

One day the three of us drove to the border near Tijuana, Mexico, and then walked across it, leaving the car in the U.S.

"You're sure getting a chance to practice your new Spanish skills, Mom," said Dawn.

"And I love it! I can't wait to learn more."

"Me, too," added Fred. "So many tourists seem to expect the Mexican people to speak English, even though we are in *their* country."

Besides looking in the shops of that large colorful city, and having a good lunch, we also took a taxi to a place where Fred could extend his ham license to operate in Mexico.

Our few days with Dawn passed quickly. We obtained a number of last-minute items that we might not be able to acquire once we left the country. We were especially glad to find the "Baja Filter," a device that would clean dirty fuel before we added it to the boat's tanks. For cruisers in Mexico, the filter was on the "must have" list.

Back at the boat, we said good-bye to Dawn, who would fly to Cabo San Lucas to meet us in a couple of weeks if all went well. Saying goodbye this time was very difficult for Fred and me. We knew we would be missing her college graduation day, but the sadness was tempered by knowing that my mom and Page would be there with her. While our absence from this occasion wasn't something that seemed to bother Dawn, it bothered me greatly. It was one of those benchmarks as a parent—seeing your child in cap and gown, receiving a college degree— and we would miss it! At this point in her life, Dawn was more excited about going to Mexico. Would she regret her decision later? Already I was having second thoughts, and it was definitely a "Kleenex" night.

Now we were ready to go. Like most of the other cruisers, we had spent too much money on provisioning the boat with food, equipment, and supplies, and knew we'd be broke if we didn't get underway soon. Surely we didn't need one more *whatever!* I had stocked *Grace* with canned and dried food before leaving Portland, and we had added more at every stop all the way down the coast. I think we could have eaten well for years on what we had tucked away in the lockers. We checked weather reports and our weather fax.

"Everything looks good," Fred said. "Today's the day—let's go!"

"I heard a guy say that a storm is coming and he was going to wait. Quite a few others have decided to wait as well," I said. "Maybe it's 'harboritis.'"

We had read some time ago about a condition that affected cruisers, where the anxiety of venturing forth into the unknown kept them finding excuses to stay where they were. Although we were anxious, we didn't want that feeling to cloud our decisions. We also thought that if we left now we might be ahead of an incoming storm, and our weather fax showed no problems in the near future.

"Yahoo! 'On the road again,'" I sang as we motored out of Mission Bay, heading for foreign countries and unknown experiences. It was December 2, 1992, and although we had been underway for months, this passage felt very different. We were leaving behind the safety, security, and comfort of our own country for something different. Who knew what we would find? We were thankful for the prayers of family and friends, and we felt we were in good hands as we sailed into the mighty Pacific Ocean.

Six

Venturing Across The Border

Once again it felt like a *beginning*. Leaving the country felt scary, exciting, and joyous. This part of the dream was now reality. The skies were cloudy, almost as if to note that we were leaving the lovely southern California sun. But there is a sun in Mexico too, right? Perhaps we should have been a little more concerned about the presence of those clouds. We set our sails and slid along, enjoying the moment and all it represented. The wind was good, and we put our usual reef in the mainsail for nighttime. I felt the return of my usual apprehension as we went through our preparations for the night passage, but I was getting rather used to it. (Not that I liked it, mind you, but *used to* it.) A few boats had left San Diego when we did, but we didn't know them, nor could we see any other boats once we were underway. I felt a little lonely and vulnerable. If all went well, we planned to make a several day run to Cabo San Lucas, Mexico. Our second day went well until about five in the afternoon. The winds had been steadily increasing all day. It was now raining and the skies looked very threatening. The seas were steep and choppy.

"I think it's time to put a second reef in the mainsail," Fred said, more calmly than I suspected he was feeling. "The winds are really getting stronger and we have too much sail up." It had become a very rough ride—rather like riding a buckin' bronco!

"I agree, but I don't like you going forward on the deck."

Although our lines were rigged to the cockpit, theoretically allowing us to handle the sails from there, the sail needed help in coming down to make the reef tight. So Fred would have to crawl to the mast to help pull it down. With the boat heaving and rolling around so much, it would not be easy for him to pull the sail with one hand and hold on to the mast with the other.

We bundled up in our foul weather gear and lifejackets. My mouth felt dry as cotton as we prepared to go out into the storm. I wanted to stay down in the cabin and hide under the bed covers, but I knew it would take the two of us to do the job and we both needed to be out there. As Fred attached his harness and tether to the jack-line and left the cockpit, I steered the boat into the wind—also not an easy task because we were continually thrown off course, and I wrestled the wheel to hold the bow in position. It took all my strength to maintain our heading. It was difficult to see the wind direction meter as the rain pelted our faces and tugged at our raingear. It helped reduce my fear to become angry.

"This wind is from the *southeast!* Where's that *usual* northwest wind?" I shouted.

Since our desired course was to the southeast, it was definitely not the wind direction we wanted, and it made our ride even more uncomfortable. Generally, it's a much easier sail when the wind comes over the side of the boat, or even behind it. I could see that the knot meter was now up to 30, and the waves were so steep and close together that the boat was violently thrown about—up and down, side to side. We had huge waves breaking over the bow, throwing *barrels* of seawater back into the cockpit, and I feared a really big wave would push us under. I was glad that Fred had wanted a boat with a small cockpit in case it got swamped. It was raining harder, and even more difficult to see.

"I *really* don't like this! I want *off!*" I shouted, only half in jest.

"Hey—this is cruising!" Fred was trying to keep his voice upbeat, but I could tell by the look on his face that he didn't like it either. I knew, after almost 30 years together, that he was trying to protect me from my fears by not adding his own. Our anxiety climbed each time we saw an increase in the wind speed.

Soon the winds were registering over 40 knots. Our sails were greatly reduced so that there was just enough to provide some stability.

The sound of the wind was frightening in itself. It had become very dark, creating an inky blackness and sense of isolation. Water continued to cascade over the bow into the cockpit. We heard a vessel try several times to call the U.S. Coast Guard on the VHF radio.

"Don't they know there is no Coast Guard down here?" I shouted above the roar of the wind. "We are more than 200 miles below the border!"

We were out in the cockpit after taking down more sail, and we decided to hold hands and pray. I was frightened. The prayer helped, and we went inside to try and dry off and to get through the night.

Fred was lying down for a few minutes and I was sitting at the inside helm seat, trying to hold on, when we heard it.

"*Mayday! Mayday!*" came the call on the radio. It was the vessel that had been calling the Coast Guard without success. I looked at Fred in desperation—what could *we* do? We were just hanging on by our teeth; how could we possibly help another boat? But we *had* to answer. When we contacted the boat, the men aboard sounded quite relieved to know that someone had heard them and they were not alone. They were in a motor vessel heading north and apparently in no immediate danger, but they were scared and, like us, feeling very alone and vulnerable.

Fred suggested that he use our ham radio to let the Coast Guard know their position, and after doing this they were much relieved. We decided to maintain VHF radio contact between our two boats every 15 minutes for as long as possible throughout the night. Hearing another voice out there in that storm provided a sense of comfort to both vessels. After a few contacts we felt like old friends! Since we were going opposite directions, we knew that at some point we would exceed the distance that radio transmissions were possible. But at that moment it felt reassuring.

We had set our sails so that we were "hove-to." (This means the sails were balanced, with one pushing slightly forward and the other pushing slightly backward.) It was a technique that allowed for safety in a storm and a slightly more comfortable ride—but not necessarily any forward progress. We had read about how to do this in books, but never in "The Dream" did we envision having to do it! We had also turned slightly seaward because we did not want to take a wave over the beam—a dangerous condition. So *Grace* was actually moving farther out to sea when all I really wanted to do was head for shore!

After a couple of hours, the conditions improved a little. Soon the wind speed dropped considerably. It became almost quiet and still. We were breathing a sigh of relief, believing we were through the storm, when a faint call crackled on the radio.

"Amazing Grace. Amazing Grace. Get ready! Winds are 35 knots from the northwest! I repeat: Winds are coming from the northwest!"

We apparently weren't through the storm after all, only in the *eye* of it. The winds would now be coming from the *opposite* direction. Although we could barely make out their transmission, we tried to hail our companion vessel and thank them for the information. Then we scurried out to adjust our sails.

Sure enough! Within a few minutes we were slammed with 35-knot winds coming from the northwest. The first blast felt like it would knock us over. Thank goodness we'd had some warning, which allowed us to prepare for the change. We didn't like to think about what it would have been like to try to change the sail arrangement after the fact. Those prayers were really working!

As dawn approached, the storm was diminishing. The winds had dropped to 20 knots, and the wave heights had decreased as well. It was possible for one of us to sleep. We were pleased that our Monitor self-steering wind-vane had worked so well throughout the storm. To hand-steer through that mess truly would have been awful.

A couple hours of sleep really helped. The storm had passed, and we decided to turn into an anchorage in San Carlos bay. It was a "roll-y" anchorage, but we didn't care. Despite the perpetual rocking motion due to ocean swells, it felt great to just "drop the hook" (anchor) and relax after that terrifying night.

"Fred, look. There is a boat approaching us," I said.

It was almost evening and we had been anchored only a short time. There were no other boats there. Along with feeling exhausted from the storm, we were apprehensive. We weren't sure what to expect in Mexico and felt somewhat vulnerable. We had heard many stories of cruising boats being attacked or robbed, and the "rule" amongst cruisers was to try to anchor in a place where there were other boats. Unlike some others, we had taken no weapons with us, for they were illegal in most countries. We did, however, have a huge can of "Bear Scare" (pepper spray) should we need some kind of defense. Fred got it out while we watched the small boat with four men in it approach.

They appeared grim. *"Buenas tardes. Por favor, necessitamos ayuda,"* they said.

After trying to tell them that we didn't speak Spanish, we finally began to understand that one man had been stung by poison fish spines while diving for lobster, and they were hoping we could offer some kind of medical help. He looked like he was in great pain but trying not to show it. I found our medical bag and did what I could, but it wasn't much. We apologized for not being able to do more. Since they spoke no English and we had very few Spanish skills, much of the communication was by body language and hand gestures. They thanked us and gave us some lobster, which we felt hesitant to accept since we had done so little. They insisted, and as they motored off we felt sad we had been so suspicious at their approach—especially when they had been so gracious and had only needed help. They also had not wanted a handout, but were proud about paying for what they received. I began to have a new appreciation for the people of this country—an appreciation that would continue to grow in the months ahead.

"I know we need to be careful when we are in foreign places," I said later to Fred. "But I hope we don't always have negative expectations— that we give people the benefit of the doubt and expect positive things to happen."

"I agree. We are guests in these countries, and we want to treat people with respect and consideration, not suspicion. When we're fearful of them, I'm sure it's communicated, and we don't want that. It's been a long couple of days. We'll do better next time."

As we went to bed that night, I thought how pleased I had been to be able to communicate a little in Spanish. I had been listening to Spanish cassette tapes all the way down the coast, and had really learned quite a bit. It felt like a game to me. If I could communicate my wishes, and understand theirs, I'd *win!* I was anxious to learn and practice more, and I was sure I would have the opportunity.

It felt *so* good to get a full night's sleep, take a shower, and eat a genuine meal. We were in high spirits the next day as we continued toward Cabo. We motored along in a light wind with just the main sail up. We had found that the boat motion was more stable with a sail up while motoring; we were not rolling so much with the waves.

Suddenly we noticed that the sea was filled with tiny creatures floating on the surface.

"What *are* they? They are everywhere. There are *millions* of them!" I said incredulously.

Looking carefully, we discovered they were tiny lobsters. We must have been in some sort of breeding grounds. We hoped they would all reach maturity. Yummm!

That afternoon we encountered a school of dolphins—perhaps 20 of them. How thrilling it was! One of them jumped straight up in the air about 15 feet! We wanted them to continue swimming with us, as they darted back and forth in the bow wake, jumping and frolicking like a bunch of kids. We had run forward to the bow to watch them.

"I've heard they can communicate with humans," I said. "Let's try singing to them to see if they will stay."

Fred's whistled version of the Notre Dame Fight song didn't work. They soon were gone. Maybe I should have tried it. Next time. This university in the sea was fascinating. What an incredible world we live in.

We continued through the night, but thankfully there was no storm. The following day we entered Turtle Bay. Our information showed that this bay had good anchorage spots and a fuel dock as well. Besides, reports on the weather fax predicted that a storm was approaching from the southwest. It was time to tuck ourselves into a good anchorage.

"This bay is really big," I said. We looked around. "The fuel dock and village are way over there. That's where all those other sailboats are anchored. There must be 10 or more."

"But look at the chart. This bay is open to the southwest. A storm coming in from that direction will send the swell right into that anchorage. I think we should anchor over here in this corner, where we'll have protection from the incoming swell and winds," Fred replied.

I knew he was right, but I had really been looking forward to some company and being with the other cruising boats. I reluctantly agreed, and we anchored by ourselves in a far, sheltered corner of the bay.

No storm or high winds came that night, and the following morning we pulled up anchor and motored over to the fuel dock by the small village. Many boats were waiting in line for fuel, and we motored around waiting our turn. The pier that extended from shore was at least 20 feet high. To get fuel, we had to drop an anchor, then back in toward the pier and throw a stern line up to the folks on the pier. When we were tied down, they would drop a diesel hose to us so we could fill our tanks. When we finished, they pulled up the hose and tossed down a jar for us to put our money in and toss back up to them. We had never seen a system quite like this and didn't relish the thought of trying it, but hey, "When in Mexico, do as the Mexicans do!"

After waiting two hours, it was finally our turn. Fred let out anchor chain while I backed the boat. We needed enough chain out to get close to the pier, but not so much that we'd run into it. It was a tricky process. After a few adjustments, we thought we were close enough. Since there was no way I could throw that stern line up to the men on the pier, Fred ran back from the bow and threw the line. Nope! Not close enough. We retrieved our line; he ran forward to let out more chain, ran back and tried it again. Finally, after two more tries, we were tied up and they threw down the hose. Fred was sweating by now!

"It's taking forever to fill the tank with this Baja Filter," I said. Fred held the hose and ran the fuel through our new filter, which I held into the tank inlet.

"I guess that's why we had to wait so long for our turn. I don't want to add the diesel without the filter. Look." There in the bottom of the filter was about a tablespoon of small gravel and water.

We continued to patiently add the diesel through the filter. Finally, we were finished and pulled anchor. Thank goodness we had managed to successfully pitch them our money, too. As we motored through the anchorage, a couple of boats called out to us.

"Hey, *Amazing Grace*. Why don't you come join us? Are you having a private party over there on the other side of the bay?" they teased.

We told them that a storm was coming from the southwest, but nobody seemed very interested, so we made our way back to our protected corner of the bay. I was sure that everyone thought we were antisocial and wouldn't want anything to do with us when we arrived in Cabo. It had taken most of the day to get the fuel and we were tired. By afternoon another sailboat had come over to join us. It was *Manana*, with a young couple we had met before, so we invited them over for dinner.

"You are right about that other anchorage," Rick said. "If a storm comes from the southwest, they will have the full fury of the ocean coming directly at them."

We enjoyed a fine evening together and turned in. During the night, we heard the wind howling and felt the boat rocking, although not uncomfortably. Sure enough, the storm was here. I was so glad we were where we were—and hoped the best for the other boats.

By morning the storm was really blowing, with torrents of rain and strong winds from the southwest. Large ocean swells barreled into the bay. Soon, about six other boats tried to anchor close to us. It was a difficult process for them in the drenching rain, high wind, and waves—even in this protected corner of the bay. They reported a horrific night, with no sleep and violent motion on their boats, which had been anchored by the village. The ocean swell and waves had pounded them relentlessly. Some of the boats had gone aground and sustained significant damage. Even the pier had been partially destroyed. They said they could hardly wait for light so they could move out of there.

After hearing their accounts we recalled that, in preparing to go cruising, we had read about the "group think" or "herd mentality" danger. Rather than using their individual observations and judgments for making decisions, boaters sometimes looked around and decided that, "if all the other boats were doing it, it must be OK." This was the case in Turtle Bay. One of the boaters who'd anchored by the village said later, "Look. One smart boat and 50 dummies, but we went with the dummies!" It was another lesson we would not forget.

Before we moved on, we waited for the stormy seas to subside. We spent the time reading, talking, and reflecting. *"Why are we doing this?"* had been a frequent comment when things were tough, although usually said with a laugh. We knew we could simply fly to these destinations in a fraction of the time it was taking us to sail, and be lounging by a pool somewhere instead of anxiously awaiting weather reports. Instead, we were going three or four days without a shower, sleeping in two or three hour shifts, being thrown around and scared out of our wits while feeling a little sick in the process! Maybe we were like pioneers crossing the prairies, or pilgrims crossing to a new world: Frontiers were there to cross, conquer, and explore. When we got to an anchorage, we certainly felt like conquerors. Then it was a real high. Fred reminded me that, in our 25th anniversary card, he'd written that I'd have made a good pioneer woman. I was not so sure!

We were invited over to *Manana* for dinner, and while there we were able to talk on their ham radio to Cheryl, a boating friend of ours in Portland. What fun! We learned that it was snowing there. (Difficult to imagine!) She promised she would call Page, who would call Mom, to let everyone know we were okay and thinking of them. Hearing Cheryl's familiar voice made me homesick. Fred gave me a big hug, which helped, but I sure missed those loved ones! *Why were we doing this?*

The following morning dawned gloriously. The sun sparkled on the water, assuring us that all was well, and soon there was a mass exodus of sailboats as everyone pulled anchor and left the bay. There were seven of us in a line as we turned south. Boy, did it feel good to be "on the road again."

"You know, the landscape here looks like what I imagine the moon's would be. There sure isn't much vegetation," I said, as we sailed along with a pleasant wind.

"With as much rain as we've had since entering Mexico, you'd think it would be greener. Maybe it's just because we're "blucky" to get all the rain," Fred said with a grin.

As we sailed into the night, the winds began picking up, and soon we were in turbulent seas again. Where was that "usual" northwest wind? It was now out of the northeast and, combined with the northwest swell, made for messy seas.

"You know, 'they' lied to us! They all said it was easy after the Oregon/Northern California coast," I complained.

We talked with several other boats during the night, and that helped. Misery *does* love company, I guess. We went through four or five sail changes trying to find something that worked. Finally, we took down all the sails because the wind was so strong, and, with only the dodger to push us, we were sailing at almost five knots. Neither the wind-vane nor the autopilot could hold the course as we were pushed around by the swell, so we had to hand-steer from the cockpit.

"Sailing, sailing, over the bounding main," sang Fred from the helm. He was trying to keep our spirits up, and it worked. We felt badly for Tom, who was "single-handing it" on *Laissez Faire*. Sailing a boat alone, with no crew, sounded just plain crazy to us. He enjoyed that we kept him company on the radio, and he often had us laughing. He was from the Tacoma area, and, although we had never met him, we had come to know him just from the sound of his voice. He reassured us that we were in "good hands."

We were now getting good use out of our solar panels (when it was not raining) and our water-maker. The effort and expense of installing that equipment was paying off. It was good to know that the water we used from our tanks was safe to drink. It was also getting hot. One afternoon I kept taking off clothes until I was down to my underwear. There wasn't anyone around to see, so why not!? I had also begun to sing Christmas carols, for Christmas would arrive in two weeks. I thoroughly enjoyed the preparations for the season when back home. It surely didn't feel the same here. I couldn't go shopping and didn't want to bake or decorate. Maybe later.

The wind and sea had calmed down, and we both felt good, although tired. Sometimes, just for fun, Fred would yell and scream like a football player gearing up for a game. I got into it, too, and laughing always helped.

"Hey, come out here," Fred yelled from the cockpit. "Look at that sunset."

"Wow! That's gorgeous! Just a minute," I replied, and ran to turn on the stereo. We had made a cassette tape of 10 different renditions of the song, "Amazing Grace." The kids thought we were crazy, thinking no one would want to listen to the same song that many times. *We* did! As we sat cuddled together in the cockpit in calm seas, enjoying the golden glow of the setting sun, with its pinks, oranges, and purples shading the evening sky, we listened to the song that always gave us "goose-bumps" and comfort, and we felt truly blucky!

"You know, we never seem to take the time to do this at home—to just sit and appreciate the sunset," I said.

"And likely it would not be so sweet had it not been for the struggles of last night," responded Fred.

"Yeah! There's some good in everything, right?" I tried not to think of the tough times that surely lay ahead of us, but just to enjoy the present.

During the night watch in calm seas, I held the kitchen timer in my hands as I curled up in a corner of the cockpit. Setting it for 15 minutes, I allowed myself to doze for a few minutes before getting up to check our progress and look for approaching traffic. It was amazing to me that virtually every time I did this I would wake myself before the timer rang. Too many times we had heard about someone unintentionally falling asleep on night watch and perilous things happening. We believed that it was okay to fall asleep *if* we first set the timer, so that we would not sleep more than 15 minutes.

"Look at that," Fred said one night. It was a huge cruise ship all lit up with hundreds of lights.

"Let's call him on the VHF," I said. Seldom did commercial boats answer us when we hailed them on the sea, but that time the ship responded.

"How's the weather down south?" we asked.

"I t'ink it not so bad," he responded in a Norwegian lilt. We invited him over to enjoy some fresh tuna we had caught earlier in the day. He laughed and said he'd take a rain check. Shortly after midnight we were contacted by other cruisers who said that our friend, Tom, on *Laissez Faire*, was in big trouble. His engine had failed, he couldn't start it, there was no wind for sailing, and he was drifting toward the rocks off Cape Lazaro. We checked the chart to find that we were 20 miles away, and it would take us almost four hours to get to him. Apparently there were no other boats closer, so we increased our speed as we motored towards his position (although it was backtracking for us, and going against the current). Meanwhile, several other boats, listening to the situation on the radio, began offering Tom suggestions on how to fix the motor. He ran back and forth between the radio and the engine compartment. Nothing seemed to work. It was a tense time for all of us, knowing that if he hit the rocks he could well lose the boat. Three hours later we were still five miles away. We heard his voice on the radio.

"Pan, pan. Pan, pan. Hello all stations, hello all stations," and we all feared the worst, as this was the second most urgent radio emergency call, just under Mayday. Our fears, however, were quickly relieved as we heard Tom say, "Hallelujah! The engine is running!"

There were shouts of joy on the radio from all of us. It was a night of calm seas, but still no sleep for most of us who had been monitoring the situation. We decided to break our safety "rule" of not entering a harbor at night when we saw on the chart that an anchorage in Santa Maria Bay was a short distance away. We called Tom and said we were going to stop there, and he decided to do the same. It had an indirect entrance, requiring us to go to the far end of the mouth of the bay to find a narrow channel before starting to enter. We breathed a sigh of relief after dropping the hook with the help of the moonlight. Tom followed shortly thereafter. But, to our dismay, he was coming straight in.

"*Laissez Faire, Laissez Faire*. Don't come any closer! You must go all the way to the south end before coming into the bay. There are underwater rocks here," we said on the radio. We could see the running lights of the boat stop, then back up and head south. Soon we heard Tom's voice on the radio.

"Good grief. I can't believe I didn't check the chart better! In my haste to get inside, I just wanted to cut the corner. Thanks again. I guess I'm tired. It's been a long night!" What an understatement.

The following morning we enjoyed meeting Tom in person as we shared a cup of coffee and heard his account of the frustrating and fearful event. He was so grateful for everyone's attempts to help fix the engine, and our coming to try to tow him to safety. We were all willing to help because we knew that any of us could find ourselves in a similar position, and dependent on others to respond to our needs. There were other boats in the bay that had shared the difficulties of the last couple nights, and was it ever good to talk with them. Once again the immediacy of situation created intimacy in relationships. We felt like old friends!

We had been listening to the ham nets, which were similar to the VHF radio nets. In order to talk on the ham radio, one needs a specific license demonstrating one's ability to use Morse code. Fred had obtained his license but had not yet tried calling someone other than the Coast Guard. He tried the next day and connected with Ralph, who ran the

Mañana net and lived in Aloha, Oregon, close to Portland. He was a delightful guy who was willing to do a phone patch so we could call Page. It worked! What a joy to talk with her. Just hearing her voice was deeply reassuring, and helped us feel closer to her. She giggled when talking with us, as she remembered to say "over" when she was done with each response. There were lots of tears for me afterwards.

Lobster fishermen came by the boats in their dugouts, which were very similar to those of early Native Americans. They usually didn't want money for the lobster but would trade for canned food or cigarettes. There were no stores nearby (so no need for cash), and they were tired of eating fish.

"I think I'll put these in the freezer for our Christmas dinner in Cabo," I said to Fred after trading some canned food for several small lobsters. "What a treat that will be."

"No turkey? It will be another 'first,' that's for sure. When you're done, do you want to take the dinghy into the lagoon? Others have done it and say it's really cool," Fred suggested.

"It's pretty tricky getting in there," I replied. "I've heard that a number of dinghies got flipped in the breaking surf trying to enter, but I'm game to try."

We boarded the dinghy and prepared to be dumped, but, after a cautious run, we were able to get through the waves and congratulated ourselves with "high fives." Suddenly the engine died. We had run into a fish net, and it was wrapped around our prop. Oh my! We had celebrated too soon, it seemed. Fred took off his jeans and jumped into the water to untangle the prop. At least the water wasn't very cold. We hoped the net was not damaged. We soon were freed of the net and moved into the lagoon and mangrove swamps. The labyrinth of mangrove roots reaching to the water and the density of vegetation intrigued me. We saw a few fishing villages composed of shacks covered with tarpaper. I couldn't imagine being in those shacks during the storms we had encountered. A few men and children were about, but we saw no women.

After returning to *Grace*, Fred got out my electric keyboard. "Why don't you play some Christmas songs?"

He knew that would please me. I played for almost two hours. However, it was difficult to get into the Christmas mood when all about us things were so different. Sometimes we longed for the familiar, even amidst the joy of seeing and doing things that were so diverse. While I played and sang, Fred checked the weather fax for tomorrow's forecast. We wanted to make our last leg to Cabo and hoped for good weather. The outlook was okay, so we decided to leave in the morning. We thought it would be about 36 hours to Cabo. If we motored, we went about five knots per hour, but if we could sail, we often did seven or even eight knots per hour if the wind was from a good direction. What we *didn't* want was wind coming from the direction we wanted to go, or "on the nose."

The following night, while underway, the winds turned to the northeast. It was blowing like "stink" and the seas were lousy. Then the wind turned again to being "on the nose" and we were really having a rough ride.

"I can't believe it. We spend hours gathering weather information, and yet we never get what they predict. There's nothing 'usual' about these conditions—yet *again!*" I groused.

"I guess this is what they mean by 'local conditions.' It seems that all reports are qualified by saying, 'except for local conditions,'" Fred sighed. Then we heard *Charlie's Girl* being hailed on the radio. They were another boat from Portland, and although we had not met, we had talked on the radio.

"What are you doing over there, Bob? Checking out the real estate?" said *Snow Goose.*

"Well, Smarty, it's a lot smoother over here close to shore than out where you are, where the waves have a chance to build up," came the answer. "I've got one foot on the boat and the other one on the beach. We're making pretty good time. See you in Cabo. We'll be having a drink by the pool by the time you get in!"

So that's the secret! We tried to work our way over closer to shore as well, but it took several hours and made our distance to travel even farther. Calling *Laissez Faire,* we found that he was well offshore in order to avoid the hazards of the coastline. However, the seas had built up to 20-foot vicious waves. He was getting beaten up, and unable to lower his sails because they were stuck. He was just holding on and trying to ride it out. He was also worried about staying on watch, because he had gotten little sleep for the last several nights. We offered to call him every 15 minutes to wake him should he fall asleep. He thought that was a great idea and we started a radio check schedule.

After several hours of such a routine, I called and said, "Tom, you should have been a radio announcer. Your voice always sounds so deep, smooth, and in control."

"Ha!" was his reply. "If you only knew that behind that smooth voice hides a body filled with sheer terror!" He always said something to make us laugh, even in awful conditions.

It was another long night, but finally we turned the corner around the Baja Peninsula and sailed past the huge rocks that guarded the entrance to the Cabo San Lucas harbor. We had arrived! What a welcome sight. It was sunny and warm and we quickly changed to shorts. Lots of boats were at anchor or on mooring buoys in the ocean just off the Hacienda Hotel. We had learned from our cruising notes that we could stay on one of their buoys for 50 dollars a week and have use of their hotel pool and grounds. However, we decided to take the hit on the budget and dock at the lovely new marina for one or two nights in order to make it easier to get some needed work done. When we got in and tied up, it was a definite "Miller Time!" It had taken 13 days and nights to reach this place from San Diego. Of the six nights we spent at sea, four were in stormy conditions. Seven days we had waited for better weather, twice waiting three days in an anchorage. We had experienced winds over 40 knots, plus we almost never had the "usual" northwest winds. But now we were here, and the weariness in our bones began to melt away in the warm Mexican sun and the anticipation of fun ashore.

"Imagine trying to make that trip in a boat other than *Grace*," Fred said.

"I know what you mean. I marvel at how sturdy she is and how well she functioned in all those conditions," I agreed. "We've really come to trust her and appreciate her. We are so blucky to have her!"

"Aye, aye to that, Admiral," was his response, with a twinkle in the eye.

The following morning we gathered all of our ship's papers and headed ashore to be cleared into the country and the port. We had heard many stories of unfriendly personnel, long lines, hassle from the officials, and even bribes that were necessary to complete the process. We had to visit each of the immigration, customs, port, and port captain's offices to have the necessary papers signed. We decided we would make an extra effort to be friendly with each of the officials, try to speak some Spanish, and show appreciation in being here. At the first office, we heard some American loudly complaining and waving his papers around. Apparently he was getting a real "run around" (as only the Mexican officials could orchestrate), and he was getting nowhere. Although we felt the American was demanding, rude, and (in our opinion) getting what he deserved, our anxiety increased as we waited in line.

Finally, we stepped up to the window, where an official asked for our papers in a bored voice, making no eye contact. We politely greeted him in Spanish and wished him "Feliz Navidad" as well. Fred had noticed a scrawny little Christmas tree decorated with a few sad ornaments on the counter. It was a true "Charlie Brown" Christmas tree. In his best Spanish, Fred tried to say that he liked the tree. Surprised, the official looked first at our smiling faces then slowly over at that sad little tree. He shook his head, but with the hint of a smile on his face. It worked! Treat people like you want to be treated and it works every time. We quickly were given our papers and made our way through the whole process without any problem.

Walking the streets of Cabo was fascinating. Of course there were the usual tourist enticements—souvenir shops, tour agencies, and hustlers on every corner that attempted to interest folks in the many "time-share" programs. Vivid colors assaulted our eyes via shop displays, and ever-present Latin music gave a "fiesta" feeling to the business area. Dogs were everywhere, and often missing large patches of hair. They were skinny and didn't appear to belong to anyone in particular. Along the dirt side streets with their crumbling sidewalks, we saw the homes and *tiendas* used by locals. They were small, but clean and neat. Everywhere the people were friendly and would smile and say "*Hola*" if we did the same. We could hardly wait to do more exploring.

There were so many things to accomplish before the kids arrived the following week. We wanted to take on fuel, wash the salt off the boat, do our laundry, and tidy up inside. The problem was that it always took so long to do any little thing. The heat was an adjustment to us as well, and we rigged all the shade awnings we had made at home to keep the sun off the deck of the boat. We found a little Mexican style, reasonably priced hotel for the kids. It wasn't like the glitzy tourist hotels, but it had lots of charm and the real feel of this country.

When we called Page, we learned that it was snowing in Oregon, and she needed to drive to the bank in Newberg to get Dawn's passport from the safety deposit box. Page and Mom would be flying to Tempe, Arizona, for Dawn's graduation the following day. Driving in the snow? Now we had something else to worry about.

We needed to take on diesel, so we borrowed extra five-gallon fuel containers from some other boats and went to the fuel dock.

"Man, these cans are heavy! I didn't realize that diesel weighed so much," I said, while we laboriously carried the containers back to the boat. I could only carry one, and then only for short distances at a time. It took seven cans to fill the tank. Once back at the boat, it was difficult to lift them aboard, and of course it was a lengthy process to use the Baja filter to drain them into the tank. It was an all-afternoon process.

By evening we were tired, sweaty, and concerned about Page driving in the snow. In addition, I decided I needed to find our Christmas decorations and began the hunt. I had carefully listed the contents of all our lockers but somehow had missed the location of those decorations. After a while, it seemed imperative that I find those elusive decorations *now!*

"Kay, slow down," Fred exclaimed, when he saw the shambles I was making of the boat as I emptied out locker after locker. "We'll find them."

"But I've looked everywhere! It won't be Christmas without them," I said, in a voice close to tears. "And besides, Dawn graduates tomorrow, and we won't be there!"

"Ah. So that's it," Fred said, with a warm and understanding smile. My being upset really wasn't about decorations. "Come here." As he wrapped his arms around me, my tears broke the dam and burst forth. After a good cry, I found the decorations, and we wearily turned in for the night.

The following day we moved the boat from the marina to one of the mooring buoys about 50 yards off the beach. It was not as convenient to go ashore but sure a lot cheaper. It was also roll-y at times, especially when the wind was from the south. We'd even known of folks getting seasick when anchored in those conditions. Ahhh—the cruising life!

When going ashore, we often stopped at one of the local bars catering to cruisers. It was a great place to have coffee (or a wonderful Mexican *cerveza*), write letters, connect with those we had met in other ports, or meet new people. Everyone had stories to tell, and we never tired of telling or hearing them. There was also the "cruiser's net" on the VHF radio each morning that shared a wealth of information, including whether cruisers or their guests were going to be returning to the States and could take mail. This was the only reliable way to ensure that letters would be delivered. Cruisers would place U.S. stamps on their envelopes, leaving them unsealed so they could be examined if needed. Once they were in the States, the traveler would seal and deposit the letters in a mailbox at their arrival airport. We all hurried to write letters when we heard someone would be a mail carrier.

LETTERS WERE AN IMPORTANT CONNECTION WITH HOME.

On Sunday, Fred and I wanted to attend a local church. We had spotted a non-denominational Protestant church on one of the side roads and went there. It was a small, unpretentious building, but people greeted us warmly in Spanish, and the pastor came over and introduced himself to us before the service.

"We are delighted you are here," he said enthusiastically in excellent English.

When the worship service began, we found that each phrase the pastor spoke was then translated into English by Maria, a young woman we had met earlier. The mixed group of locals and visitors could all understand. The singing was joyous, although many of the songs were new to us. We felt surrounded by warmth and caring, which we greatly appreciated.

Browsing through the many shops on the streets of Cabo was an adventure in itself. We wanted to get something for ourselves and decided on a small nativity set carved of whalebone. Of course we negotiated the price, which is an expected part of a purchase. We had made and mailed shell Christmas ornaments as gifts for family and friends while still in the States. We had seen something similar in a boutique shop selling for an outrageous price, but we knew we could make our own. This year we had decided that the "rule" for the family exchange was that no gift could cost more than five dollars and they were to be bought here in Mexico. It was a challenge to find something for each person, but lots of fun as well.

"Hey, look at these sandals," Fred said. "The soles are made of old tire treads."

"What a great idea." I said. "The Mexicans are really creative with recycling."

Talking with people in the stores was great fun for me; I had the opportunity to practice Spanish. It was always amazing how people would warm to my efforts and go out of their way to help me learn more. They did not care that it was imperfect but seemed to greatly appreciate my attempts to speak their language. There was usually lots of laughing in the process. While in the marina, I had befriended a 17-year old employee who loved trying to help me, while I helped him with English. It was a great trade off.

One night there was a "Cruisers' Christmas Party" at the local hangout. There was special music from local as well as cruising singers, and a street juggler from San Francisco who was single-handing on *Adventura*. He had even performed for the queen of England and practiced by juggling bowling balls, which he carried on his boat. He would take the balls in his dinghy to the beach to practice. We never saw him drop one! The party was great fun, but a little bittersweet; we all missed family and loved ones back home, and it really didn't seem like Christmas.

When Dawn and Page arrived the following day we were ecstatic. They looked *so* good! My face hurt from the constant grinning. It seemed that everyone tried to talk at once and there were never too many hugs. Steve arrived the day after that, and we delighted in showing them this charming town and area. Of course we missed Lance terribly, but we were glad to hear that he was enjoying Vail and the "ski-bum" life.

"Look at what Lance sent me to bring here," Dawn said. In her hands was a package that contained small gifts for all of us.

"That is absolutely incredible. Lance is the original 'last minute' kid. For him to have planned ahead to do this was nothing short of a miracle!" I replied. We could hardly wait to taste all the gourmet foods he had sent.

The girls loved the little hotel we had arranged. They also enjoyed the beach and pool time and wanted to take home a nice tan. Page and Steve attended one of the many time-share presentations so they could get the free promotional gift of a parasailing experience or a free restaurant dinner. We had taught them well how to stretch their money and get "good deals." We moved *Grace* back into the marina so that it was easier for the kids to come to the boat for meals and down time. The sun and heat took some adjustment for them as well.

On Christmas day we had our traditional "hunt" for hidden gifts for the kids. On the boat there weren't many places to hide them, but we made do. It was fun and meaningful to have some of our family traditions to express the holiday when so much was *so* different. Fred had sent the girls shopping for my gift, and I'm sure they spent more than the limit on the beautiful traditional Mexican lace blouse I received. But I loved it! We laughed at the five-dollar gifts we had all found here in Mexico. After going to church on Christmas Eve, we decided that it was too hot to cook in the boat, so we barbequed a turkey, cut it up, and made turkey tacos—or Christmas dinner "a la Mexico." We also cooked the wonderful lobster tails from our freezer another night.

"Did you know that we got these eight lobsters for three pairs of sunglasses, two packages of cigarettes, and one baseball cap?" I inquired of the kids.

"They are delicious," said Steve. "You've got a spear gun. Can we go get some more?"

"Only the locals can use spear guns to get the lobster. We want to respect the law, so we must get them by trading or buying them. That's harder to do here in town because the fishermen sell to the restaurants. It's easy when we are in more remote areas," Fred replied. "But let's take the boat out for some fishing."

Our fishing trip was not so successful. Steve managed to catch a 39-inch skinny fish that none of us recognized. Later, back at the dock, a local told us it was a "needle nose" but not good for eating. Oh well, it looked great in a picture! While on our fishing excursion, we also had the opportunity to do some snorkeling in one of the areas well known for its colorful fish and coral reef. Later, we swam ashore from *Grace* and enjoyed the dollar margaritas from one of the many *palapa* beach bars. Beautiful weather, gorgeous beaches, clear ocean water, good snorkeling, fabulous *cerveza*, dollar margaritas, and being together: How blucky we were!

The days passed too quickly, and soon Page and Steve returned home. It was *so* hard to say goodbye, for this time we did not know just when we would see them again. It helped that Dawn was staying another week.

"We'll see you sometime this summer, right?" Page asked tearfully.

"Well, we hope so," Fred said. "If we can find a safe place to leave the boat, we'll fly home for a couple of weeks. We don't know where or when that will be right now."

We moved *Grace* back out to a mooring buoy and slowed our pace considerably after they were gone, but Dawn didn't complain.

"Hey, I don't mind sitting in the sun," Dawn said. "I have to return to the 'real world' soon enough and hunt for a job now that I'm through school."

"We used to call our life in the States that," I said, "but our thinking has changed. Hanging on in the middle of a storm or sitting in the cockpit watching a beautiful sunset—now *those* things seem truly 'real.' What you're going back to is 'the *other* world.'"

Before we left Cabo, we wanted to call my mom, because we knew it might be some time before we would be able to do that again. We had encountered difficulties trying to get a phone patch through one of the ham radio operators. Finally, we tried a local phone. Now that was an experience! The few public phones available for long distance calls were usually outdoors, in a hot and mosquito-filled area, with long lines of people waiting to use them. The operators often spoke no English. But persistence paid off, and we finally made contact with her. Chuck, her husband, was having many medical problems, but they were receiving good care where they lived. They both encouraged us to enjoy our dream. I wondered if I would have had the courage to be so supportive if I were in their shoes.

Dawn's time to return home came all too soon, and we tearfully bid her goodbye. Each of the kids looked forward to joining us in some other exotic port. They also gave us great support to continue our journey. Buoyed by that, we set aside the sadness of her leaving and began to prepare for our next passage.

"Lots of cruisers are heading north to winter in the Sea of Cortez," I said one evening. "There are many advantages to doing that, and La Paz is an interesting area of Mexico."

"I know. It's a difficult decision whether to see the Sea or go south, but I'm thinking Costa Rica," Fred replied.

For us, there was great allure in the idea of cruising on to Europe. However, it would take an additional year to get there if we went up into the Sea, because weather patterns dictated when boats could travel in certain areas. Many boaters had waited out the hurricane season in the northern part of the Sea of Cortez only to become so comfortable with the lifestyle there that they never moved on.

"Do we want to do that?" Fred asked.

"You're right. Let's go south. I'm anxious to see that 'Gold Coast' we've heard so much about. To avoid hurricane season we need to be south of Mexico by the end of May, right?"

That gave us five months to explore Mexico from the Pacific coast side. Out came our next set of charts for crossing the Sea of Cortez from the Baja peninsula to the Mexican mainland, and along with the charts came the familiar (yet still uncomfortable) anxiety of an upcoming ocean passage.

Seven
The Cruisers' Gold Coast

"Did you hear those folks say that Isla Isabella is a mile and a half away from its charted position?" Fred asked as we prepared to leave Cabo.

"Yeah, comforting, eh?" I shook my head and chuckled. "Apparently that will be the problem all throughout Mexico and Central America. The GPS will give us our exact location, but all the charts are a little inaccurate. So I can plot a course to a certain bay and, if we follow the GPS, we will end up a mile or two *inland.*"

"Hey—it just makes for more adventure. We are sailing 250 miles across the Sea of Cortez to a tiny island that isn't where it's charted to be. If it was easy—*everybody* would do it," Fred said with a laugh. That had become a favorite saying when we lamented the more difficult aspects of cruising.

The weather information from our fax looked favorable, and we had decided to leave the following day when into the harbor sailed *Ossuna.* It was *so* good to see them.

"Maybe we should delay our passage to spend more time with *Ossuna* and see the football game," I said to Fred.

"I don't think so. You know, we can always find reasons to stay— good ones at that. If we give in to that kind of thinking, we will never leave. We'll see *Ossuna* today, and we'll see them again down south," Fred replied gently. He was right—it was only an excuse to stay.

As we left Cabo San Lucas harbor about noon, friends yelled to us, wishing us safe seas. The crossing of the Sea of Cortez was often a rough one in strong winter winds, but we were hoping for good weather. The skies were cloudless, the sun warm, and the sea a little choppy. While there would be a number of boats heading our direction, none were going that day.

After 10 hours under sail, the seas smoothed out and the ride was nice, but I worried about the ominous clouds overtaking us from the west and blocking out the moon. It was so much more enjoyable if there was moonlight at night.

"I so badly want just *one* pleasant night at sea," I said to Fred when we changed watches in the middle of the night.

I was to get my wish that night, and was I ever grateful. The wind was strong enough to push us along at a reasonable speed, but the water remained calm; *Grace* enjoyed an easy, flowing motion. The air was fairly warm, even this far out to sea, and occasionally the moonlight peeked through the clouds. It was almost perfect.

We continued sailing the next day, glad to be using our water-maker and keeping the batteries charged with our solar panels. We didn't like using the water-maker in the harbors, but at sea it was great, even if it only produced about 1.4 gallons per hour. Always we conserved water, sometimes even using seawater to cook with while at sea. Showers were short, and really *could* be called "spit baths."

Sailing our second day was roll-y due to the strong northern swell, but we were not complaining. It could be *so* much worse. We saw no other boats.

The second night I was sitting in the cockpit enjoying the gift of a beautiful dawn slowly advancing in the eastern sky. I decided to throw out our fishing line since it was almost daylight. Over time, we had developed quite a technique for catching fish after a cruising friend had given us some unique tips that we adopted. Prior to that, we had a huge mess from trying to kill our catch by clubbing and bleeding large flopping fish. Such efforts left blood and fish scales all over the cockpit and stern deck. Now, our large fishing line was tied to the stern of the boat and connected to a rubber "stubber." When the stubber stretched, we knew a fish had taken our lure. The "drill" began when one of us would yell, "Fish on!" Fred would then pull the fish toward the boat until he could grab it by the tail and bring it aboard, holding it upside down over a large bucket. Meanwhile, I ran to get out the knife and fill a plastic ear syringe with an ounce or two of cheap tequila. When the fish was upside down over the bucket, I squirted the tequila into the gills of the fish, and instantly it would go to sleep! No thrashing about, no blood and scales all over the cockpit! Fred would then bleed the anesthetized fish into the bucket and fillet it so that we could freeze some of the meat.

Sometimes filleting the fish in a roll-y or bouncing boat caused Fred to go a little "green around the gills," but he got the job done. Our drill worked fantastically, and there was virtually no mess to clean up—other than the bucket. Many people insisted this was a "fish tale" when we told them about it, but it was absolute truth. Besides being good for us, it was good for the fish, and they died blissfully! We had great success with fishing in the Pacific and could almost guarantee a catch if we put out our line. The fish were big, too, often weighing 20 pounds or more.

I was quite pleased with myself that morning as we approached Isla Isabella. I could see it off in the distance, and it reminded me of the movie, *South Pacific*, and the island, Bali Hai, with its mountainous interior. We had slowed our approach so that we would arrive in daylight, and though Fred was sleeping at the moment, I knew he would be awake shortly. So I put out our line and soon afterwards saw the stubber starting to stretch. I knew I could not bring the fish aboard by myself, so I thought I'd drag it for a while, which would likely kill it, and we could pull it in and cook it. A short time later, Fred appeared in the companionway, rubbing his eyes and stretching.

"Hey, look! I caught us a fish for breakfast," I said with great pride. But when Fred pulled it in, the only thing left on the lure was the head of a rather large fish.

"Looks like something else ate our breakfast treat," he laughed.

Not a good idea to drag a fish too long, I reflected, shuddering to think about how big the fish (shark?) must have been that ate my catch.

"Let's try again," he suggested, and sure enough, in 15 minutes we had another fish on the lure and hauled in a 30-inch, 15 to 20 pound skip jack tuna. While we preferred other more flavorful types of tuna, this kind was acceptable once in a while. I had learned different ways to cook it so that it tasted good.

We were excited to drop our anchor in the little bay of Isla Isabella mid-morning. Located 20 miles off the mainland coast of Mexico, the island was a nesting ground for several kinds of birds, including the blue-footed booby. Turning off the engine, Fred triumphantly announced, "It's 'Miller Time!'"

"Absolutely," I replied, and ran to get two cold beers to celebrate our successful passage. By now this had become our ritual at the end of each leg or passage, and we relished that cold beer regardless of what time of day it was, feeling we had certainly earned it. We never drank alcoholic beverages while we were underway. It didn't help the "queasies," and we wanted to be at our best for any possible emergencies. There were eight other sailboats in the bay, which was deep and had a very rocky bottom. This made it difficult to get the anchor set, and we tried a couple of times before we felt good about it. If a storm were to come up, we definitely did not want to drag anchor and be blown ashore.

"I sure hope we can get that anchor up when it's time to leave," Fred said.

I wasn't worried about leaving at that point; I was just enjoying arriving.

We were tickled to see the boat with the folks who had hosted the baptism in San Diego. The skipper rowed over and we spent three hours talking. We marveled again at the relationships that develop with others sharing the same dream. Many also shared the same values, and with those folks bonds were established quickly and deeply.

The next day we went ashore and hiked around the hilly island that is covered with rocks and scrubby bushes as well as a few trees. Some places have huge banana groves and sugar cane in the wild. It was very hot as we climbed, but, reaching the top of a hill, we felt a refreshing breeze and could look down at the sailboats anchored in the small bay. The various blue colors of the sky and water were glorious, and fluffy white clouds dotted the sky—it looked like a picture postcard. Walking around the top of the hill we could see many bird nests on the ground. It was amazing to wander amongst the nests of those crazy blue-footed booby birds, and there seemed to be hundreds of them.

"I've never seen so many birds," I yelled to Fred. "There are eggs everywhere, and look at those darling little chicks."

"They sure don't seem to mind us being so close," Fred responded. The boobies are an awkward bird when walking on land. We laughed as we watched them and, sure enough, their feet were bright blue. We tried carefully not to get too close to the nests, although the birds acted as if we weren't even there.

"Look at those frigates—they are flying six feet over my head," Fred exclaimed. "There are terns, gulls—birds everywhere! This is incredible."

On the way back to the beach, we lost the trail and were scrambling through scratchy bushes, sweating and tired. We felt like we were in an Indiana Jones movie. I had blisters on both feet, and there were bird droppings *everywhere*. Finally, we made it back. Down on the beach were a few shacks housing the fishermen when they were ashore, but they were empty at the moment. We grabbed our dinghy and rowed back to the boat. We could hardly wait for a refreshing swim or shower. The water felt wonderful, although I admonished Fred not to go swimming. He had an angry red sore on his leg from hitting it on the rigging. The ocean water was so warm it incubated many organisms that could develop infections in open sores. He complained, but hey—I was the nurse.

That night there was a potluck dinner on the beach for all the boats in the bay. It was fun to meet the other folks and hear their plans and stories. It was our first opportunity to meet Cindy and Reed, on *Yobo,* and we liked them instantly. While we had planned to stop first at San Blas on the mainland, 30 miles from our present location, we had heard reports on the radio of vast numbers of "no-see-ums" there at this time of year. These were tiny flying insects that were difficult to see. They bit and left a welt that itched for many days, or even weeks. I had seen a cruiser's legs covered with angry red marks from these little critters, and it wasn't pretty! Several boats decided to skip going to San Blas and head directly for Puerta Vallarta. That sounded just fine with me. Mosquitoes adored me, and I often had numerous bites and welts while Fred had none. Maybe it was because he was so hairy, or my blood was sweeter. Nevertheless, I got out the bug repellent that night—just in case.

It had been light when we left the boat for shore, and it was dark when we returned.

"Wow. It really gets dark quickly," I said, climbing into our dinghy. "It's almost like someone turns a light switch off. No twilight."

"Thank goodness we have our anchor light on, and it's a little different from the others," Fred said.

"Indeed. It sure makes it easier to find our boat. Look at the incredible number of stars." The sky was brilliant with myriads of lights, and we searched for the North Star, which we always felt connected us with home and family. The sky was so clear that viewing the stars was very different than at home.

One night, while having dinner on another boat, we saw strange lights and shapes in the sky. The lights seemed to hover in one spot for a time and then zipped away at incredible speed. We all had our theories as to what those lights were, and they ranged from ionized gases to a strong conviction they were UFOs!

"Boy, am I glad that anchor came up easily," Fred said. We were ready to leave and waiting for *Yobo*.

"It looks like *Yobo* is not so lucky," I added. We watched them in the early morning light, trying to recover their anchor. After many attempts, Reed finally dove into the water to release it by hand.

"I bet that was an invigorating swim," Fred laughed, and we motored out of the bay.

As the sun raised its golden head in the eastern sky, we felt its invasive rays and knew the day would be a warm one. There was no wind, so we motored along, making about five knots per hour. We caught two fish, the first being a skip jack tuna, which we released, and the second a dorado, or mahi mahi—sometimes known as a dolphin fish.

"Man, are these good eating," Fred exclaimed, pulling the 34-inch fish aboard.

"Oh, but look. It's changing colors as it dies!" I said incredulously. "What a shame to kill such a beautiful creature."

As we watched, the fish turned to vivid yellow, chartreuse, and then bright blue. We had read about this phenomenon but had not seen it before. What a wonder of the sea!

Later in the day we talked on the ham radio with cruising friends from Portland. They were still in San Diego, having been pinned in by frequent storms, and it looked as if it would be at least another four days before they could get away.

"Cruising in the Pacific in January presents some problems," Fred remarked.

"In mid-winter it can be a problem even here in Mexico in the Sea of Cortez," I added. "I'm so glad we got away when we did, although that ride down the Baja wasn't very pleasant. Now *this* is cruising as we pictured it in the dream."

About three in the afternoon we pulled into Chacala, a little bay on the mainland, north of Puerta Vallarta. Palm trees lined the shore, along with small *palapas* (thatch roofed huts) that were open to the air, usually with sand or dirt floors. Verdant green foliage was everywhere; it was a genuine tropical paradise, in vivid contrast to the dry, brown, and sometimes desolate landscapes of Baja. Close to the white sand beach, the ocean waters were a vivid turquoise, and gentle white lines of surf rolled ashore. What a visual treat! Five other boats were there. Going ashore after we were securely anchored, we walked around the small village nestled near the beach. A narrow cobblestone road led up a hillside. Hundreds of coconut trees were heavy with their green and yellow globes.

"Look at these houses," I exclaimed. "The walls are just slats or tree limbs with openings between them, and they have dirt floors. Some have a single light bulb for lighting, and they're all so open. It seems like we have stepped back in time. This really looks like the Mexico we studied in school when we were kids."

"Those slat walls are really functional because they let the air in to keep the rooms cool," Fred added. "The people sure seem friendly."

Everywhere we walked, people greeted us warmly, and, stopping at a beach *palapa* for a cold drink, we were able to practice more of our newly acquired Spanish skills. Again, like in Cabo, dogs roamed everywhere, and I had learned not to put my legs under the tables—fleas congregated there.

The following day we spent on the boat, doing chores and maintenance jobs. Fred worked part of the day trying to correct an interference problem with the ham radio; I studied Spanish. Besides the many night watches I had spent listening to a cassette tape to gain more vocabulary, I also used the Spanish textbook we had aboard. We went ashore in the late afternoon and had an inexpensive shrimp dinner at a beach *palapa* restaurant while we watched the sun slide beneath the sparkling blue ocean horizon in a blaze of gold, red, purple, and rose. Gentle ocean breezes gave welcome relief from the day's heat. Now *this* was cruising!

We were the only *"gringos"* ashore that evening. Later, a retired American came in who lived in Chacala during the winter and volunteered at the local health clinic. He was also teaching English language classes on the beach in the evening and invited us to come help. Getting ready for bed that night, we reflected on this charming place.

"I could easily stay here for month," I said.

"It would be tempting, but remember, there are lots more places to see," Fred responded.

"Well, let's at least stay here for another few days."

In the morning I organized a "Happy Hour Potluck" with the other four boats now anchored here. Fred and I went ashore and hiked a half-mile over the hill to another secluded little bay lined by coconut trees—our own private piece of paradise. Fred watched some local men harvesting the coconuts and then asked if he could help. In return, he got a drink of the sweet coconut milk and made some new friends. Swimming in the warm, almost hot, ocean water was a delight, and the palm trees provided much needed shade from the sun. I tried to talk with a little girl on the beach, and drew a picture of Mickey Mouse in the sand. She laughed with delight as she said, "Mickey!" The other boaters arrived and we shared food and stories for many hours.

Back on board *Grace*, Fred continued to struggle with the ham radio that was still acting up, and another cruiser came over to help, but no luck. It was frustrating, to say the least.

"Hey, here come some more kids," I yelled to Fred. A number of 10- to 12-year old boys would sometimes swim on inner tubes out to the anchored boats and ask for candy or pencils. They were fun, good kids, but we also had a concern.

"Do you think we are teaching them to be beggars?" I asked Fred after they had left.

"I wonder about that. We want to help them out, but would their parents want them to be doing this?" Fred replied. "They are proud and concerned parents. We don't want to undermine them."

"Maybe we could share some of the school supplies we brought with the English classes," I suggested.

"Good idea. We could also call other cruisers on the ham and ask them to bring school supplies to the village. They surely need them." And so we did.

One day Cindy and Reed asked us if we'd like to go into a nearby town with them. A local taxi bus left in the morning and returned in the early afternoon. What an experience that turned out to be. The "bus" was an old VW van with the door fallen off. We sat on wood benches and talked with a lobster fisherman as we rode along. He spoke no English, but we kept asking him the names of different trees and crops as we bounced along the 9-kilometer potholed and rocky dirt road. There were orchards of mangos, pineapple, limes, and bananas. Finally I laughed and said to him in Spanish, "You are a professor!"

"Oh no," he replied. "*Un pescador* (a fisherman)."

"*Ah, si, si! Quatro estudiantes* (four students)," and I pointed to the four of us asking so many questions. We all shared a good laugh.

The small town of Los Varos was an absolute delight. There were many small shops, each selling different items, along cobblestone streets. The houses were neat and clean, and of a much higher economic standard than Chacala.

"Look," Fred pointed. "I don't know whether to feel safe or intimidated." Outside the local bank were armed guards, each holding a machine gun. Security was obviously taken seriously here.

After a wonderful shrimp lunch, we bought fresh vegetables, fruit, bread, and the magic ingredient for making margaritas: *Controy.* It was the Mexican version of the much more expensive Cointreau. Although we had asked the time of the return bus and where to catch it, it was an hour and a half late in arriving. Many others were waiting but not upset by the delay. It was *mañana* time, and we laughed as we learned that "Mexican time" is not at all like U.S. time. Thank goodness there was so much to see we didn't even mind the wait—as long as we were in the shade.

Late that afternoon, while safely back on board and reading in *Grace's* cockpit, I saw our "professor," the fisherman who rode the bus with us. He and a young man were motoring across the bay in a *panga* (fishing boat). I waved and yelled to attract their attention.

"*Hola, amigos*!" I yelled, and motioned for them to come alongside. In stumbling Spanish, I invited them to come aboard for a coke. The young man, called Chewie, was 14 and the "professor's" son. What fun we had asking about their family, showing them pictures of ours, and telling them how much we enjoyed their country. Their warm smiles, hearty laughs, and gracious manners epitomized all we had seen and experienced from the Mexican people. At one point, when asking the ages of Mardalleno and his wife, we discovered they were the same ages as Fred and me. I laughed in delight to tell him of the similarity and said that Fred's birthday was in four more days.

"I think Mardalleno said he would bring us some lobster," I said to Fred later. "I'm not sure, though. It's always a guessing game at translating what they say."

"You are really doing well with the Spanish," Fred responded. "Chewie said he was going to attend the English class on the beach tomorrow. Let's go in to help. I think they enjoyed our visit as much as we did. It's just what we wanted from visiting other countries—to interact with the people, not just see the sights."

Sure enough. Early the following morning, Mardalleno and Chewie came by our boat with three small lobsters. We insisted on paying for them, but they were adamant in refusing the money. They were on their way home but would see us at the English class that night.

Cindy and Reed joined us that night for class. About 10 to 12 young people came, and it was great fun. I led a couple of songs. Chewie smiled brightly when he saw us. We had brought a few small gifts for him and his family, but afterwards we couldn't find him. Since we were planning on leaving the next morning, a couple of other boys said they would take us to his home. So with our flashlights in hand, Cindy, Reed, Fred and I climbed the little rutted dirt road in the dark, following the boys who were excited about being our guides.

When we arrived at Mardalleno's home, a small shack on a trail up the hillside, he appeared quite pleased, and was eager to introduce his wife. She invited us to stay for coffee and immediately said something to one of the children, who ran to a neighbor's shack and came back with a jar of instant coffee. We declined their kind invitation, hoping not to offend them in doing so. There were a number of neighbors standing around watching this group of visitors, seeming to find it an exciting occasion. We did not want to stay long, and in order to leave graciously, I thanked them for their hospitality and tried to say in Spanish, "My husband is an old man and needs his sleep, so we must go." All, including the neighbors, laughed heartily, and I began to wonder if I had said something to the effect that my husband was a dirty old man and wants to go to bed! We'll never know!

"Those people live simply but seem happy and content with their families," Fred said when we were back at the boat.

"They sure do. But Mardalleno wants Chewie to learn English. I'm sure there are many more opportunities for jobs and a different lifestyle if one can speak English," I responded. "I heard there might be a big resort built at that little bay north of here. What a shame to change the natural beauty and serenity of this place."

"True, but it would provide lots of jobs for the folks around here. I guess we all want better opportunities for our children. The life of a lobster fisherman must be hard at times. Would change and progress be good for these folks? It's a timeless debate."

Early the next morning, as we reluctantly motored out of that charming bay, we saw Mardalleno and Chewie coming toward us in their *panga*. With lots of smiles and greetings, they held up a sack of three lobsters for us, saying something about "mother." We had included a sewing kit for her in our gifts last night. We again offered to pay them for the lobster and again they refused, saying, *"un regalo"* (a gift). I tried to say that we would miss them. I thought they understood. As we waved our goodbyes, we heard them yell, *"Feliz Cumplianos."* They had remembered that the next day was Fred's birthday! We were touched and incredibly sad to leave this lovely place and charming, generous people. Now *this* was cruising!

As we rounded the rocks to turn into Banderas Bay, we saw spouts of water shooting up from the ocean just a few feet from us.

"It's whales," Fred cried. "Look at them, there must be at least a dozen!"

"I've heard they come down here from Alaska to have their babies," I said. "Don't get too close. I've also heard they can ram a boat in defense.

I don't want to make them mad—they can sink a boat that way." We watched the pod in awe, again amazed at the wonders of nature.

Rather than go directly into Puerto Vallarta, where there was no place to anchor and the marina costs were high, we anchored along with about 25 other boats at La Cruz, a little town on the northern side of the huge bay. It was a typical, small, working town, with a few shops and on the bus line to PV, if we wished to go in from here. Again, there was a local VHF radio net in the morning, and Fred asked if anyone had ideas on how to fix the ham radio problem. Several cruisers had come to the boat, two that were electrical engineers in "the other world," but no one could solve the problem. Today he tried again and discovered that if he simply unhooked one of the accessory units the problem went away.

"What a birthday gift! Countless hours have gone into fixing that one little problem. We have more than a birthday to celebrate today. I think I'll fix Lance's Christmas gift tonight," I said.

It was Fred's birthday, and a perfect time to enjoy the package of gourmet foods that Lance had sent us via Dawn. We savored each new taste, trying to discover which one we liked the best. They were all wonderful! I had invited ten other cruisers to come over later for cake and the praline coffee from Lance. It was a special time, sitting in the cockpit under the starlit skies, enjoying the cool of the evening in spite of the warm breeze blowing.

We had come to know a number of the cruisers, and we identified quickly with many (although not all) of them. Like any big group, it had its diversity. Just as the boats themselves ranged greatly in style, age, the way they were maintained, cost, and appearance, so too did their occupants. The folks we gravitated toward varied a good deal in age. Some were the ages of our children, but that mattered little. They shared the same values and dream. It was late in the night before we turned in, feeling very blucky.

"Hey, *Amazing Grace.* Do you want to come into Bucerias with me tonight for dinner? Its Fiesta week and I'll be taking a couple of friends from the States who are visiting me." It was Tom, our friend from Tacoma. He had rowed by our boat on his way to shore.

"Fiesta? I thought all those fireworks were for my birthday," Fred laughed. "So they really were to celebrate the fiesta?"

We had discovered that the Mexican people loved fireworks—lots of them, and very late at night, or very early in the morning. The first time we heard them, we had imagined gunfire and visions of a revolution occurring!

Later that afternoon we traveled about 10 minutes on the local bus to a small town on the way to Puerto Vallarta. It seemed that each town celebrated a special fiesta each year, often honoring the town's patron saint. The festivities usually lasted a whole week, with parades, rodeos, carnivals, street dances, and, of course, fireworks. We had known that the Mexican people worked hard, and we now saw that they partied with the same zeal. Much of the celebration involved the whole family. Little girls were dressed in their finest frilly dresses, with fancy bows in their hair, looking like precious dolls. With obvious delight, they danced with their fathers, while the young boys danced with their moms.

"Does the music ever stop?" one of Tom's visitors inquired.

"Never," Fred responded, yelling to make himself heard as the parade danced by. The music was infectious, and we couldn't stand still as we got caught up in the spirit of the celebration.

"Look, they're dancing right into the church," I said. "Would that *we* had that much enthusiasm upon entering a church."

We found a nice restaurant on the beach, but as we prepared to order, both Fred and I became extremely uncomfortable and embarrassed by the behavior of Tom's visitor. He insisted that the young waiter speak English, complained about the prices, and was generally rude and demanding. He was the "ugly American" tourist. Looking at Fred, I knew that we both were considering leaving, but I also knew that Tom was in a difficult position. Waiting a bit, Fred and I both tried to interject our own perspective of being guests in another country and praised the hospitality and graciousness of the people of Mexico. It wasn't a direct confrontation, but I think we made our point and things settled down a bit. It nearly spoiled an evening that had been fun until then, but it helped us understand why Americans often have a bad reputation in some countries. We had seen ourselves as "ambassadors of good will" and wanted to represent the U.S. in a positive way. We made extra effort to talk with the young waiter, trying to distance ourselves from the "jerk" at the other end of the table. We learned that the young man had ten siblings and his father owned the restaurant. He seemed appreciative of our interest in him and our willingness to struggle with Spanish.

"Say, isn't that our waiter over there?" Fred pointed to a man climbing a coconut tree just outside of the restaurant. "Do you suppose he's getting a coconut for the Coco Loco you ordered?"

Sure enough. The waiter soon returned with our drinks—*and* the bright green coconut. As we waited for our meal, we saw the restaurant owner walk out on the sand when some fishermen beached their *panga* just in front of the restaurant. As we watched, he looked over and selected several fish and some oysters and carried them back into the kitchen. Talk about being *fresh!*

The following day we rode on the bus to PV, about a 30-minute trip. It was fun to be in a big city again—really the first since San Diego. We explored the marina area and talked with several friends who were staying there, including *Yobo,* who had needed the shore power to do some sail repair with their sewing machine. We checked on places to get copies of some charts, did some shopping, and went to the bus stop for our return. Twice, young men came up to us to chat while we waited. One spoke no English, the other spoke excellent English. They wanted nothing from us and were just being friendly.

"This is incredible," I said to Fred. We had just boarded the bus. "Do you think that if these folks were in our home town, or any city in the U.S., their experience with U.S. citizens would be similar to what we are having?"

"Sadly, I doubt it," Fred replied. "It makes me rather ashamed of the stereotypes I have had of Mexicans in the past. When I compare the hospitality they give to strangers in their country to what they would likely receive in ours, they win, 'hands down!'"

"For sure," I agreed. "To be fair, though, when we see someone with dark hair or dark skin walking down the street in our towns, they could be fourth generation Americans. There are so many races and cultures in our 'melting pot.' Here, for the most part, we stand out and are pretty obviously visitors or tourists. Regardless, they surely teach us something about hospitality."

Our days in Banderas Bay were full ones. Occasionally we took a "day off" and stayed on the boat to relax, read, and do chores. Rowing ashore, walking in the heat, catching buses—it all was tiring.

"I'm really getting the hang of this 'siesta time,'" Fred said one afternoon. "It sure makes sense to snooze for a couple of hours in the early afternoon when it's so hot and then be more active later at night when it's cool."

"Absolutely. Everything ashore is closed from noon to three anyway. Maybe that accounts for why all the little kids stay up so late too. Thank goodness for all the fans we installed before we left. The heat would be unbearable without them," I added. We especially liked the two fans in the aft cabin that made sleeping more comfortable either in the afternoon or at night.

It was a problem trying to keep the boat cool while maintaining security. We liked leaving the hatches and doors open for airflow, but it also meant that someone uninvited could board, particularly at night. We had an alarm system so that we could leave the main companionway doors open, and if someone stepped onto the cockpit floor pad, an alarm would sound. We also had a "panic alarm" button in our aft cabin by the bed. But we had no way to secure the hatches at night, so we used a number of fans for airflow. We always locked the boat when we left it, feeling that it was our responsibility not to create temptation for others.

Marinas certainly made life easier, and here in La Cruz the anchorage was often very roll-y from the ocean swell, so that sometimes we didn't sleep as well. It also took effort to balance ourselves when trying to do anything on the boat. We didn't relish the idea of getting seasick while at anchor! It was one of the reasons we tracked the weather and storms even far out in the ocean, for they affected the swell that came into the bay.

After about a week in La Cruz, we decided to go into a little marina at Nueva Vallarta. It cost much less than PV, but had few amenities, and although not far from PV, it was not an easy task to travel there and back again.

"It feels good to be 'on the road again,'" Fred said. We were making the 3-hour trip over to Nueva Vallarta across the bay. Tying up in the little marina, we thought about the many things to do.

"I'm anxious to get the salt washed off the boat," Fred said. "It's *everywhere.*"

"I can hardly wait to do laundry," I replied. Clothes became sticky with sweat just minutes after we put them on, so fresh clean clothes became something of a luxury. We rushed about trying to do everything at once. We also enjoyed the ritual of reconnecting with other cruisers we had met in previous ports.

A "HIGH" MAINTENANCE JOB FOR FRED.

The following day we felt we had enough of the work done to venture into PV. Another cruiser was moving his boat to the marina there and asked if we wanted to ride along with him. It was good to see the harbor and entrances from the sea because we planned on entering with *Grace* the following week.

"One of our priorities today is to find that water filter," Fred said. The water in this area was safe to drink, so we wanted to fill our tanks, but there was a lot of sediment in it, thus the need to find a special ceramic water filter. We found that, like other Mexican towns, each store carried only a limited number of items, and it meant going to many stores before finding one that had what we wanted. It took all day to find the filter, but it was fun to interact with people at each place.

"Hey, we'd better get back to the boat. It gets dark by 6:30, and we don't know exactly how long it will take us to get to the marina," I said.

"Ask these folks how to get to the marina and what stop to take," Fred suggested. "See how long it takes, and if we can take a taxi."

"Fred!" I said in exasperation. "I'm lucky if I can get across the bare essentials, let alone understand their responses. You always want too many details!"

The bus driver assured us that we were on the right bus and that he would let us off at the stop closest to the marina. We were the only *gringos*, and people smiled kindly at us. Stepping off the bus, we felt a little anxious as nighttime was fast approaching and we knew we still had to walk a couple of miles to the marina. We started out, hurrying as much as possible. All too soon it was dark.

"Man, it is *really* dark. Where are the stars and moonlight when you need them?" Fred said. It was difficult to see the road ahead as we walked in the thick black air. There certainly were no streetlights. There were, in fact, no lights of *any* kind.

"We must have walked at least two miles, and I don't see anything like a marina—not even houses!" I replied a little shakily. "I don't like this. Are we even on the right road? We haven't even seen any cars go by."

Finally a car approached and we anxiously waved it down. It was a taxi, and the driver said we were on the wrong road. Alas for the cruising budget that had us using buses rather than taxis. It was a quick decision to get in the car and let him take us to the boat. We jumped inside, actually grateful to be spending the extra money. Arriving at the marina, we walked down to the dock from the parking lot.

"Oh boy, does *Grace* ever look good," I said.

"Yeah," responded Fred. "Who knows how long we would have had to walk. This was definitely an 'M.E.' for the books!"

"What's an 'M.E'?" I asked.

"You know, *Mexican Experience*," he said with a laugh, and thus began a new code for the many adventures ahead.

I awoke during the night to the sound of rain. For a moment I thought I was back in Oregon listening to the patter of the rain on the open-beamed ceiling of our house. We had only experienced a couple days of intermittent showers on our trip since Cabo. I recalled Lance writing that when it rained in Colorado it made him homesick. I guess we were true Oregonians.

The rain continued the following day and it gave us time to do a number of "ever present" maintenance jobs. How we appreciated the cruising community when we got stuck on those projects. On the morning radio net, people would often tell of a problem and other boaters would offer ideas, items, and assistance. It felt like a big family. We supported others, knowing that "what goes around comes around." Dale, from *Windborne*, came over to help Fred remove the engine zincs.

"Wow. These zincs are almost gone," Fred said with concern. The zincs protected the engine from electrolysis damage, which can occur much more quickly when the boat is in salt water rather than fresh. "We'll have to find some replacements before we run the engine, because I have only one and we need three."

The next day we got a ride into Puerto Vallarta and began the hunt for the zincs. We must have gone to at least 20 hardware stores, and *finally* we found what we needed. The people in the stores all wanted to help us, and we enjoyed trying to talk with them even though we feared we would have to make the zincs ourselves. We decided to rest from walking all over town and get a margarita in one of the beach bars that advertised "Happy Hour—2 for 1!" When it came time to pay for the drinks, we thought the price was a little high and inquired about the "2 for 1" deal.

"*Si, si, senor*," said the waiter. "Two for one."

"But we ordered one, and you have charged us for two," Fred said patiently.

"*Si. Dos margueritas*," was the reply, and the young man looked concerned and called for another waiter to help. The conversation was repeated, and a third person was called. Over and over we repeated our confusion and received the same answer. By then, Fred and I could hardly keep a straight face. It was a little like the old joke about "Who's on first?" Finally, we understood that "2 for 1" at that place meant that, if you ordered one, they would bring you two, but you still needed to pay for two! Something seemed to have been lost in the translation of an American custom.

"Well, those were expensive margaritas, but the 'entertainment factor' was priceless!" Fred said.

"I'll say. That was truly another M.E." We both had a good laugh and started for the bus home.

The final Sunday in January came: *Superbowl Sunday!* We had been tickled when our Canadian friends on *Ossuna* pulled into Nuevo Vallarta a few days previously. Along with them and many of the other cruisers, we walked to a local hotel and restaurant to watch the Superbowl on television. There had been no televising of other American football games, and we were all ready for a "football fix." What a fun afternoon! It made us think of home, and how much Fred missed watching football games. Of course, the commentary was all in Spanish, so we made up our own as the game progressed. It was late when we returned to *Grace* and went to bed. About 12:30 a.m., we were awakened by the sound of knocking on our hull. Concerned that something was wrong, we jumped out of bed only to find Harvey standing on the dock in his underwear, holding out a loaf of bread.

"It's just out of the oven. I made it myself!" he pronounced proudly. We all laughed about the craziness of cruisers and enjoyed the midnight snack of yummy, fresh hot bread.

The following day we took *Grace* the short distance over to Puerto Vallarta and the huge marina there. I'm glad we had seen it before, or we could have gotten lost in all the rows of boats. We were sent to a dock where there were several other cruisers that we really enjoyed being with. Some of them had decided to go back into the Sea of Cortez for the summer and fall before heading south. One other was heading on to Costa Rica. Our friends on *Kacheena* were leaving for the South Seas. Others, who had less time to cruise, were going on to Hawaii.

Knowing that Bob from *Charlie's Girl* was alone, we invited him over for dinner. His wife, Charlotte, had flown home to Portland to take care of some business. She was to bring back our mail if Page could get it to her.

Since we had moved *Grace* to a different port, we needed to check in with the Port Captain here in Puerto Vallarta. Fred and Reed did that the next day while Cindy and I went shopping for groceries in old town. After meeting the guys for lunch, we returned to the marina and went to the pool for a swim. There was to be a dock potluck party that night.

"It will be fun to see Charlotte again," Cindy said.

"Bob is really worried about her getting through customs since she is bringing back so many items for other cruisers," Reed added.

"Yeah," agreed Fred. "Those things are supposed to be duty-free since we are boats in transit, but it could mean huge hassles with the customs authorities."

Later, we learned that Charlotte was a resourceful woman. She had packed a lot of those items in one bag and then put all of her "undies" on top. When the customs official opened her bag, he looked at a few bras and underpants and then snapped it shut!

The dock party was bustling. One long dock held many of the transient boats, so in the late afternoon sunshine we had filled the area with tables of food. Charlotte was there with a package of mail for us and told about meeting Page when she delivered it. We could hardly wait to get back to *Grace* that evening to read all our mail.

Of course, getting mail also meant pangs of homesickness. Feeling joy and sadness at the same time always felt a little crazy. Most of the time we were deeply enjoying what we were doing and the people with whom we were sharing this dream adventure—yet we were sad to think of the loved ones back home who were so far away. It was another lifetime, it seemed. Such moments usually led to a few tears for me, and a comforting hug from Fred.

Marina life was not all parties and pool time. Having shore power meant an opportunity for fixing things. Fred was adding insulation to our little refrigerator after finally having found the foam material he needed. We had gone to many little hardware stores looking for this particular product, and trying to explain what we needed with our limited Spanish skills was always a hoot. Usually a group of men encircled us, trying to understand what we wanted. Finally, after many attempts at different stores, one young man excitedly exclaimed, *"Si, si!"* and with his hands mimicked pressing the top of a spray can and then made a loud "Phoosh" sound while his hands showed something expanding. We all laughed and pointed to him with a resounding, *"Si, Si!"* Success at last, but oh, how much fun was the process to obtain it.

I had taken my little red folding wagon to the supermarket close to the marina for more supplies and was weary upon returning to the boat in the heat of the afternoon. When entering the cabin, I saw cushions askew, lockers open, supplies all over the floor, and virtually no uncluttered space to walk or set the groceries. What a mess! Working on any project in such a confined space meant moving things about in order to access certain areas—disrupting the entire boat. That made it difficult for both of us to find what we needed because things weren't where they usually were. For some projects it meant allowing caulking or glue to dry overnight, so we would wake up to the same disarray the following day. It made me grumpy, and the constant heat added to my irritable mood.

"Why don't you go take a shower?" Fred suggested. "I'll finish up here and put away what I can."

That sounded good to me—although it was a huge marina, and, to get to the showers, we had to walk all the way around the perimeter of the marina bay. The transient docks were usually the least convenient of all the docks. It was a good 20-minute walk, but we usually stopped to talk with other boaters on our way, or enjoyed looking at the many different types of boats. At least a shower refreshed me and lifted my sagging spirits. Coming back, I saw the huge motor vessel owned by the widow of the McDonald's hamburger chain. Reported to be worth 13 million dollars, it had a crew of six or eight, all of who wore matching attire. I watched a florist van deliver several huge bouquets of flowers, which the crew carried aboard. They must have been expecting either the owner or guests. Another enormous sailboat was for sale for only six million dollars. Wow. It was amazing what money could buy. But, coming back to *Grace*, I felt content with her—at least when she was picked up and orderly now.

"Hey, do you guys want to come with us to Mismaloya? Karen has a car and invited us and you folks to drive down there," yelled Cindy from her boat. That sounded like an offer we couldn't refuse, and we quickly got ready to go.

Leaving the city, we drove up into the hills and jungle, where we hiked over rocks and a small river to a waterfall. It felt cooler there, but more humid because we no longer had the ocean breeze. It was strange to be away from the ocean and beach. Here, we were surrounded by the lush green of tropical vegetation. Reed did a fair job of imitating Tarzan as he swung on a vine far out over the water below the falls. I wasn't ready for a swim just yet, so I passed on the opportunity to play Jane. This was the area where parts of the movie, *The Terminator*, were filmed, and we could still see some of the props peeking through the jungle foliage.

Climbing back in the car, we drove on to Mismaloya Beach, the area made famous by Richard Burton and Elizabeth Taylor when Puerto Vallarta was just a sleepy little fishing village. There were hundreds of people sitting on lounge chairs along the beach. Umbrellas or small *palapas* made of palm fronds provided shade from the blazing sun. The chairs belonged to the various beach restaurants surrounding the bay. We found six chairs and negotiated the price for their use with the waiter, who assured us there were "none finer in all of Mismaloya!" He solicitously seated us and encouraged us to try their special: Coco Locos. Of course, there were "none finer in all of Mismaloya!" *Why not?* we thought—and we enjoyed the afternoon even more after the second round!

I soon needed to find a bathroom. Asking for the *baño*, I was directed behind the beach bars to a busy area containing a raised platform. On it were a number of toilet stalls, each with a plastic shower curtain rather than a door. Since there was no running water on the beach, several older men stood in front of the platform with buckets of water. Urgency prevailed over being choosey and, after paying them a few pesos, I climbed the stairs to the "stage," used the facilities, and watched as they went up and emptied the bucket into the toilet. Quite an ingenious system for flushing—definitely another M.E!

Late one afternoon a number of couples climbed the steep hillside streets that overlooked Puerto Vallarta's old town—a charming area typical of older Mexico. It contained a meandering river for washing clothes, great restaurants and bars, and a gigantic public market that filled a city block. We found the restaurant we were looking for and climbed up the stairs to a roof terrace bar. Here we enjoyed one of the most beautiful sunsets we had ever seen. The golden sinking sun and its rays slowly turned the sky to a brilliant rose and deepening purple. The magnificent colors saturated both the sky and the sea over the large expanse of Banderas Bay. The ocean breeze felt refreshingly cool, and we all became increasingly quiet as we soaked up the panorama before us. Caught in the moment, we were transfixed. Suddenly, we saw it—the elusive "green flash," that split-second burst of light that occurs just as the sun dips below the horizon. When we had first heard about this phenomenon, we thought it was some mariner's myth. That night it truly was a spiritual, magical moment that gave us goose-bumps!

Reed then led us on a hunt through the old town streets to find a particular taco stand. These street stands were on almost every corner—and mid-block as well. It took some time before we found "Tres Hermanas" tacos, though. Reed had befriended these three sisters the day before, and they were delighted to have him return with all his friends. Several people gave up their chairs, which were in the street next to the stand, while others went to neighboring houses to find more for us. The guys bought beer at the corner grocery store, and we gorged ourselves on tacos, quesadillas, and that all-time favorite—Mexican *cervesa*. What a feast! And it cost us less than five dollars.

After our week of luxury in the PV marina, we left to go once again to La Cruz.

"What on earth is happening?" I exclaimed to Fred. The boat was rolling violently at the La Cruz anchorage.

"It's sure not like it was two weeks ago. Maybe these swells are from that volcanic eruption out at the Socorro Islands. Even though they are 400 miles from here, there's no land mass in between to diminish the impact," he replied. "I don't think we should go ashore—it's too rough."

We spent a sleepless night "rockin' and rollin'" in the bumpy seas. We were able to do a few projects, but all that boat movement made us tired. It took forever to do anything. We did manage a trip to shore in the dinghy for some fruit and vegetables. Our plan was to leave at four the following morning, cross to the other side of Banderas Bay, and round the cape beyond.

"Hey, look. Here come *Yobo* and *Kacheena*," Fred said with delight. They were going the same way as we were, and we were tickled.

"Why don't you leave later tomorrow and we'll join you," Reed yelled from their boat. "Four o'clock is way too early for me."

"I want to get around the cape before the winds and seas build," Fred responded. Despite our desire to travel with friends, we decided to pursue our original plan and leave early. "See you on the Gold Coast."

The area south of Banderas Bay was filled with wonderful little inlets, as well as many bays and delightful places to anchor, and was affectionately called "The Gold Coast" by the cruising community. As we left before daylight the following morning, the seas continued to be lumpy, with big swells coming at us. But there was good wind, so we were happy about being able to sail. We threw out the fishing line and caught a nice yellow fin tuna—one of the better tasting fish. About noon the wind died, so we fired up the "Iron Genny" and motored on. We saw a sailboat standing still in the water, and we heard a boat trying to call us on the radio. He didn't answer our response. That seemed odd. As we approached the boat, we called out and found a man who was single-handing whose engine had died. He had worked a long time but was not able to get it restarted. Fred tried to talk him through the process of bleeding the engine, but without success.

"Do you have a swim ladder?" Fred called out. "Put it down, and I'll swim over to help you."

Oh no, I thought. That meant I would be on the boat *alone*!

"Just circle his boat slowly, and remember to put the gears in neutral when I swim back," he told me.

Nervously, I watched him jump into the water and swim to the other boat. I couldn't remember ever being on the boat all by myself when it was underway. Anxiously, I put the engine in gear and began to move about the drifting boat. I soon found that I was doing just fine. In fact, I was just beginning to rather enjoy the drama of the moment and my being in charge of our vessel when I heard the sound of the other boat's engine starting, and the guys reappeared from the cabin with huge smiles. As Fred swam back to our boat, I heard the man yell, "*Amazing Grace,* I'll never forget you!" Another saved by amazing grace!

As we continued on, we were treated to another "acrobatic show" by a pod of dolphins. They jumped and dove under the bow wake in an intricate dance with incredible grace and speed. When I went forward to watch them, I sang to them. We were sad to see them finally leave, and Fred was sure that his whistling this time had worked. There were also whales sounding in the distance, and then a huge marlin swam by, only a few feet from the boat. At one point we even saw a large manta ray jump completely out of the water. We could hardly believe our good fortune in seeing all those gorgeous creatures of the deep.

When we found a quiet little cove to anchor in, we were tired from getting up so early. Fred attempted a swim, but before I could get in, he was stung, likely by a jellyfish. Angry red welts appeared across his stomach, and he said it hurt considerably. The vinegar treatment suggested in the dive book seemed to be effective, but I decided to forgo the swim. Instead, I cooked some freshly caught fish, and it was yummy.

For several days we enjoyed making short hops and exploring little bays and coves. These anchorages provided a feast to the eyes. Waving palm trees beckoned us ashore, and the light blue water reflected the hues of the sky. Sometimes a protected corner provided the quiet motion of a gently rocking cradle. The relaxed, tranquil pace in these places was deeply appreciated after the busyness and excitement of PV. We were happy to be by ourselves after all the social opportunities we had experienced in the marina. We lazed in the sun when it was not too hot, and spent time reading or enjoying the sunsets. We went ashore and took long walks along the beach or in small villages. This often meant we returned to the boat hot and sweaty.

While we had a shower in the head, and hot water from a propane heater, we much preferred to shower in the cockpit using a large, heavy black plastic bag that we had earlier filled with water and placed in the sun. When this solar-heated water bag was suspended from the boom, its attached nozzle provided an adequate shower spray.

"I love these secluded anchorages," I said to Fred. I had rigged our shower bag in the cockpit and was anxious to use it. "We can actually have an outdoor shower standing up, and the breeze feels so good on my skin."

"It's a lot easier on clean up out here than down below in the head," he responded. "Save some hot water for me."

In crowded anchorages we hung towels on the lifelines and sat on the cockpit floor for privacy. Sitting down for a shower was less than ideal, but boating is about compromises, right? The cockpit shower was also useful after swimming. While we enjoyed taking a dip in the sea, it meant our bodies would be covered with salt when we dried in the sun. A quick rinse in the cockpit or on deck took care of the salt.

Not all swimming was planned, unfortunately. One day we decided to go ashore for some necessary groceries. Since we were close to shore, we rowed the dinghy rather than using the five-horsepower outboard engine that we carried on *Grace's* stern railing. After completing our shopping, we walked back to the beach and got ready to row out to the boat. While I put our groceries in our waterproof bag, Fred carefully observed the surf.

"This might be a little tricky," he said. "Those swells are pretty big and close together."

We had come ashore many times, so I felt no real anxiety as we got ready to push the dinghy into the water. But the Sea Gods were out to get us that day! As Fred attempted to row those first few strokes, one of the oars popped out of the oarlock. By the time he scrambled to get it back in place, a wave pushed us sideways. That was all it took. The next wave hit us broadside and heaved us upside down in a flash. I looked up to see the dinghy coming down on top of us, and thought, *Gee, someone could really get* hurt *out here!*

Coming up out of the water, sputtering and wiping our faces, we saw all the dinghy's contents floating on the water and quickly tried to retrieve them. We were fortunate to have received only a few scratches, but our egos were certainly bruised. One of the local young men came running over to help us get the boat righted and out of the surf. Likely there were a number of other folks, including some fellow cruisers, sitting at a nearby beach restaurant having a good laugh at the not so uncommon spectacle. Finally, we were ready to try it again. This time, I was truly anxious and my adrenalin was pumping. The young Mexican who had helped was standing alongside, watching the surf.

"Está bien?" (Is it okay?) I asked, hoping he would be able to tell us when it was best to launch the dinghy and get through the surf.

"No, no," was his quick reply, as he continued to watch the waves, and we waited a couple of minutes before asking again.

"Está bien?" we said several more times, and received the same negative response.

Finally, he said excitedly, *"Ahora, ahora!"* (now, now) and we quickly jumped to get into the dinghy while he helped push us out into the water. Rowing like crazy, Fred got us through the surf into calmer water, and we exchanged high fives, yelling our thanks to the young man.

As we unloaded our things when safely back on *Grace*, I suddenly realized I had lost my expensive sunglasses that had special significance to me. When we had purchased them, they became a symbol of our desire to be in tropical areas—as well as our desire to protect our vision and bodies. I was crushed to lose them. We considered going back to look for them but thought it would be a lost effort. They would surely be buried in the sand by now. Then I saw a local *panga* boat carrying four young men to shore. On an impulse, I yelled and waved my hands; they came alongside.

"Por favor," I said, and tried to explain in Spanish what had happened. Either they had seen us flip or understood my pantomime, for they nodded when I asked if they would try to find my glasses. I held up a peso bill equivalent to about 20 dollars, offering it as a reward. Off they went to shore, and we could see them walking around in the shallow water. In only a matter of minutes they returned with my glasses in hand. What luck!

"Gracias, gracias," I said with delight and handed them the money. We offered them a cold beer, but when I saw the youngest, who appeared to be about 15, I wagged my finger and said, "No cervesa. Coca-cola!" and we all laughed. We continued talking with them and showing our pleasure at the return of my sunglasses. They weren't even scratched.

We deeply enjoyed these interactions with the Mexican people. They were friendly and caring, and they always appeared glad for the opportunity to talk with us. We almost always initiated the conversation, but their responses were enthusiastic. As we learned more, we gained more respect for their culture and lifestyle. We hoped, too, that their impressions of us—and Americans in general—would be favorable.

Yobo had joined us in one of the anchorages. Cindy and Reed were always up for some kind of adventure, so we decided to go snorkeling. We got in their dinghy and rode to a nearby beach. The surge of the waves was still high and strong, so we quickly decided that it would not be wise to snorkel there. Waiting for a lull in the waves in order to leave, we all began to wonder if we would be stuck on this remote, secluded little beach. We remembered, all too well, our "turtled" dinghy trip. Finally, we were able to get off the beach and return to our sailboats. Apparently this big surge was happening all along the coast. It sure made for uncomfortable sleeping at night when the boat would sometimes rock violently as it lay in the trough of the waves. A stern anchor made for a more pleasant ride, but it took time and effort to set and was sometimes difficult to retrieve. Always a compromise. Many aspects of cruising were not easy—cooking a meal, finding gear we needed, all the bending, twisting, or stooping to put things away, dealing with insects, worrying about weather, wondering if the anchor was holding—but we realized it was the price we had to pay for that incredibly rich experience. I sometimes had huge mood swings: from utter euphoria about our trip to being just plain mad that *Grace* wouldn't stop rockin' and rollin.' I guess if it weren't for the bitter, the other wouldn't be so sweet.

Along with *Yobo*, we sailed about 10 miles the following day to the lovely little bay called Bahia Careyes. Eighteen years earlier, we had stayed at the Club Med there. We had sailed every day in small boats, and less than a week after returning home had bought our first sailboat. We chuckled as we watched Reed make four or five attempts to anchor. Finally, it held.

"Are you ready to go ashore?" I yelled to Cindy and Reed. We jumped into their dinghy and headed for the beach at Club Med.

"Look, there are security guards on the beach waiting for us," Reed said. The men were friendly but asked us to accompany them to the office. As others looked on, I felt a little like a criminal being led to the gallows! At the office we purchased a ticket for dinner and the evening's entertainment. It was a heavy hit on the cruising budget, but we had really looked forward to returning to this place. Going back to our boats, we decided to do some snorkeling and take a nap so we would be ready for our much anticipated and expensive night at the Club. Because sometimes traveling in the dinghy meant being sprayed with seawater, when we were ready to go that evening, we put our fancy clothes in a waterproof bag and changed in a restroom when we got ashore.

The evening did not disappoint. After a five-course dinner with all the wine we wanted, we headed for the musical show, followed by an outdoor trapeze show, and then moved on to the disco. If only our kids could have seen us! We danced up a storm—although I'm sure there must have been some folks wondering what kind of dance step we were doing. (On prior occasions our kids had just shaken their heads in disbelief while affectionately calling our unique steps "The Freddy!") We had a glorious time. It was three o'clock in the morning when we finally arrived back on *Grace,* tired but happy. We had certainly gotten our money's worth!

The following day we weren't moving very swiftly, but Fred did manage to go diving with Reed, using Cindy's tank. Fred was a certified diver, and we had a Hooka system aboard that allowed him to dive with a compressor and air hose. Since it wasn't wise to dive alone, and I didn't dive, he had not used it much. It was great for cleaning the hull, however. As Cindy and I sat in the dinghies while the guys were underwater, we noticed *Ossuna* coming into the bay. Later, we all joined together on *Yobo,* along with a couple we had met at the club the night before.

Heidi wasn't feeling well, so Fred and I took her to see the doctor at the Club Med Clinic. Poor health was an ongoing concern of all cruisers. We discussed the situation as we got ready for bed.

"It's scary to think about being ill while cruising," I said. "We could be far away from adequate medical care and completely vulnerable."

"You're right. Even if we could find a doctor, we wouldn't know what kind of training he or she had," he replied. "I'm glad you were a nurse before you changed careers."

We had brought with us a large selection of medical supplies, along with some good reference books. We hoped we would not need to use them. We went to sleep that night praying for the gift of continued good health.

The next morning I realized that it was Sunday and there was no church (nor any towns or bus service) close to us.

"Time for church, eh?" Fred laughed, when I started playing some Sandi Patti cassette tapes we had brought along. It had become our custom to play the tapes on Sunday mornings, and I loved singing along to the old familiar hymns, as well as the newer jazzy ones. Fred wasn't much of a singer, but he enjoyed the songs as well, and the music always had us feeling incredibly thankful for this awesome adventure.

Later, along with *Ossuna* and *Yobo*, we went ashore for a long hike up into the hills surrounding the bay.

"Oh, what a gorgeous view," said Cindy when we got to the top. "Our boats look so idyllic—so peaceful at anchor down there in the bay."

"Yeah, you'd never realize from here that they're actually rollin' like crazy!" responded Reed.

"That's right," said Fred. "Kay and I were trying to hug this morning in the cockpit, and we had to do a little dance to keep from falling over!"

On our way back down the narrow, rutted, and rocky dirt road to the boat, we stopped to pick wild limes, bananas, mangos, and coconuts. We had seen other cruisers with whole stalks of bananas hanging from their boats' riggings. We didn't want to try that because all the bananas ripened at once—far more than two people could eat.

We left Bahia Careyes and had a fast and exhilarating six-hour sail down the coast to a protected and *calm* anchorage. After dropping the hook, we were ecstatic to see the boat lie quietly in the water.

"We really enjoyed that warm, fresh loaf of bread you brought us last night," I yelled over to *Ossuna*, anchored nearby. "Why don't you come over to help us eat the yellow fin tuna we caught on the way down?" Our little freezer couldn't hold much, so it was fun to share the catch with others. After stuffing ourselves that evening with the fresh fish and more of Heidi's homemade bread, we all turned in early for a much-appreciated quiet night of sleep. No more rockin' and rollin.' Ahhhh!

After "cleaning house" the next morning, we decided to tackle the dinghy trip. Exploring areas in our small boats was a favorite pastime for all of us. It took us only a few minutes to set up our dinghy and get it into the water by using the spinnaker halyard from the mast and a special sling that Fred had made. We could also raise and lower the heavy outboard dinghy engine by another sling and pulley system that was attached to the radar pole.

Just inside the surf line, in the corner of the bay, was a lagoon filled with mangroves. Despite its tricky entrance, we and three other dinghies were able to enter and proceed up a small stream to another nearby bay.

"This is marvelous," I said to Fred. We motored under the canopy of mangroves, which created something like a tunnel of foliage over the stream. "Look at all the egrets." Beautiful white birds flew gracefully over our heads.

"They can't get out through the mangroves overhead, so they just fly ahead of us—like they're leading the way," he said. "There are some large cranes over there, and look at all those orchids growing on the trees." I had not seen orchids growing in the wild before.

After about three miles, we pulled the boats ashore to eat lunch at one of several *palapa* restaurants along the beach. Hammocks swayed alongside the tables and chairs on the sand, and the kitchen was very basic—a small cement room with a sand floor, wood stove, and sink. The owner was apparently glad to see our group, and kept bringing us free little appetizer dishes until we decided to stay there for a shrimp dinner.

A FAVORITE CRUISING PASTIME—BEACH DINING.

"Was that ever delicious," I exclaimed as we got ready to leave. "Those folks said that, on Wednesdays, all the locals come for the house specialty—*chile rellenos*. We should come back."

As the afternoon quickly slid by, we realized that we must get back through the lagoon before the mosquitoes came out in force. They continued to be a constant problem for me, and I tried to carry repellent, especially when I knew we would be out during dusk. I had made cloth insect screens for all of the opening hatches on the boat, and we faithfully put them in place every evening. We even had made screens to enclose the entire cockpit, as well as our bed. When we were on the boat, the mosquitoes were less troublesome if the wind was blowing from the sea.

We motored back through the lagoon and held our breath as we crossed the surf line, watching the incoming waves carefully. When we were finally well off the beach, we breathed a sigh of relief and headed for home—another wonderful day in paradise.

"Are you ready to try the Hooka?" Fred asked one morning. I wasn't very excited about hauling out all the equipment stored all over the boat. I wasn't very excited about being underwater, either, but I did want to learn to use the system for underwater diving. When we jumped into the water, I tried not to let my anxiety get out of hand, as it sometimes did when snorkeling and I got water in my mask or snorkel. Fred was patient and supportive. I didn't want to go very far away from the boat, so we cleaned the bottom, which kept my mind busy and away from the fact that I was breathing underwater—even if only at a depth of 12 inches! It was a start.

That night, *Yobo* and *Ossuna* came over to *Grace* for an informal potluck dinner. Since each boater's supply of liquor was limited, it was the custom for cruisers to bring their own drinks, as well as something to eat when gathering on someone's boat. After dinner I brought out my guitar. I had spent countless hours playing and singing by myself in secluded anchorages but had not yet played for others. Harvey adamantly told us that he didn't sing, but the rest of us started a sing-a-long of old favorites, and, before we knew it, he was belting them out with the rest of us. What a kick! He wailed. He waved his arms. He even started dancing a "Newfy" jig—all in the cockpit!

"What on earth is a 'Newfy' Jig?" we all asked.

"It's what we do in Newfoundland," he patiently explained. "That's where I grew up!" We all laughed and sang that night until we were hoarse.

The next day was Wednesday. We had decided to skip the return to the beach restaurant for *chile rellenos* until Harvey and Heidi insisted we come with them in their dinghy. Later that night, we were glad we had changed our minds. So many local people had come to that little restaurant that they had to send someone to the market for more peppers. They were delicious! I wanted to watch the cook make them, so I stood by the little kitchen doorway and talked with the women cooking. Soon I asked if I could help beat the egg whites, and they grinned enthusiastically and gave me the whip. I watched as the cook swiftly took the skins off the peppers, likely burning her fingers but smiling all the while. Then the young girl who was assisting cut them open, and they were stuffed with cheese and deep-fried in an egg batter. The owner, who was the cook's husband, was delighted with my interest and told his friends about the *gringa* who was helping in the kitchen. When Fred tried to ask him what kind of meat was in the tacos, we could not understand his reply. Finally he snorted and grunted, and we laughed as we realized that the meat was pork!

When we tried to leave, we again learned about the instability of dinghies and the trickiness of the sea. This time the boat was swamped even before we got in it. The restaurant owner's young son came running out with a bailer for us to dump out all the water. Finally we were ready to try it again, and this time we were successful. Thank goodness for waterproof bags!

After a few days in an anchorage, we started to get "itchy feet." The call of unknown places and adventures pulled us onward. We hoisted anchor and, after a delightful sail in light winds, tentatively approached the lagoon entrance at Barra de Navidad.

"The cruising notes say to enter only at high tide, and it's already two hours before *low* tide," I said apprehensively. "Do you really think we should try it? Some boats can't even get through on high tide and have to wait several days for the tide depths to increase."

"Ahhh. But they don't have a *swing keel*," Fred said with a twinkle in his eye. "We have it—so let's use it."

We pumped up the keel so that *Grace* only drew about three feet, then we cautiously slid through the entrance. We made it easily and anchored in a calm, protected area surrounded by the construction of a new resort. Shortly after dropping anchor, we saw a dinghy approaching.

"Hey—what you guys just did was *miraculous*," a young cruiser said from his dinghy. "A number of us were watching from the hotel over there, and we were sure that you were going to run aground at any moment. How did you *do* that?"

We laughed and told him about our marvelous lifting keel. After we tidied up the boat, which always became cluttered during a passage, we lowered the dinghy and crossed the lagoon to go ashore.

"Wow—this is great. The hotel has a sea wall to tie up the dinghies. No more going through the surf," I said.

"It feels like a luxury, doesn't it," Fred replied. "I hear this hotel caters to cruisers. They offer some great Happy Hours and let folks use their pool and outdoor showers."

It wasn't long before we (along with the others) carried our soap, shampoo, and towels into the hotel, and, wearing our swimsuits, lathered up in the showers by the pool, knowing our kids would be totally embarrassed by the whole scene.

After finding a local woman to do our laundry and checking out the town, we returned to the boat and spent a quiet evening onboard. We loved reading after dinner, something we seldom seemed to find time to do in "the other world," and we didn't mind not having a television. Many boaters had them, but for now we enjoyed the quiet. I also found that picking up a book enabled me to have some "private" time. Fred and I were together almost 24 hours a day, and often others were around as well. It was all good, but I needed my private space too. The aft cabin of our boat helped, for it allowed us to be out of eyesight of one another.

Cindy and Reed arrived in the bay outside of Barra. Fred went into the entrance channel in our dinghy to measure water depths so they could get inside without getting stuck. When they were safely anchored, we showed them the town and all bought tickets for our planned bus trip to Guadalajara. The bus would be a big, modern, Primera Plus. It had air-conditioning, movies, and a hostess who served coffee and cold soda. No "chicken buses" on this trip! (That was the term we affectionately used for local buses, which were very old, brightly decorated, school buses. They were almost always stuffed with people who sometimes carried chickens, small animals, and large bundles—and they were always hot inside.) This bus to Guadalajara would be a luxury! We were all excited. It would be a big change of pace and environment.

Getting ready to leave the boat for a week meant eating up everything in the refrigerator. We also wanted to turn off the batteries before we went. Our emergency pump would remain operational, but all other systems requiring electricity would be shut down. We had good friends who had experienced a huge fire on their boat when they were away for several weeks. It had started with an electrical short. We felt good about the calm, protected anchorage, and other boats close by had offered to keep an eye on the "vacant" boats. While we had not encountered any theft thus far, we knew it was a universal problem, and leaving large boats unattended was an invitation for crime. It felt good to know that the "family" would help keep them safe.

"Ohhhh! I can't believe the bus driver is passing that car," Fred exclaimed. "That's suicidal!"

The road over the mountains to Guadalajara was steep, narrow, and winding. There were no shoulders alongside, and a gigantic drop-off loomed for much of the trip.

"I can't watch," I said. "I much prefer looking at the countryside. It's sure good to see something other than sea, sand, and palm trees." Our scheduled five-hour trip turned into six and a half hours as we wound our way inland, and we were all glad to finally arrive.

For five days, Cindy, Reed, Fred, and I played "tourist" and discovered the sights and sounds of Guadalajara, the Garden City—and learned a little about the delights and passions of the two million people who live there. In the center of old town we rented rooms in a large Spanish home that had been converted into a funky *posada*. It only cost 15 dollars a night, was mostly clean, and the landlady was a real kick. From there we walked for miles and miles, and then walked some more. We quickly became aware that we were a very visible minority, and children (and sometimes their parents) stared at us as we passed.

I loved seeing the children. The little girls were dressed in fancy dresses and looked so precious as they walked with their families around the plazas and gardens. When I smiled at them, and then at their moms, the parents would beam with pride. How like parents everywhere! We all enjoy attention being paid to our children. The women dressed with great style, not like the poorer folks of the beach villages. I felt I could have been in New York. There seemed to be 20 shoe stores on every street. We learned of one street that had 70! One day we found the local market, reported to be the biggest in the world; the prepared food area had at least a hundred stalls and counters, all filled with locals. When we walked in and found a place to sit, *everybody* turned to stare at us!

One of the special times that warmed our hearts was whenever we stopped to look at a map or appeared confused about directions. Someone *always* stopped to offer us help! Of course, the conversations were all in Spanish because very few residents spoke English, but Reed and I did pretty well with the language when we accompanied it with our "charades" act.

"Let's go to Telaquepaque and Tonala tomorrow," Reed said one night. We were sitting on the steps surrounding a plaza, listening to one of the many strolling Mariachi bands. "I've finally learned how to say the names—so I can ask for directions."

"This is unbelievable," I said as we got off the bus at the market town of Telaquepaque. "There are truly *thousands* of stalls and shops along every street. It goes on for miles. There's no way we can see it all!"

And we didn't. After hours of shopping, there were many streets yet un-traveled, but we finally had to call it quits.

After five active days soaking up the sights and culture of this huge metropolitan city, with its contrasts of old and new, we were glad to be on our way home. At each bus stop, as we rode back over the mountains, folks would come on briefly to either sing and play a guitar for a tip or sell some kind of food item. Just like on the beaches, the kids would sell Chicklet gum.

"Man, does it ever feel good to be back home," said Fred as we wearily climbed aboard *Grace*.

"It really *does* feel like home, doesn't it?" I replied. "And everything looks just like we left it, thank goodness."

More and more boats kept arriving for the upcoming fiesta week. About 12 sailboats were able to get into the lagoon at Barra; the rest were anchored at nearby Melaque. That town's patron saint was St. Patricio, so they hosted a huge "St. Patrick's Day" party and cruisers all along the Pacific coast of Mexico arranged to come for this event in the middle of March. There were to be daily parades, rodeos every night, and a carnival/midway that was sure to bustle with music, colors, fun, and excitement. The food vendors would tempt us to try all the Mexican delights. It was not a week to be on a diet. We hopped on a local bus to Melaque and in 15 minutes were making our way down to the beach.

"Look at the boats rocking," I said. The cruising boats had anchored just beyond the breakers and were rolling in the ocean swells. There were probably 30 of them swinging on their hooks. "I'm *so* glad we were able to get into the lagoon! Let's go over to Philamina's."

Philamina was a legend amongst the cruising community, and her beach restaurant and bar catered to them. She was a large, gregarious Mexican woman who loved to have fun and enjoyed the friendship of visiting cruisers. We found a number of friends there, planning for the "Cruiser's Parade" on the last day of the fiesta.

"Wait 'til you see our sand sculpture," I teased. "It's going to win the prize!" Philamina was sponsoring the contest on the beach in front of her restaurant. Since the prize was a shrimp dinner for two, we were motivated to win. There would be many more silly contests that would draw mostly cruisers. We walked downtown with Cindy and Reed to check on the festivities and eat some of the goodies from the many food booths.

"Wow—I bet everybody in town is here tonight," I yelled to Fred over the blaring, joyful music.

"And most of the neighboring towns as well," he said. "Look at that mechanical bull. I haven't seen anybody remain on it for the whole ride."

"I think they turn it up to go faster for the adults, because some of the kids have a more gentle ride. But you're right—everybody gets thrown off. Good thing there's lots of padding on the ground around it. Want to try it?" I joked.

"Are you kidding?" he replied with a laugh. "I value my neck too much."

The fiesta atmosphere was electric—and intensified by typically loud Mexican music. (Even when there wasn't a fiesta, someone was always playing music, from early morning until late at night.) We often thought the local music had a beat similar to the Czech "oompha band" from Fred's heritage, and the rhythm made our feet tap and bodies sway. The town's outdoor basketball court was filled with lively dancing couples, including children who danced with their parents or by themselves. While we watched, we heard some shrieks from down the street.

"Look out!" someone yelled. "Here comes *El Toro*!"

"A bull? Here on the streets?" I asked anxiously. The yelling and screaming had become louder and people were laughing and starting to move aside. No one looked frightened; even the kids were excited.

"It's a man wearing a bull costume," said Reed. "He shoots fireworks from the headdress into the crowd. We don't want to be too close—it seems pretty risky to me."

Sure enough, running down the street was a man pretending to be a bull. The fireworks appeared to be small rockets that blazed from the horns on his costume.

"This is insane," I said, as we ran for cover. "Someone could really get hurt." The threat of real danger added an unusual spark of excitement, but the crowd was laughing, enjoying the local tradition.

Later in the evening, Fred and several of the other cruising men helped the locals erect a 40-foot tower made of bamboo and strapped with all kinds of fireworks. It was quite a feat just to get it to an upright position. When the fireworks were lit, they shot off in all directions, again making an incredible (although dangerous) display. Children carried cardboard on their heads for protection from the rockets and competed with each other to see how close they could come to the tower.

We marveled at the difference between the Latin culture and our own regarding exposing our children to the types of danger we had seen this night. Certainly these parents loved their children just as much as parents in our own country loved theirs, yet they had a different approach to experiencing risk. Perhaps it was the awareness that we can't protect our children from everything: Here parents let their kids learn some lessons in how to keep themselves safe. Even allowing the cruisers to help erect their tower runs counter to the behaviors we are accustomed to in the States, where fear of lawsuits and litigation prevent such "helpfulness." In our spontaneous effort to assist—and to respect and appreciate the culture we were in—we had become a part of it; our sense of shared humanity at that moment transcended national and/or societal "boundaries." We wished we could have talked with someone more on the subject, but this was definitely neither the time nor place.

Walking over to the carnival area, we heard Bob from *Charlie's Girl* bet Reed 20 dollars that he couldn't stay on the mechanical bull for an entire ride.

"You're on," Reed said with a laugh, and hurried over to take a turn. While we all watched, along with dozens of locals, Reed climbed aboard the big machine and began "hamming" it up. He waved to the crowd, held a hand over his head like the rodeo riders, and whooped and hollered. His blond hair and infectious grin, along with his Hollywood bravado as he bounced up and down, lurching 'round and 'round, soon had everyone laughing and yelling encouragement. When the ride was over, he climbed off the bull, bowed to the crowd's applause, and walked over to Bob for his 20 dollars. We couldn't believe he had done it! Only later did we find out he had told the ride operator in Spanish that he would pay double if the ride would go *"Muy despacio!"* Since Bob didn't speak Spanish, he hadn't understood the arrangement—or that it meant "Very slow!"

Late that night we returned to the lagoon and prepared to row out to our boats. Reed was again savoring the telling of his victory ride and winning bet. With the flair of a victorious matador, he stepped fearlessly into his dinghy, which was rocking gently against the harbor wall. Suddenly his foot slipped, and, with a loud splash, he ended up head first in the water. Undaunted, he came up spitting water, shook his head, displayed that familiar grin, and said, "You can't win 'em all!"

"Come on, no rest for the weary," Fred said the next morning when I wanted to sleep in. "We said we were going to paint the wall today."

In several countries it is the custom of the cruising boats to paint the vessel's name (and sometimes a logo) on a town wall dedicated for that purpose. These colorful walls record the journeys of mariners over many years. Barra de Navidad had such a wall and we wanted to be a part of it. Some of the artwork looked very professional, and we wanted our painting to look good. We had decided to use a large sun, similar to that used by Sun Valley resorts, for our logo. We had labored one whole morning to make a stencil so we could use spray paint, creating the same results wherever we painted it. Needing to get the job done before the wind came up, we had set our alarm for sunrise. We worked for some time and finally had it finished.

We were proud of our efforts.

126

"It looks great," I said. "Do you think anyone will get the connection of 'The Son/sun' symbolism along with our boat name?" Our desire had been that the sun would represent our Christian faith in the Son of God, and that it was only through His amazing Grace that we were here in this place, doing what we were doing. The longer we cruised, the more we felt this as a certainty.

"Maybe *they* won't get it," Fred replied, "but it means something to *us*."

Fred insisted on touching up areas of the painting that I thought were okay, and I became impatient. On such a joint project, we frequently had different approaches, and getting the job done always involved a process of communication and compromise. I often thought that working together should get easier after almost 30 years of marriage, but not so. Seeing things differently and having distinctive ideas has been a challenge—but also a great benefit many times. We knew we were a good team. So I thought I'd keep him around, and was I ever glad he continued to endure me!

On the day of the sand sculpture contest we toiled under the blazing sun for several hours, creating our new logo in three-dimension.

"I don't know, Fred," I said, as I viewed our completed design. "It looks a bit like an octopus with many arms."

"No way," he responded. "It's better than all the rest of the entries." And the judges agreed. Shrimp dinner here we come!

One afternoon we went to the rodeo. The events were all bull riding, but the party in the grandstands had the most action. There were live bands playing continuously, dancing in the aisles, a constant stream of food vendors, and buckets of beer. We were the only *gringos* there, and people all around offered us soda, food, or beer; they also explained what was happening or what we were eating and generally included us in the fun. We were guests at the party! When the band started a new song, many would squeal with delight and start dancing—and boy, did they have the moves. Would that we could dance like that!

Suddenly, a huge fight broke out in the arena between the younger men, who were riding, and the older, more seasoned, *macho caballeros*.

"Wow—these guys are really going at it," Fred said.

"Look! Here come the police. They have shotguns!" I exclaimed. Soon things settled down, and shortly thereafter the young men walked over to shake hands and make peace with the older cowboys. Everyone laughed and clapped as if it were all an expected part of the afternoon fun.

On the final day of the fiesta, we arrived in Melaque just as Mass was finishing and the Blessing of the Fleet was beginning. Many of the cruisers who were anchored there had brought their dinghies to the beach, and the priest, choir boys, and nuns climbed aboard. The flotilla of dinghies went to each of the anchored boats, where a priest sprinkled Holy Water and offered up prayers and a blessing. It was some time before they arrived back at the beach, with their vestments dripping and delighted smiles on their faces.

The Cruisers' Parade was the final event of the week. Never before had the *gringos* participated in such a parade, and we all dressed in green and white and carried balloons and banners. Some had borrowed horses, and Phil provided music. We walked through the town to the church and threw candy to the kids along the way. The townspeople waved and cheered and were pleased that we had joined in their celebration, particularly when we placed large flower bouquets on the church's altar following the evening Mass. It was truly a feeling of international *companerismo*.

Before leaving Melaque, we finally connected with friends we had not seen for some time. They had traveled down the coast several months after we had. How different their cruising experience had been! They had taken longer passages rather than short hops, usually stayed in large city marinas rather than anchoring near small villages, and had never taken their dinghy to shore through the surf. While in port, they spent much of their time on the boat. They were outraged at having to drink instant coffee in restaurants, and they spoke no Spanish. They were not impressed with Mexico, thinking it a "third world" country that had nothing to offer other than its scenery. They had interacted mostly with other cruisers or Americans but seldom with the locals. They had not eaten from the street food stands, fearing the food and water, yet still had experienced the "*touristas,*" which added to their negative impressions. We were saddened to hear all of this. Had we been in different countries? To our thinking, they were missing the best parts of Mexico by not sampling the culture and lifestyles of the Mexican people. We reminded ourselves that there were "different strokes for different folks," and renewed our determination to look for the positives in new and different situations.

Finally, it was time to move on to new harbors and new places, and we left Barra in the company of *Yobo* and *Lamorna*. Costa Rica was calling! It felt glorious to be out on the sea again, with the breeze in our faces, the sun warming our skin, fluffy clouds floating overhead, and nothing but water surrounding us. Light winds from the northwest allowed us to sail blissfully along, savoring the relaxed and private time. We found a small cove in which to anchor for the night. I had a good deal of work to do in preparing our navigation routes from the charts and reading about upcoming ports from our cruising notes, but I decided to curl up with a book instead. The work could wait until *mañana*. We were feeling the need for some "down time," so we all stayed on our own boats and turned in early.

After so much time playing, there really was a lot of work that needed to be done. The main head hadn't been pumping well, which created a flushing problem. So Fred started emptying out the large storage lazarette in the cockpit to get to the pump. At times like these, I was grateful for having two heads aboard.

"I'm *so* glad that this is a 'blue' job," I joked. "You never even complain about working on it."

"Gotta be done," he said stoically, from deep down in the lazarette. "Hey, today is Sunday. Go get the tapes." I hurried to play our Sunday morning tapes and began to sing along. Soon equipment littered the deck and moving about the boat was difficult, but the project was going well so I didn't complain. At least I wasn't squished down in the hatch with the heat and the smell! I continued with the navigation work and then put things back where they belonged later that day.

The following day we entered a bay near the resort of Las Hadas.

"Look at that," I said. "This is where they filmed the movie *10*, with Bo Derick." Looking like giant steps ascending the hillside, the huge mega-resort glowed a brilliant white in the sunshine.

"The hotel looks beautiful *and* expensive," Fred replied. "But those boats in the marina are sure getting banged and jerked around by the surf. Let's go anchor outside the breakwater with those other sailboats."

After getting settled, we prepared to go ashore to complete the obligatory paper work. Checking in with the Port Captain meant going first to the marina dinghy dock, climbing the hillside through the resort, and then taking a bus into the city of Manzanillo. Roaming the narrow streets of the old part of downtown, we finally found the offices and completed the necessary forms. It took most of the day. It was hot, and we were tired and anxious to go for a swim, so we decided to return to the boat by taking a shortcut.

"Who told you about this route?" Fred asked. He was irritated. We had walked on a golf course for a while and then climbed over a low barbed wire fence.

"The folks on the boat anchored next to ours," I replied. I wondered anxiously if we were going in the right direction. After working our way around some construction, we were relieved to finally see the dinghy dock and hurried to *Grace* to put on our swimsuits. Going back to the resort, we went directly to the huge swimming pool.

"Ahhhh! Now *this* is the life," Fred exhaled, as he reclined in a lounge chair beside the beautiful pool, which had small islands built throughout the water. They were full of large tropical plants, flowers, and palm trees. More manicured lawns, wandering paths, and vibrant gardens surrounded the entire area. It was an oasis and we relaxed, soaking up the beauty and luxury of that elegant place.

"Look! There are iguanas swimming in the pool," I said in disbelief. "They look like a miniature version of some pre-historic monster or huge, ferocious lizard."

"Sure enough. Must be feeding time," Fred said. We watched as a worker laid out lettuce and vegetables on the lawn.

"The iguanas live on the islands in the pool," said the man. "They don't come into the water when people are swimming. They won't hurt you," he added. Maybe not, but they sure looked scary and I didn't want to get too close to them. Some were three or four feet long, with large spiked points around their necks. I was glad to hear they were vegetarians.

The following day we made our way to a large supermarket and loaded up with supplies. Taking a taxi back to Las Hadas, we discovered that the ocean surge had all the boats—both in the marina and at anchor—bouncing and rolling violently. When we arrived back on board *Grace*, we pulled up the anchor and motored about an hour to a nearby bay for calmer anchorage. We still had all our new supplies to put away before we could call it a day. I soaked all our fresh veggies and fruits in an iodine water solution so we would not pick up any unwanted bugs or bacteria. Anything that was sold in cardboard we transferred into plastic containers and returned the cardboard to shore. We were told that cockroaches lay their eggs in the glue of the boxes, and these hatch when stored on the boat. Keeping the cardboard off the boat helped keep those critters from tagging along. An infestation of cockroaches was difficult to eradicate. So far we had been lucky and had no problem with them. Now, if only we could solve the problem of the mosquitoes!

During the night I realized I had developed a urinary infection. I began taking some antibiotics we had aboard but quickly realized I would need additional medication. The following day we returned to the anchorage at Las Hadas and rode a bus to a pharmacy. In our halting Spanish we explained the problem to the pharmacist, who then suggested a medication. He was caring, patient, and knowledgeable, and made sure we understood how to take the medicine as well as drink plenty of fluids. Our anxiety about getting adequate care decreased, and we were appreciative of the ease of access to the medical system here.

"That guy was really helpful," Fred said. "He certainly went 'the extra mile.' I'm glad we were able to buy more of the malaria prevention medicine, too." Once again, we found the people of Mexico to be quick to help, and caring in response to us.

Walking back through Las Hadas in the early evening, we stopped for a glass of wine at a beautiful plaza within the resort and listened to an accomplished flamenco guitarist. Sitting at a table in the elegant and romantic setting, with the hauntingly lovely music and the cooler night air bathing us in comfort, we were surrounded by a feeling of pampered luxury. A full moon shone down from the clear, starlit sky. It was a fairytale moment. As we sipped our wine, we savored the ambience—such an incredible contrast to many of our rough and tumble experiences on this journey. That night, sitting on the terrace of Las Hadas, I felt like a *lady*—and I had even worn a sundress instead of my usual shorts and T-shirt. Such a feeling didn't last long, however, as we later rowed back to *Grace* and climbed aboard—not the easiest thing to do in a dress. At least the anchorage was calm.

"We need to get diesel before we leave," Fred said the next morning. "It's still rough in the marina, so I think we should borrow gas cans and take the dinghy in rather than try to tie *Grace* up to the dock."

"I'll call on the radio to line up some cans," I said, but I was dreading the backbreaking procedure that I knew would take most of the day. As I grudgingly prepared for the task, I again remembered Fred saying, "If it was easy—everybody would do it."

When we left the following morning, we got the news about our friends on *Kacheena* who had come to visit us in Melaque. Kier had experienced a ruptured appendix just before they were to leave Puerta Vallarta and was hospitalized. It looked like their trip to the Marquesas would be canceled due to complications. Our worries about getting sick on this trip returned, as well as the feeling of gratitude for good health thus far.

"I want to try and call the kids," I said to Fred. "After hearing about Kier, I need to hear that they are all okay."

We switched off the engine to make a ham radio call to Lance and Dawn. What luck! We were able to get through to both of them.

"Hey—what's up?" said Lance, when we were patched through to him. "I'm planning on coming to Mexico the end of April and want to sail with you to Costa Rica. Can I bring my windsurf board and a quiver of sails?"

Of course! How thrilled we were! All was well on the home front, and we grinned all afternoon.

The sun was low in the sky as we motored into a bay for the night. Since we had a clear view of the horizon, we quickly got out the binoculars and put on our "Amazing Grace" cassette tape in preparation for the sunset and its "green flash." Although it was often difficult to see, we had discovered that, when we watched with binoculars, we could spot it almost every time—provided there were no clouds in the sight line. That night it was spectacular! The golden glow of fading sunlight gave way to the brilliant momentary flash of green, signaling the end to another gorgeous day.

Since we had heard the anchorage was often roll-y, we put out both a bow and stern anchor to try to keep the bow pointing into the waves.

It didn't help much. We were tossed all night long, getting virtually no sleep. The up and down motion was manageable, but the side-to-side movement was so irritating and relentless that when we got up the following morning we were more tired than when we went to bed. Ah well; there has to be some minuses with all the pluses.

One day we were motoring not far from a large industrial port. I was down below and heard a horrendous thudding sound, like something hitting the hull or keel. Instantly, I could feel the adrenalin racing through my body and my heart began to pound. I dashed up on deck.

"What in the world was *that*?" I said. "It sounded *horrible!*"

Obviously, we had hit something. Hitting a submerged container that had fallen from a ship was every cruiser's nightmare. There was no way to see something floating just beneath the surface, and there could be huge damage from such a collision—even sinking the vessel. We looked behind us, and Fred thought he saw something moving away.

"Maybe it was a whale," he said, "or an oil drum from that port we just passed. Or it could have been one of those huge turtles, like the ones we saw earlier today."

We knew that three-to four-foot turtles sometimes took "naps" in the water, with only a small portion of their shell above surface. Sometimes a seagull would stand on the shell, so we knew to avoid what appeared to be a bird standing on water. We anxiously checked for damage but could find none. Again we were aware of how much we were in God's hands and depending on His grace and protection.

We had not stayed at a marina since Puerta Vallarta and needed to get some work done on the boat, so, after a great stop in the anchorage at Isla Grande, we decided to take the hit on the cruising budget and visit the new marina at Ixtapa. The docks and facilities were not yet completed, but boats were able to stay there. When we arrived just outside the rock entrance jetties, it was low tide, so we partially pumped up the keel to make sure we wouldn't run aground. We carefully watched the ocean waves approaching the jetties for several minutes. All looked good, so we proceeded through a narrow entrance, well marked by buoys.

We were just into the channel, when, to our horror, we found ourselves in *breaking* waves. However, because of the restricted space, we were unable to turn around. We knew that if a wave were to break under us, it could turn the boat sideways and we would be thrown against the rock walls of the jetty. The thought was terrifying. Our only course was to get through the entrance as quickly as possible.

I had been down in the cabin studying the charts. As I came up into the cockpit, I saw the water behind us rising to tower over us. "Oh *no!*" I yelled to Fred. "Go *fast!*"

Fred quickly glanced over his shoulder to see a 15-foot wave heading our way. "Oh *shit!*" was his only reply, as he jammed the throttle as far forward as it would go, hoping to outrun the oncoming wave. I stood there frozen with fear as I watched the water rise threateningly above us, lifting up the stern of the boat while the bow remained down in the trough. Fred handled the vessel like a champ, and we flew through that entrance at a 45-degree angle, surfing down the front of the swell. Once inside the marina, the water quickly dispersed to a calm, flat sea, and we motored to a safe place.

"I don't think I have ever been so scared," I panted. "I can't stop shaking!" My hands and body continued to shake for another 15 minutes. It felt like forever before my heart rate returned to normal. By then, we were securely tied into a brand new dock slip, telling others about our harrowing entrance. No one else had experienced such a problem, but no one else had tried to enter on low tide either.

As we looked about the new facility, we saw that it was very well protected from the ocean swell, and we relaxed, believing we were finally in a safe place, at least for the time being. Little did we know . . . .

What a joy it was to get out the hose and wash all the salt off the boat—and to use as much water as we wanted. The following day we walked by the modern resort hotels of Ixtapa and boarded a bus to the neighboring town of Zihuatenejo, about 15 minutes away. We completed the usual port check-in procedures and explored the charming small town. It was a typical, working class Mexican town, with many small shops, narrow cobbled streets, and traditional style buildings with red tile roofs. It nestled around the large bay, and a number of sailboats were at anchor just off the fishing pier. Lively Mexican music could be heard just about everywhere. Dogs roamed freely, and friendly people greeted us on the streets. How different this was from the "tourist-oriented," large, and rather impersonal modern architecture of the Ixtapa resorts.

Our evening entertainment involved sneaking around the docks just after dark with some kids and another couple, trying to spot "the crocodile." The marina area used to be a swamp that contained several hundred of the big creatures, but they were caught and "relocated" when the marina was being built. One or two remained, we were told, but they only came out at night and swam away if they spotted people or heard noise. Sure enough, we hid behind the dock boxes and saw a couple of them, about eight to ten feet long. It was a daunting task, however, because we were in the meantime eaten alive by myriads of mosquitoes.

We spent a couple of days working on *Grace*. A continuing problem with the head had Fred announcing he needed to go in the water and clean the barnacles from the through-hull fitting. I was incredulous.

"You can't go in this water," I said. "There are crocodiles in here!"

"Ah—they only come out at night," he replied. "I won't be under for very long." Despite my vociferous objections, Fred jumped in the water and dove under the boat to fix the problem. I stood on the aft deck carefully watching the water for the feared beasts, knowing I could do little but yell if I spotted one.

Fred was gone only a couple of minutes. Just before he climbed up the swim ladder, we heard a man yelling, "*Señor! Señor! Muy peligroso, muy peligroso!*" (Very dangerous!) He continued to yell as he ran our way. "*Cocodillos!*"

Just then, we spotted a menacing 12-foot crocodile swim toward the stern of our boat. The monstrous critter stopped about 20 yards away, partially submerged his huge body near another dock, and ominously remained there for the next two hours. Fortunately, there was no "free lunch" for him that day. I was so shaken and angry with Fred that I wasn't about to fix lunch for him, either. He could jolly well make his own. And we had thought this marina would be *safe*!

On Palm Sunday we attended a Baptist church in "Z" town, anticipating a celebration service. After 45 minutes of listening to someone talking, we thought perhaps we had misunderstood and were actually in some sort of class. Disappointed, we headed to a nearby restaurant, only to have a good deal of difficulty trying to order. Usually we ordered "the plate of the day," which would be the most economical selection. Apparently this place had three such entrees, and the poor waiter couldn't seem to make us understand that we needed to choose one of the three. Back at the boat we had a couple of young women come to talk with us about doing our laundry, only we could not figure out the cost. It was fun to talk with them, but the day's experiences made us realize that we really needed to learn more Spanish. I could express myself pretty well for the basic things but got totally lost when folks responded. They spoke so rapidly! I got out the Spanish dictionary and Spanish cassette tapes and resolved to spend more time in study each day.

When we heard that some cruisers were heading back to the States, we spent almost an entire day writing letters, making copies of our monthly newsletter ("The Awesome Adventures of Amazing Grace"), and addressing envelopes.

"It looks like our supply of U.S. stamps is dwindling," Fred said.

"We'd better add that to the list of things we want Lance to bring us when he comes," I replied.

As we returned from the mail drop, we reflected on the couple that was headed home and their obviously stormy relationship. I had seen in them many of the same issues that were evident with couples in therapy when I worked in "the other world." I was concerned for them and believed that alcohol was a part of the problem.

"Remember when we were preparing to go cruising? We were warned that alcohol abuse was prevalent with a number of cruisers," Fred said.

"Yeah—I guess because it feels like every day is a vacation; or it often seems like a time to celebrate, especially after some of the difficulties," I said. Contributing to this problem was the cruising community's tendency to congregate at a bar near the anchored boats. Here in "Z" town, the cruising hangout offered beer that only cost the equivalent of 33 cents—cheaper than a soda or water, as long as you returned the bottle. On top of that, with the heat, one was often thirsty. We tried to be cognizant of the potential for problems and carefully limited ourselves, generally, to one beer and one drink a day—often omitting the drink.

Before leaving the marina and heading over to "Z" town with the boat, we again needed to fill up with diesel. We took *Grace* over to the fuel dock and watched as two men laboriously carried over a 50-gallon container of fuel.

"That has to be incredibly heavy," I exclaimed. "How will they get it in our tank?"

"They siphon it out with that rubber hose," said Fred. As we watched, the men lifted the weighty container aboard with some difficulty and attached a hose. In order to get a siphon started, they took turns sucking on the hose. It almost made me gag to watch them. I guess there are many ways to get the job done, and we had seen some very creative solutions here in Mexico. Soon our tank was full and we were ready to leave. Apprehension gripped me as I remembered our entrance through the jetties, but our exit was thankfully uneventful, and we proceeded on our day trip to Zihuatenejo.

"I'm too tired to go in with the others tonight," I said to Fred after we had anchored. "Let's have dinner aboard instead."

"Sounds good to me," he responded. "It's been a busy day, and I'm tired too." I had been trying to make big meals for Fred so he could gain back the 10 pounds he had lost since leaving home. No such problem for me—without my daily running, I struggled *not* to gain weight. It didn't seem fair!

Sometimes, when we were in a port with a number of other cruising boats, there would be a semi-organized meeting. Such was the group who met one day to discuss sailing from Mexico on to Costa Rica. A lot of information was shared, particularly about crossing the infamous Gulf of Tehuantapec, on the southern tip of Mexico. That stretch of water was feared by almost everyone. My anxiety level started to rise again as I heard about fierce winds that raise huge, choppy seas when they blow from the Gulf of Mexico—intensifying as they cross over the small land mass of southern Mexico and into the open waters of the Gulf of Tehuantapec. Once again, the suggested course was to either "keep one foot on the beach and the other on the boat" while crossing the gulf, so that you could throw out an anchor if conditions got really bad, or else cross it about 500 miles offshore. We walked back to the beach to get our dinghy, thinking about the meeting and what lay ahead.

"You know, the sailing has been so easy and anchorages so delightful here along the central and southern coast that I dread the thought of difficult conditions, storms, and frightening passages again," I said.

"I hear you," he replied. "There were also those reports of increased security problems in Costa Rica. So far we've heard of little theft, but there are apparently lots of things being stolen from boats at anchor further south. I'd sure like to have some way to secure the boat while keeping the hatches open at night."

"Yeah, it gets too hot to close them," I added. "It would also be great to leave the hatches open when we are gone from the boat." We had the alarm system, but we now felt like we needed something more. Like Scarlet O'Hara in *Gone with the Wind*, though, I vowed to think about all those anxiety-producing issues "tomorrow," and continued that day to enjoy the Golden Coast of Mexico.

It was Good Friday, and in the evening we headed for town and the Baptist church. Again, it was not a worship service, so, feeling disappointed, we walked to the Catholic Church. It was crammed with people overflowing onto the streets. We stood with the crowd for a while but could not see or hear any of the service, so we left, again feeling disappointed. How we missed our church family that night! We stopped for dinner and later watched families dancing in the town square. Ready to head back to the boat in the dark, I stood in shallow water holding the dinghy in place while Fred started the engine. With the incoming waves, it was difficult to keep my dress from getting wet while holding the boat with one hand and my skirt with the other. Finally, I gave up and just stuffed the skirt into my underpants and marveled at the many ways I had changed!

"Fred, come here. It's *Takamami*," I yelled one morning. I had just entered the cockpit after awakening. Anchored beside us was a boat whose owners we had come to know in the yacht yard in England when we were both purchasing our sailboats. They were a Japanese couple that had been cruising internationally for the last five years. Sitting in the cockpit was the husband, waiting for us to wake up and come on deck. They had heard we were in the area and came looking for us, anchoring sometime during the night. What fun it was to get together, renew our friendship, and hear of their travels. It truly was a small world!

On the morning VHF net we heard from a boater who had been living on his boat in this town for a long time. He reported that the Port Captain had asked all cruisers to stop paying the young boys by the dinghy landing area to "watch" their dinghies. The boys had been suggesting that someone might harm the dinghies if they were left unattended. A few boats had been filled with sand or turned over. Giving them money to "watch" the dinghy was a practice we didn't like. Even though the boys were playful, it was a form of extortion, and though the boaters paid only small amounts to the boys, the money added up by the end of the day. Sometimes the boys would return to their homes with more money than what their fathers had earned working all day. It was creating family problems; thus the Port Captain had intervened. It certainly made us think about how our actions could seem innocent enough but impact others and have rippling effects on the places we visited. We certainly didn't want to create problems. We all agreed to no longer pay the boys.

Days were now often spent getting ready for our continued trip south. There were cruising notes to read and organize, charts to be studied and catalogued, and navigation points to be entered into our electronic systems. Other cruisers offered to let us copy their charts. We were glad there were copiers available that could handle the three-by-four-foot charts. Many were charts not available in the U.S. The copies were much cheaper—but not as easy to read as the originals. I penciled in the shoreline, which helped.

While we waited to use the copier one day, a young woman who worked at the shop sat and talked with us on the steps for about 20 minutes. When we were ready to go, she came over and gave us a small lighter with "Zihuatenejo" written on it.

"This is so you will remember me and my town," she said. We were touched.

Another time, Fred was trying to get some special kind of wire to install an additional lightning grounding system. Four men came over to him in the hardware store and spent many minutes trying to help him figure out what was needed. These small acts of kindness humbled us and left us with an ongoing feeling of awe for the gracious hospitality we continued to receive.

On our final day in "Z" town, Fred went ashore to do the necessary "check-out" procedure with the Port Captain and copy one more chart. Meanwhile, I enjoyed the time to myself and puttered around making cookies and doing a little laundry by hand. We had gotten quite wet in our dinghy the previous night, and the pesky thing about salt water is that, after it dries, it leaves cloth feeling stiff, or it reabsorbs moisture from the air at night and feels clammy.

That evening we met several other couples at the cruisers' favorite "Blue Porch" restaurant for dinner. It had oilcloth tablecloths and some of the plates were chipped, but for less than two dollars we could get a good meal. These fun and inexpensive places allowed us to save our money for boat repairs and trips home. They were also places where the local folks ate, thus we knew the food was good. A number of us sat at the outdoor tables.

"I'll be right back," Fred said to me. "I want to check on the dinghy."

As I watched him walk down the street, I whispered to Cindy, "I think I know where he's going. We're celebrating our 30-year anniversary in a week, and we were looking at some beautiful gold peso bracelets today. I bet he's going back to get one. At least, I hope he is!"

When Fred returned, I winked at Cindy and pretended to be deep in conversation with our friends. We would see if, after all these years together, I knew him as well as I thought I did.

"Ahhh! It feels so good to be out at sea. 'On the road again,'" I sang to Fred the following morning.

"It sure does—and that high cloud cover feels good too. Not so hot," replied Fred. "I'm glad *Yobo* left this morning as well. We should be able to do those 40 miles to the next anchorage easily."

What joy it was to put up the sails and revel in the comfortable ocean breeze! We were filled with a renewed sense of freedom, and we giggled like kids filled with anticipation and excitement. The ocean was calm and we sailed along quietly. New ports and places were calling our names, and we were a'comin.'

When we anchored that night, friends on *Melinda Lee* came over to visit. They were a family with two young children: Ben, age two, and Annie, age six. We enjoyed playing with the children but thought later how different cruising with kids would be. There would be so many more things to consider—not to mention so much more work for the parents. But what a great learning experience for the kids!

We continued sailing south along with Cindy and Reed, the four of us planning a trip ashore to explore Papanoa, a small village in the bay where we had anchored. Soon the four of us were walking along a dirt road that wound up a hill to the village. It was hot and dusty and we were beginning to wonder if this was a good idea.

"*Buenos Dias.* Do you want a ride?" asked a man, stopping with his pickup truck. *Of course!* The four of us climbed in the back and bounced our way up to the town. We found a pool hall and played a few games while visiting with some of the locals. One young man recommended a restaurant down by the bay and we went there later for a yummy seafood dinner. As we were eating, the same young man walked into the restaurant.

"The shrimp boat just came in," he said. "Do you want to buy some fresh shrimp?"

Fred and Reed went over to the boat, climbed down in the hold, and came back with a bag of gorgeous jumbo shrimp. The young man accompanied them, apparently wanting to make sure they got what they wanted and had no problems. He even bought us all a beer back at the restaurant and would take nothing we offered in exchange for his help. Those small-town folks were the greatest! Many were eager just to talk with us.

"Where's the *baño*?" Cindy asked, when I returned to the table after asking for the location of the bathroom.

"Believe me, you don't want to know," I laughed. "It's a large area behind this building with a plastic tarp stretched around it for walls. There are no toilets, only flat ground. And it's dry and hard as concrete."

"You're right. I guess I can wait," said Cindy with a pained look on her face. It was definitely another M.E!

Charmed by Papanoa, we reluctantly pulled anchor about seven that evening for an overnight sail to Acapulco. We were hoping to arrive there late afternoon of the following day, before it got dark. As I came out into the cockpit after a nap, I looked at the sky.

"Oh my," I exclaimed. "Look at all those stars. There are *myriads* of them!"

"And look at how low on the horizon the Big Dipper and North Star are," Fred added. "As we keep going further south, we will eventually not be able to see them at all."

"I'll hate to see them go," I said. "They're a connection to home. But maybe then we'll be able to see the Southern Cross."

Sitting there in the cockpit as we motored along under those beautiful stars, I felt so small. It was difficult to think that we were really significant in the grand scheme of things. Yet I believed we were.

"Look at the phosphorescence in the water behind us," Fred said. Turning around, I saw thousands of sparkling diamonds shimmering and dancing in our wake. It left a trail that led far off into the distance. Any splash or disturbance of the water caused it to glow from the microscopic organisms it contained. In my imagination it was "fairy dust," and it was beautiful. My watch that night was glorious.

Another beautiful day dawned at sea—serene and majestic. It made me think of our beautiful Dawn, and I wondered how she was doing getting a new job and apartment.

As we approached Acapulco later that day, we heard a radio call from *Yobo*.

"Our engine died and we can't get it going. We don't have any wind here. Do you?" asked Cindy.

"Give us your position, and we'll turn around and come back to you," Fred said.

It was about four miles, and they were dead in the water. While they worked on the motor, we practiced our "Man Overboard" routine using just the sails to maneuver the boat. Fred was beginning to think about how to give *Yobo* a tow when, to everyone's great relief, the engine started and we all headed toward Acapulco. It was times like this when it was good to be buddy-boating.

The bay at Acapulco was crowded with all kinds of boats, water skiers, and jet skis. We found mooring buoys and tied up, but were too tired to go ashore. Tomorrow. Thankfully, things quieted down as evening came upon us, and we were grateful for a good night's sleep.

"Acapulco. We are in Acapulco. Doesn't that sound exotic?" I said. We were going ashore that morning, and I was excited.

"They even have a yacht club, but there are apparently no slips available," Fred responded. "At least we'll have a place to dock the dinghy rather than having to go in through the surf."

While many ports had all the offices for check-in procedures located in one place, such was not the case here. We had to take the bus to places many miles apart, and it took most of the day. We at least got a good look at that huge city in the process. It was also easy to get a little (or a lot) lost. Many times we asked for help and felt like we were being told different directions each time. It was all in the translation. Again I resolved to work harder studying Spanish. We tried to look for parts for the repair work we were doing. Often we couldn't find what we wanted and began to look at other ways and materials we could use to do the job. Finding no stainless steel cable for locking our gear to the deck, for instance, we began to look for electric cable as a substitute. We felt very "Mexican," using the "necessity is the mother of invention" practice just like the locals did.

That evening we found the large *zocala* (plaza) in the old part of town. It was Saturday night and the streets were packed with locals. Almost anything you could imagine was being sold in the little stalls peppering the plaza. All about us blazed the colors and decorations of traditional Mexico, as well as the style of dress and products of modern society. Music, kids, noise, and dogs abounded. It felt like a party! The old Spanish-style buildings surrounding the square made us feel like we were part of another century, and my imagination was going wild. We saw *no* other *gringos*. Walking into an old, domed church, we watched a wedding ceremony for a while before heading back to the boat. We sat in the cockpit with a brandy and savored the multitude of twinkling lights all about the big, busy harbor. It looked like a giant Christmas tree. The cruise ships were decked out with thousands of lights, shining skyscraper hotels ringed the bay, and lights sparkled all over the hillside surrounding the city. This was utterly unlike the fishing villages to which we had grown accustomed.

"Maybe we should spend a night in a hotel for our anniversary," Fred suggested. Oh, what luxury! The idea of fresh, clean sheets, air-conditioning, showering naked and standing up, no getting wet going ashore—what a treat that would be! We began to inquire about costs. Ouch! They were all so expensive. Finally, we decided to go into the marina for a night or two. Semi-luxury instead.

"Happy 30th Anniversary," Fred said the next morning when we awoke. "What were you doing 30 years ago today?"

"It's hard to believe that it has really been that long!" I said. We reminisced for a few minutes on all the experiences we felt so grateful to have had together. So many blessings!

"Enough of that. Time to get to work," Fred said with a laugh. "We're going to the marina. No more waking up every hour or two at night when we bump into this doggone mooring buoy." It had been another long night, and despite everything we tried, nothing seemed to prevent the loud, frequent thudding sound.

Indeed, being in a marina again meant time for lots of work. Fred set up our snazzy hand-wringer on the cockpit pedestal, and, having all the water I needed, I began to wash everything in sight. We had sheets, towels, clothes and underwear hanging all over the boom, lifelines, and deck. We looked like a gypsy vessel! Even with the wringer, it was hard work handling those big items, and I began wishing that we had taken them to a laundry.

I'M ONLY SMILING BECAUSE THE JOB'S ALMOST DONE!

Everything dried quickly in the midday sun, so we washed the boat, not knowing when we would have another opportunity. I also borrowed Cindy's sewing machine to make more "courtesy" flags for each of the countries we would be entering. It was required that we fly each country's flag from our spreaders while we were in their waters. I also made a new awning for the bow of the boat. Finally, finished with chores, we showered and got ready for our big night on the town.

We had invited *Yobo* and *Raporiga* to come over to *Grace* to share a bottle of champagne we had bought at the plaza. As we were opening it, a local man came to try to repair our autopilot.

"That's not champagne," he said when he saw the bottle. "That's sparkling apple juice." Oh dear! Reed quickly went to *Yobo* and returned with the real thing, and we all had a good laugh.

"A little something to remember this day and where we are," said Fred with a twinkle in his eye as he handed me a small wrapped box.

"Ohhh! The gold peso bracelet and a ring that matches," I exclaimed with delight. "They're gorgeous. I love them!" I winked at Cindy as I tried them on. I guess I *did* know him pretty well. Hugging Fred, I felt incredibly *blucky!*

We had a lovely evening. Dinner at a Polynesian restaurant reminded us of our honeymoon in Hawaii. Walking back to the marina, we stopped to call Page. What luck—Dawn was there as well. She was going through a tough time resettling: beginning life in the adult world and missing all her college friends. We knew she would be fine, but we missed being there to give her support. She was turning to Page and Lance for that, though, and that gave us pleasure. Perhaps it was better we were away.

"Here's something for all the boats in the fleet," said Cindy the next morning on the radio net. "You are all invited to a dock party tonight in honor of Fred and Kay's 30-year anniversary." What sweeties she and Reed were—and what a surprise!

That evening dozens of people crowded onto the docks, each bringing something to eat and drink. They offered a nice toast to us, and there was lots of laughter amidst the funny stories, shared ideas for fixing things, and talk of ports further south. Some folks were going to stop in El Salvador, which had recently opened to cruising boats. Others were leaving their boats in Guatemala to do some inland travel. Our ears perked up. How we'd love to do that if we could find a safe place to leave *Grace!* Frequently the conversations of those heading south turned to their apprehension at crossing the Gulf of Tehuantapec.

"Are you going to stay offshore?" someone asked.

"If you do that, you almost need to head straight south from here. It's a long sail before clearing the Gulf."

"What happens if a 'Tehuanapecker' comes up when you are only half way across?"

"I sure hope we can get some weather info from Herb on *Southbound II* so we'll know when there's a window for the crossing."

Everyone had something to say. It made me think that anxiety loves company.

When Susie brought out her guitar, Fred went to get mine, and Tom, who had been a professional drummer, produced drumsticks and a funny box that made a real drum sound. We managed to fit 14 of us on one boat and we sang and played well into the night. Fred was going strong on the tambourine, and several others played the spoons. We were sure we were ready for the recording studio!

Staying at the marina was nice, but with the strong ocean surge, the boat continued to dance around, tugging violently on the dock lines and boat cleats. We decide to return to a mooring buoy, but first we wanted to do some major provisioning. While Fred and Reed made a fuel run, Cindy and I went to the big supermarkets where we could get many prepared or specialty food items that wouldn't be available in small villages further south. We knew we could always buy fresh produce, meat, fish, and bread in the villages. Anything else was unlikely. We loaded up our carts and returned to the marina.

Fred and Reed came along about the time we had everything aboard. Great timing for them! When we finally got out to the mooring buoy, it was evening and, too tired to find a place for all the provisions, we climbed over and around them until the following day.

It was an all-day affair to reorganize and stow everything. We put up our new awning and hoped the fabric would endure the harsh rays of the sun. With it up, we could leave the forward hatch open when it rained. We knew we'd be getting lots of rain in Costa Rica. As the day grew hotter and more humid, we wished we could cool off by jumping in the water. But this bay was so dirty that it wasn't an attractive or healthy option. We were grateful for the shade in the cockpit provided by our bimini, and the awnings that attached to it, as well as the new bow awning. They all made the boat ever so much cooler.

"The renters are behind in their rent," said Page, in a phone patch through the ham radio. "The property manager has been ill, so I don't think he's doing much." I began to feel even more anxious about our finances.

"The stock is still doing well," Fred reassured me. "Not to worry." (He checked the stock market each time he could find an English newspaper.) Since most of the other cruisers were also on tight budgets, we were all in good company.

One night, five couples went ashore to see the famous Acapulco cliff divers. We took a bus, and then hiked up a steep hill. Stopping along the way, we could see the divers in the distance. Finally getting closer, we watched from the side of the road, along with hundreds of other folks, as the men climbed up the jagged rocks of the high cliffs. Reaching the top of the cliffs, they poised on the edge, crossed themselves, and then one by one dove for the water far below. They needed to throw themselves far out from the cliff to avoid landing on the boulders directly beneath. Such a daring feat: It surely wasn't for the fainthearted!

One morning I asked about an English-speaking church on the radio net, only to find that it no longer existed. Later, we got a call from *Valiant Lady*, who suggested that maybe some of us could get together for our own worship time. While we felt a little nervous, we also felt nudged to do that, so I gave an open invitation on the radio net to anyone who wanted to attend. While there were only five of us from three boats that following Sunday morning, and the faith practices of the others were somewhat different than ours, it was a spirit-filled time in which all of us felt richly blessed. The folks from *Valiant Lady* were both pianist and organist, so they played my electric keyboard for some wonderful music. It was a nice connection with "family."

Time to be "on the road again." We completed our check-out procedures with the various officials, cleaned the barnacles off the bottom of the dinghy, loaded it aboard, and got ready for a two day passage. Three boats left the harbor with us, while *Yobo* stayed to fix some of their boat systems. We had an opposing current, so we were not making great time, but it was an enjoyable day. The cabin was *very* warm with all the hatches closed, but we didn't want to risk opening any for fear of a "rogue" wave; so we stayed in the cockpit as much as possible and were glad for the shade from our bimini.

On the second afternoon, we approached a small anchorage and carefully made our way into it, for we had little information about the conditions there. Inside, there were big swells and breakers. It didn't look good, but we were tired and dropped the hook anyway. The other three boats arrived and planned to go ashore. But Fred and I decided, because of all the motion, we would just eat and rest, then continue on rather than spending the night. We later heard that the others didn't sleep at all due to the violent rolling.

"Sorry to wake you, but we need to take a reef in the main," Fred said during the night. "I've been seeing lots of lightning in the distance, and it smells like it will rain soon."

I stumbled out of the sea berth and put on my life jacket. It soon would be time for my watch, anyway, so we completed the task and Fred went below to try to sleep. I settled in to my favorite corner in the cockpit. That night I had difficulty staying awake, so I held the kitchen timer in my hand, just in case. The buzzer never went off, but it sure felt good to close those peepers for even a few minutes.

When dawn came, so did the dolphins. Their playful cavorting brought me some energy for the new day. About nine in the morning we approached Puerto Angel. But, to our chagrin, the autopilot started going awry. It kept veering the boat to the right. How we'd hate to be without that "little guy." It was like having another crew member onboard.

"Look, here comes the Navy," Fred said, only moments after we anchored in the little bay where two of our sailing friends were already at anchor. A small military motorboat was approaching.

"It looks like they plan to board us," I said apprehensively. They pulled alongside roughly, bouncing into our hull. Ouch! We hurried to put out fenders to protect our boat, as they had none on theirs. Five men in fatigue uniforms, with heavy black boots and automatic weapons slung over their shoulders, immediately climbed aboard our boat. No one was smiling.

"*Buenos Dias*," we said, with as much friendliness as we could muster. None of the men spoke English. They pulled out a number of forms they were intent on completing, and roamed freely around the boat. Few made any eye contact, and there wasn't any friendly chatting. At one point they asked if we had any marijuana onboard, and I laughed while replying that we did not. Finally, after 30 tense minutes, they said they were done and left. Black marks from their boots were all over the decks.

"Well, we finally found a flaw in Mexican hospitality," Fred said, and we both laughed.

Several couples had gathered on a boat one evening when, just after dark, we saw another boat entering the bay. "It's *Yobo*," we exclaimed with delight, and went out in the dinghy to help them anchor.

"Finally, all of our systems are functioning," said Reed when they were settled. "What a job. I'll never buy an older boat again!"

Various breakdowns on a boat were not uncommon, particularly with older boats. Since we were concerned about our autopilot not working correctly, we decided to leave the next morning, when there was plenty of daylight. If necessary, we could ask Lance to bring a new one down when he came.

As we left Puerto Angel that Sunday morning, the conditions were close to perfect when we raised our sails. We were in just about the most beautiful and regal cathedral that could possibly be imagined. The wind speed was right; the wind direction was right; the sun, sky, and water were right; and we sang along with our cassette tape: "Even so, it is well with my soul." Even the autopilot was working. So many times we experienced "fluky" winds and had to motor sail. Not that day. It was gorgeous. The ocean lapping at the hull sang to us, the sails billowed before us, and *Grace* slid gently through the shining water. After awhile I got out my guitar and relished playing and singing.

"Don't stop," Fred said. "I'm enjoying it." And I knew (that he knew) that it was just what I wanted to hear.

Such a day deserved a good Sunday dinner, so despite the heat of the cabin and the rolling of the boat, I managed to present a first class fish specialty. As we arrived that afternoon in the harbor of Huatulco, we saw that its anchorage was well protected and the water inside was calm. Terrific! Five other boats were anchored there.

"Looks like everyone is waiting for that weather window and full moon to cross," Fred said. This port was the "jump off" place to begin the crossing of the dreaded Gulf of Tehuantapec. Several days earlier, three boats had made it across safely and had sailed the entire way without incident. We were envious.

"I can't wait to see Lance," I said after we anchored.

"Yeah—it's been nine months since we've seen him. And you'll have to wait another four days," Fred replied. "We've got a ton of stuff to do in the meantime."

The next few days were busy ones. Fred spent hours trying to pick up different frequencies on our weather fax, but none either came in clearly or included information for this particular area. We attached our storm jib and storm trysail so they would be ready for use if needed. It took a good deal of time to review the rigging, lines, and how to use them.

"I *so* hope we don't have to use these," I said.

"Me too, but we're ready if it gets rough," he replied. "I called *Yobo*, to have them tell the rest of the fleet in Puerto Angel that I heard a forecast of 35-knot winds for tomorrow in the Gulf. We'll get the fringe winds here."

By afternoon we were ready for a break and went ashore. There was a lovely new marina in the bay, with a dock for the dinghies. A great deal of construction was underway; the government was trying to make this area into the "Cancun of the Pacific." The small, shack-like houses around the bay had been destroyed and families relocated inland in order to clean up the appearance. A planned community begun in 1985 was a short taxi ride away. It had *sidewalks*, many new buildings, restaurants and hotels. While wandering about town, we saw the owners of *Valiant Lady*. What a horror story they had to tell!

When coming ashore a week ago in their dinghy, they were run over by one of the large, heavy *panga* boats. Local fishermen often rode through the bay at high speeds, causing the bow of the *panga* to elevate and thus making it impossible to see in front of them. Dick had multiple stitches on his arms and shoulders from contact with the propeller of the large *panga* motor. They could have been killed! The Port Captain was furious with the fishermen because he wanted to maintain a good reputation with the cruisers; it was important to the developing tourist industry. He now required one person to ride in the bow of the *pangas*, as a lookout, to prevent this from happening again.

When we got back to the harbor, we learned that all the boats from Puerto Angel had arrived. They had been concerned about the weather report Fred had given Reed. Huatulco was a much safer harbor. There were now 15 boats anchored here, all waiting for the "crossing." We stopped in a beach bar that catered to cruisers and talked with everyone until it was dark.

"Oh dear," I cried, as we climbed into our dinghy. "Where is *Grace*?"

"Darn it! We forgot to turn on our anchor light when we left. I guess we didn't think we'd stay ashore so long," Fred replied. I could hear the concern in his voice.

"Wouldn't you know? There's *no* moon tonight, and it's so dark I can't see anything! It's really disorienting. How could it be so black?" I said. I felt the tension rising within me.

We knew the general area of the harbor where we were anchored, and we slowly motored in that direction. But we were a long way from shore, and the further we went, the less sure we became about where we were and the more anxious I became about finding the boat. The night air now felt cold with the ocean breeze blowing over the water. Would we end up going out to sea? The inky blackness surrounded us, making me feel small and vulnerable, and the lights on a few boats seemed a long way off. We nearly ran into a number of boats without any lights, but since they had anchored after we left, they provided no clue in helping us locate *Grace*. Finally, after what seemed like hours, we slowly approached a hull and discovered our beautiful boat. What a welcome sight! I surely had not wanted to spend the night in the dinghy. One more lesson to add to our list: turn on the anchor light *whenever* we go ashore!

One afternoon Cindy and I went to a hotel close by our marina that had a swimming pool. We asked if we and our friends could come buy a drink at their pool bar and then go for a swim. "*Si*," was the quick response. So about 20 of us spent the rest of the afternoon escaping the heat by playing in the hotel pool. It felt *wonderful*! Fred stayed in the water so long that his fingers became wrinkled as prunes.

Finally it was the day for Lance to arrive. It cost 40,000 pesos to get to the airport by taxi, and three pesos by bus. That was a "no brainer" decision. We had to transfer buses; wait on a hot, barren, and dusty roadside in the middle of nowhere; and it took more than an hour. But it was worth it all when we saw that smiling, blond head coming through customs. I couldn't stop grinning, jumping up and down, and hugging him. He laughed and looked a little embarrassed at all the motherly display of emotion, but I think he secretly enjoyed it.

"Oh my gosh!" we gasped, when we picked up his "luggage." There was one large backpack and one small one. Then there was his large windsurf board in a case. There was also a six-foot duffel bag for a "quiver" of sails. How would we ever get all of it back to the boat? We had to walk about three blocks on a dirt road to the bus stop, carrying all the gear. A number of taxis stopped and asked if we wanted a ride, but we could never have gotten all the gear aboard. When the bus finally arrived, the driver grinned and quickly said, *"No problemo!"* A man jumped down and opened a door in the back of the bus to load everything. When passengers wanted to get off, they calmly jumped or crawled over all the things lying in the aisle and smiled as if it was an every day event. It was quite the introduction to Mexico for Lance!

Arriving back at the marina after carrying the gear another three blocks from the bus stop, we found a note on our dinghy from *Yobo.* They had left their dinghy next to ours, thinking we may need it to get Lance's things aboard. How thoughtful! We *definitely* needed it. By the time we had everything aboard *Grace,* we were all hot and tired, and we could see Lance beginning to wonder if this trip had been such a good idea. There was so much to talk about and put away, but we couldn't do it all at once. A cold beer and nap revived him, and later we headed in for a special cruisers' Happy Hour at a beach restaurant near the marina.

Two days before, a tragic accident had occurred in the harbor on a large shrimp boat. After the boat had anchored, a member of the crew had climbed the rigging and attempted to dive into the water for a swim, but had hit the deck and died. Several cruisers had observed the event, and although witnesses risked being delayed by all the "red-tape" of legal proceedings, they testified to the Port Captain about what had happened. This cleared the crew of the shrimp boat of any wrongdoing, and the boat captain was so grateful that he had given huge amounts of seafood to the restaurant to cook for all the cruisers that night.

About 30 of us gathered on the beach enjoying the free food, camaraderie, and the opportunity to relax before the dreaded crossing. It was a fun way to welcome Lance into the cruising community.

"Wow—are you ever *white!*" was the comment we frequently heard when we introduced Lance to our friends. His neck and face were tanned from skiing, but his fair body stood out in a crowd of suntanned folks.

While Lance slept the following morning, we had an opportunity to read the mail.

"They will be more excited to get the mail than to see you!" Dawn had told Lance before he left.

Not true, but it sure was good to hear from home. We finally stowed all his gear, lashed the windsurf board to the boat's lifelines, and gathered around to hear the cruising weather reports from Herb on *Southbound II*. Herb was an amateur meteorologist that lived on his boat in Bermuda. Every night he had a net on the single sideband radio. He gave the most concise and accurate weather information needed by mariners for all of the Caribbean and areas of the Pacific and Atlantic oceans. That night we finally got the word we were all waiting for!

"There will be a 36- to 48-hour weather window for crossing the Gulf of Tehuantepec, starting tomorrow morning," Herb said. "The window will then close and a 'Tehuantepecker' will follow." Perfect! We anticipated that it would take between 48 and 60 hours to make the crossing.

All around the anchorage we could hear shouts of excitement and the sounds of dinghies being brought aboard and anchor chains being pulled up. We decided to wait until daybreak to leave the harbor, but we worked quickly in the dark to get our dinghy aboard, everything battened down, and ready the vessel for a potentially difficult passage. The tension and excitement were palpable, and we knew there would be little sleep for any of us that night.

About half of the 18 boats had already left when we motored out of the harbor the following morning, about five o'clock. There was lots of radio "chatter" as we all checked on positions, wind, and sea conditions.

"It feels good to be finally underway," I said. "I hope we have enough wind to sail."

"I'd be happy if these darn booby birds wouldn't try to hitch a ride,"

Fred said, moving forward to the bow pulpit where two of the big birds had perched themselves. They each had a wingspan of about four feet, and they seemed to love decorating the boat with their droppings. As Fred actually pushed one of the birds off the pulpit, Lance used a boat hook to dislodge another atop the radar pole.

"Stay there," Lance called to his dad. "They keep trying to come back." Finally the boobies gave up and flew away.

Conditions were good and we sailed along, keeping alert because we were close to the shore. The Tehuantepeckers, those furious storms that we all feared, were notorious for springing up with little or no warning, so none of us were truly relaxed and we all wanted to clear the gulf as quickly as possible. Lance was doing fine and had no problem with seasickness, as he had feared.

"I can take a night watch," Lance said, as evening approached.

"True, but one of us will be on 'standby' and rest in the cockpit with you while you are on," Fred replied. "There are just too many things for you to remember after being away from it for so long. It will help to just have another pair of eyes."

In the morning, while dragging our fishing line, we noticed a booby bird caught in the hook. We hadn't noticed it until it was drowned. Lance had always been a sensitive kid, and he felt it keenly. He was delighted, however, when the dolphins came to play. As evening approached we again listened to *Southbound II*.

"The window is closing. I repeat: the window is closing! You must be east of the 93rd parallel by tomorrow morning," the forecaster said.

While we could not see or hear any other boats around us, we imagined all the boats in the gulf starting their engines to get across the magic "safe" line as quickly as possible—just like we were doing. No more gently sailing along with the breeze. Now we were employing both sail and power to push us swiftly across the gulf. Throughout the night we carefully monitored our progress on the charts, believing we would be in the safe zone in time but anxious to have the miles behind us. Nothing was a certainty until it was over. We listened to the other boats on the radio, everyone checking positions, wind strength, and sea conditions. The wind dropped to less than 12 knots; we were getting less pull from the sails than we would have liked. Our speed through the water slowed. None of us liked that. Flipping on the radar, we frequently scanned the screen, looking for any indication of the approaching storm. The skies had become overcast, and I ached for the lost light of the moon. I willed our beautiful *Grace* to go faster. None of us slept much that night.

By daybreak we knew that we would cover the necessary distance and we began to relax a little. After two and a half days, we dropped anchor about noon in the tiny harbor of Puerto Madero, on the southern tip of Mexico.

"We made it!" I squealed with delight.

"Let's go ashore and celebrate," Lance suggested. And so we did, along with the other eight boats in the basin. Eight more boats later joined us in the tightly packed east anchorage.

"There's really only room here for four boats," Fred remarked, but we were all so pleased with having the gulf behind us that no one gave it much thought. About midnight, that changed dramatically.

We had all turned in early, tired after the stress of the passage. We awoke to the sound of explosive thunder and strong winds whistling through the rigging. There were constant flashes of lightning. We realized that we were in the fringe of the Tehuantepecker. Shouts from other boats, waves splashing, and a deluge of rain on the deck assaulted our ears. *Grace* was swinging wildly at anchor, jerking violently when the chain became taut.

"Look," I said, peering through the rain-splattered window. "Is that a boat aground? It's listing badly."

"I'm going to go start the engine," said Fred, as he pulled on his foul weather coat. "There are way too many boats in this anchorage, and they're swinging into each other. I'll try to keep us from hitting someone."

"I'm coming with you, Dad," said Lance, and I handed him a rain jacket. How I loved that Lance was here and it wasn't me that was going out in the storm to help!

Many other skippers were doing the same thing. As night wore on, the tide changed to ebb, and another boat too close to the beach went aground. Several men in their dinghies attempted to pull it free, but it was stuck tight. Finally, they were afloat, and the skipper cut loose his anchor and chain after being unable to retrieve it. They moved out of the harbor to wait it out in the sea until daylight, hoping the storm would pass.

"Wow! What a night," Fred said, as he and Lance came down into the cabin after things had calmed down. Removing their wet jackets and sitting down, Lance toweled off his wet hair and looked at his dad with an intense expression of concern.

"You know, Dad, this really isn't what I had pictured for your retirement!"

Fred simply smiled, looked at me with one of those unspoken understandings that come after 30 years of marriage, and gave me a wink. We had promised Lance excitement, and he was surely getting his money's worth! And we weren't ready for the rockin' chair just yet!

The following day, Fred and Lance dove down to dig out the anchor that our friends had not been able to retrieve during the storm. It had wedged itself deeply into the silt of the harbor, and it took a good deal of effort to free it. Having had their morning swim, they then needed to go to the airport 10 miles away to check out of the country at the Immigration office and later get fuel. I worked on the charts to get ready for our trip to Costa Rica.

"*Buenas tardes*," I heard coming from outside. Going into the cockpit, I found two pretty *señoritas* swimming in the water. They asked if my son was aboard and seemed highly disappointed to learn he was not. Word sure traveled fast around that place—especially when this platinum blond "hunk" was so visible in a crowd! When the guys returned, the *señoritas* were gone, and we were ready to leave this much loved country.

Eight
Central America Calls

"On the road again," the three of us sang. After many enjoyable months, we finally sailed out of Mexico bound for other countries that beckoned to us. Although we had the requisite navigation charts, some of our most important information came from notes of prior cruisers. Guatemala, El Salvador, and Honduras were countries that many cruisers had avoided in the past, partly due to civil unrest and less than favorable reactions to having boaters in their waters. We had few notes on these areas and knew little about what to expect, but we wanted to stop there if we could.

Shortly after leaving Mexico, we realized that our autopilot was permanently defunct, and we were even more grateful to have Lance aboard to help with steering the boat. When there was moderate wind, we could use the wind vane to steer, but often we were motor-sailing in light winds in that area and the vane did not work well in those conditions.

"Look at those dark, foreboding clouds south of us," Fred said that evening. "It looks like we're going to have another big squall."

"I can see the storm on the radar," I said from the cabin, where I was watching the radar screen. "It's not very large, but it's coming our way."

Sure enough. It had just turned dark when we were slammed with ferocious winds, buckets of rain, and continuous flashes of lightning followed by booming thunder. The adrenalin started to flow, and my tight stomach and dry mouth had now become a familiar, if unwelcome, feeling. Lance's eyes were large, but he anticipated what was needed, asked the right questions, and thought things through. He was a great help, and we were proud of him.

"Man! This lightning is *close*," Lance said. "It's almost simultaneous with the thunder!"

We had thrown a special cable into the water to add to our grounding system in the hull of the boat, but who knew if any of it was effective in diverting a lightning strike? We felt very vulnerable with that tall mast sticking up into the sky, the only potential lightning target within miles. Despite the foul weather gear, we were soaked, and *cold*! It was hard to believe, with all the sticky heat of the day, that at night we felt so cold in the wind and rain.

As we watched the radar, we knew we were traversing through the squall, and that helped keep the anxiety from escalating. It was also easier to handle the boat at sea than when it had been at anchor. Nevertheless, there were lots of prayers offered.

Approaching Puerto Quetzal, Guatemala, the following day, we saw the Guatemalan Naval Station that had recently opened up to transient boats. It cost 100 dollars for a five night stay there, which we opted to do, and we "med-tied" *Grace* to a cement wall. This meant bringing the stern of the boat back to the wall, rather than the "side-tie" of many docks. It was a tricky maneuver, and made it more difficult to get on and off the boat. But it was required here. We felt reassured that, with the protected harbor and security of the navy, we would be safe from ocean storms as well as thieves. The water was calm behind the breakwater, and there were about eight other cruising boats tied up with the navy vessels. By using this facility, we could safely leave our boat for a few days of travel inland to Guatemala City and Antigua.

Our first agenda item was to make a ham radio phone call to Dawn, so that she could arrange to purchase an autopilot from a marine store in San Diego. Friends of *Yobo* were flying in to join them in two days and were willing to pick it up for delivery. Dawn handled all the details efficiently and anticipated potential problems we hadn't even considered. She knew the urgency needed to make it all happen, and we were deeply grateful for her help. That girl was going places! We were also delighted to hear that Page would be able to come to Costa Rica after her medical school board exams. Lance had said she was incredibly busy, and it would be a good break for her. We wished Steve could come as well.

"Now it's time for some of the fun of cruising," I said to Lance, as we settled into lawn chairs under the deck awnings, enjoying our arrival "Miller Time." "You've already seen the scary and difficult part."

"Well, I've learned a lot too," he laughed. "Wait until dark so you can take a stand-up shower in the cockpit; throw a bucket of sea water on your head to cool off; and savor the times when you can sleep *all* night. Oh yeah, and avoid ice cubes!"

Lance and I had picked up a bit of the "*touristas*" and thought it must have come from the ice cubes in the Coca Cola we drank in Puerto Madero. We knew better than to have ice in our drinks: the water used to make it may not be safe. But we were so hot and thirsty at the time! Fred had also had ice cubes but no diarrhea symptoms, so it was difficult to tell where the "bug" had originated. I was soon feeling better, but Lance was not. We wanted to travel inland, but we knew that we all had to be in good shape in order to do that.

When *Yobo*'s guests arrived, we were ecstatically thankful they had brought the all-important autopilot.

"Hey, man. We really *owe* you!" Fred said, when we met them. They both worked for the America's Cup Sailing organization and knew a great deal about sailing. It would be fun to learn from them.

"All the cruising boats are invited to a pizza party at Jose's restaurant," I said, after talking with friends.

"Isn't that the place that's air-conditioned?" Fred asked.

"*Air-conditioned?*" Lance jumped to his feet. "That sounds awesome! I hope they have a bathroom close by."

The heat was really getting to him, but he didn't complain. We joined the other eight boaters but came home early, as neither Lance nor I were feeling tip-top. The following morning, Lance wanted to begin our planned inland trip. But after he made several trips to the bathroom, we reluctantly said, "No way."

"We will be riding a local 'chicken' bus, crammed with people," Fred said. "There are *no* rest stops. When we get away from the ocean, it will be even hotter, and it's a three-hour ride to Guatemala City. There's no way you can do that now."

We all felt disappointed as we lay around the boat in the sticky heat. A local man had told us of a remedy for the "*touristas*" last night at the pizza place: Eat a quarter cup of uncooked white rice. Lance was so desperate he was ready to try anything. He poured the rice into a cup and, with some difficulty, gulped it all down.

Whether it was the rice, or whether the thing had simply "run its course," by the next morning he was better and we were ready to go. Off for adventure! Rick and Helle, from *Manana*, traveled with us, which was fun for Lance since they were closer to his age. It was a great experience riding the old school bus. At every stop a "driver's helper" would jump down and help folks climb on with their packages, putting big things—like crates of chickens or large bags of flour or grain—outside on the roof of the bus. Three adults sat in each of the small seats, with children often sitting on their laps. Still, the driver stopped to take on more passengers. Apparently the bus was *never* full! Lots of folks stood crowded into the aisles, but no one fussed or complained. Mercifully, as we headed up into the highlands, it became much cooler, with no humidity.

As the bus wound along the narrow road, past many villages and shacks, sometimes there would be cattle blocking the way. The driver would simply lean out the window and whistle at them, and they would eventually wander off to the sides of the road. How things changed when we approached the huge city! The road became a several lane highway. Traffic was everywhere. Cars and trucks whizzed by us. We could have been in any large city in the U.S.

Arriving at the bus terminal in the center of Guatemala City, we were amazed at the huge market surrounding it. Hundreds of small stalls sold household goods, jewelry, hardware, clothing, music cassettes, and anything else imaginable. Indian women walked by, carrying huge bundles on their heads and wearing their traditional, brightly colored costumes. Indian men hurried along, stooped over with huge loads on their backs. There were buses parked everywhere in a large dirt lot, with hawkers calling out their intended destinations and urging people to board. It was colorful, chaotic, and noisy as we searched for the bus to Antigua, a colonial city about an hour's ride away.

Antigua was charming! It had once been the capital of Guatemala, and we loved stepping back in time by exploring the tidy streets and plazas. It was also well known for its cultural events, Spanish language schools, and nearby active volcano. We met a friendly local, who suggested an old, inexpensive Spanish hacienda style hotel and later offered his services for a tour of the area. Standing in the back of a pick-up truck, the five of us rode around seeing the coffee plantations, a couple of small villages, a great old Spanish style church, and the homes of women weaving their gorgeous, brightly colored, traditional Guatemalan designs. The little girls learn to weave at age six, and we loved seeing them, although they were often too shy to talk with us. We wanted to stay longer, but we had to go back to the boat after two days, hoping to return to this remarkable place someday.

While riding in a taxi to get from one bus station to another in Guatemala City, we stopped at a street light and were surprised when a man on the sidewalk came up to the car and warned us, in Spanish, not to leave the windows down. "*Banditos*," he said, and showed how they would reach through the taxi window and grab watches or bags. We thanked him as the light changed and the taxi moved on, and thought about what had just happened.

"I guess people might get robbed like that in Los Angeles or Miami just as easily," I said, feeling a little shaken about the interaction.

"But would anybody take the time to stop and warn a tourist?" Lance looked thoughtful.

"I wonder," added Fred.

We arrived back at the boat shortly before another squall hit the area. It went from almost no wind to 30-knot gusts in a matter of seconds. We hurried to close hatches, take down the windsock, and secure anything that might get blown over. Apparently these storms were a frequent part of the early evenings during that time of year.

"I can't believe how many things you need to do to be ready to go to sea," Lance exclaimed as we left the boat basin about three in the afternoon.

"Those preparations pay off if it gets nasty," Fred replied. Fortunately, the weather appeared stable and we had a pleasant two-day sail under the hot, cloudless sky. Lance was thrilled to catch three fish—although, since they weren't very good eating, we threw two of them back.

LANCE'S CATCH IS TOO BIG FOR THE BUCKET.

As we were making our way along the coast of El Salvador, we heard a call from *Yobo*, who had left Puerto Quetzal about four hours before we had with their two guests aboard.

"We are having trouble with our transmission. We can't get the engine into forward gear," said Cindy. "We are sailing at the moment, but the wind is light. I don't think we can make enough headway to get into the Gulf of Fonseca for repairs." Cindy didn't rattle easily, but she sounded scared.

"Give us your position," I said. "We'll come see what we can do."

162

They were about 16 miles ahead of us, and it was late at night when we finally arrived at their position—just as a huge lightning and rainstorm hit. With the strong winds, both boats could sail with the storm toward the direction of the nearest port. But it was impossible to see *Yobo* through the pounding rain and fierce wind. Since our boat was faster and could sail closer into the wind, we tried to slow our progress to stay near them. Even so, by morning we had passed them by about seven miles.

It had been a tense night, and we had slept in half-hour segments. I was feeling very frazzled. The wind had died, and it was incredibly *hot*! We were all tired, and I was feeling very sorry for myself, even though I knew Lance and Fred had been through the same things.

"Why don't you go below and have a nap?" Fred suggested. "We'll head back to where *Yobo* is."

"It's really too far to tow them to a port, isn't it?" said Lance. "They're bigger and heavier than we are."

"I'm not sure what we can do," Fred responded, "but we can't just desert them."

Motoring against the current, it took almost two hours to reach them. They were happy to see us, but had drifted back to the position they were in five hours before. After some discussion, and relying heavily on the considerable knowledge of their guests, we decided to tow them in the calms and then release the tow and sail whenever the winds came up. We were told to keep the rpm's of our engine low, so as not to damage our own transmission. The process worked well enough, and we crept down the coastline. We knew, when we offered to help, that it would likely delay our arrival in El Salvador by 24-36 hours, but we also knew they would've done the same for us.

By that evening, another storm had arrived. With great concern we considered the rough wind and sea conditions in consultation with the folks on *Yobo*. We anxiously decided *not* to cut loose the tow, as *Yobo* would likely be blown off course again and we'd have to go back to get them and make up the distance yet again.

The wind howled. The rain was driven by 30-knot gusts that slammed into the boat and heeled it over. Lightning punctuated the skies every few seconds, followed by incredibly loud thunder. *Yobo* had hoisted two small sails to ease the strain on our boat, and we had our sails up and engine going as well. We were making only about two miles per hour in the desired direction.

"I think I could *walk* through Central America faster than this," Lance said with a smile. His sense of humor and capable assistance were invaluable—even though it was *still* a long, wet, tiring night. During the worst of the squall, the guys sent me below to nap beneath one of the fans, as the cabin was still stuffy and hot. I did manage to nod off for a while—sleep was an escape from the unpleasantness of the moment! By three in the morning, the storm was mostly over and it was time for my watch. I felt much better after the nap; now the guys were tired and cold. It was difficult for Lance to sleep, though, and he tried the floor and different berths, all with little success. By six, Fred awoke refreshed, and Lance tried to use the sea berth.

"I sure hope Lance doesn't jump ship when we get to a port," I laughed. "This hasn't been much fun."

"He says it's what he expected," Fred said, "and we had warned him that this leg could be tough."

Several other cruisers in El Salvador had been monitoring our situation via the radios and called to say they had found a mechanic in La Union who could fix the transmission, and that the El Salvador Navy would take over the tow when we entered their waters in the Gulf of Fonseca. That was the first good news in a long while! It was offset, however, by learning that our planned anchorage for a night of rest before we reached La Union in the Gulf would be on a lee shore—one that would be especially dangerous in the nightly storms. So we altered course to head directly for La Union. No rest for the weary!

Finally, we entered the gulf waters and saw a gray motor vessel.

"Hey—here comes the navy boat," Lance yelled. We waved and watched as they stood off our beam by several hundred yards. We waited, expecting them to come in and take *Yobo* in tow. They made no effort to come closer.

"It doesn't look like they are going to do any towing," Fred said finally. "I guess it's still up to us."

We had been reading in our piloting book about strong currents in a very narrow pass through which we needed to navigate. This could be especially problematic depending on the tides at the time we were in the pass. In addition, there were many shifting shoal areas in the gulf. The crew of *Yobo* assured us that one of them would climb the spreaders as we entered the pass to watch our progress, and another would be at the bow with a knife in hand. If it appeared at any time that *Amazing Grace* was in danger, they would cut the tow in order for us to get through safely. Of course, this meant they would likely founder on the rocks! Many silent prayers were offered throughout the day.

Reed had a wonderful way of breaking the tension of that long, tense passage. One time he called on the radio, saying, "You know, I don't think we'll get our transmission fixed when we get to port after all. Yeah, we've decided that this works really well. We can sail when there's the right wind, and we save a whole lot on fuel costs when there is none." Right!

The navy boat continued to follow along with us.

"Amah-sing Grah-say, Amah-sing Grah-say," came the radio call. *"Mas izquierda, mas izquierda!"* (More left, more left!) It was the navy boat! Apparently they wanted us to move further to the left to avoid shallow waters. We all laughed at the Spanish pronunciation of our boat name, but we were also glad they were keeping an eye on us.

All went well. We obtained six knots going through the narrow passage but had *no problemo*. Those prayers were working. When we got to the anchorage, we did a nifty job of first anchoring *Yobo* and then gratefully dropping our own hook. Whew!

"It's definitely 'Miller Time,'" I said. We poured a beer to celebrate our incredible journey and arrival. Cindy and Reed and their friends soon came over, heaping appreciation on the three of us.

"So much for you owing us for the autopilot," they said happily. "We owe *you*, man!"

Going ashore at La Union (a town of about 57,000 in El Salvador) was a unique experience. Since few cruisers ever stopped in this port, people would often stop and stare at us, as if we were some kind of oddity. Everywhere there was evidence of extreme poverty, and we encountered many who begged for money or food. Unlike Mexico or Guatemala, there were also many dirty faces and dirty clothes.

"It takes money to buy soap, Mom," said Lance.

If we talked to someone, they were friendly and helpful, but when we stopped walking, people would often crowd around us.

"Let's sit down for a few minutes here in the plaza," I said to the guys. A woman immediately sat on the ground near our feet and began to touch the blond hair on Lance's legs.

"Hermoso (handsome), *hermoso!"* she crooned softly. Lance looked embarrassed and got up.

"Ella es loco (she is crazy)," said a man standing nearby.

We were all uncomfortable and moved on, while children followed us down the streets. After working our way around the town, we stopped at a beach restaurant where we met some of the other cruisers from the six cruising boats that were anchored in the harbor. Much of the talk was about the evening storms, called *Chubascos*. During these storms, an El Salvadoran Navy boat circled around the anchored cruising boats, and we assumed they were ready to help if needed. We all appreciated that gesture. The restaurant owner was also friendly and helpful, offering to drive us to the gas station to fill our jerry cans with diesel. Terrific!

The following day, when we went into town for some groceries, Lance chose to stay aboard. He did not like the attention he received with his very blond hair, and he likely needed some private space—something hard to come by on a boat.

Fred and I went into the navy station and talked with some of the men. Apparently the naval boat dock was not strong enough for their boats to remain tied up during the evening *Chubascos*, so they had to take the boats out into the gulf. And we thought they were out there to help us!

Coming back from town to our dinghy, we found the tide had ebbed and the dinghy was sitting on the mud, a long way from the water.

"Yuk! This is gross," I grumbled. We were walking through ankle deep mud and warm water, trying to push the dinghy to water where it would float.

"I thought mud baths were a beauty treatment," Fred laughed. "Think of trying to get those local dug-outs through this mud." We had seen a number of fishermen in this area using the large, hollowed out log boats. It was like looking back in time to another era.

THE CATCH OF THE DAY—AN OCTOPUS.

We realized that La Union was only a small sample of El Salvador, and while we had some very favorable interactions with some locals and the Navy, it was not our favorite place. Lance was anxious to move on to another port, and I was too. As we pulled out of the anchorage we could hear him singing, "On the road again." He was becoming a real *cruiser.*

After a three-hour sail, we arrived in the harbor of Isla El Tigre in Honduras, just across the gulf from La Union. Three countries—El Salvador, Honduras, and Nicaragua—all have harbors in the Gulf of Fonseca.

"Look. There's the mountain that's pictured on the money of Honduras," said Lance. We had just anchored close to the town of Amapala.

"You're right. I'd like to go ashore, but here come the *Chubascos.* We better get those hatches closed," I said.

We actually preferred the nightly storms to come early. That way they didn't wake us up, nor did we have to jump out of bed to close windows and hatches to keep out the downpour and then get up again to open them after the storm had passed.

"I set out buckets to catch some of that rain tonight," Fred added.

"We have more protection here, so the wind is less than at La Union." Still, the rain came in deluges, and the lightning and thunder occurred every few seconds. We had begun to move some of our electronic gear away from the "nav" station during these storms, hoping that, if we were hit by lightning, our electronics might be spared. By morning, we had seven or eight inches of rain in the buckets, and even more in the dinghy. Every time Fred stepped into the dinghy to begin bailing, it started to sink. He finally devised a way to get the water out, and we all went ashore.

Several locals approached us as we tied up the dinghy, including a drunk and an assertive ten-year-old boy named Ramon. The men said they would "watch" the dinghy. We agreed, knowing they would want to be paid when we returned. Ramon wanted to be our guide, and he was fun to talk with, so we headed out for our "tour" of the town, giving him a pair of sunglasses and laughing when he put them on and strutted along like he was "top dog." Again, we were struck by the poverty of the area. Buildings made of dried mud lined the narrow cobbled streets. There did not appear to be any electricity, window openings had no glass in them, and the rooms looked cramped and dark inside. Chickens and pigs roamed freely, and dogs with large patches of missing hair searched for food. When we checked into the country with the Port Captain, we learned we were only the fifth cruising boat to stop here, and the only one at the present time. Continuing our tour with Ramon, we walked up a hill. He tried to talk slowly, for he knew our Spanish was limited.

"What did he say?" I asked Lance.

"I'm not sure, but it's something to do with soccer, I think." Lance shrugged.

Sure enough, when we came over the hill we saw a soccer field where there was some sort of school tournament, with several teams competing.

"Wow! These kids are really good," Fred said.

"They get lots of practice. They're always kicking the ball around in the streets," Lance said. "It's likely the only sport they can afford—all it takes is a ball. Some of them don't even have shoes. Amazing!"

In the afternoon, Lance had a chance to do some windsurfing, but when we headed back to the boat we were greeted with more rain. He brought his large surfboard down into the cabin, not wanting to leave it on deck. This meant salt and sand and water all over the place. Walking around the main salon was almost impossible.

"Are you sure it's all right, Mom?" Lance asked. He was nervous when he saw the mess it created.

"I've given up trying to keep out the salt and sand—it's a boat!" I said. "After the locals have seen you using the board, it probably isn't a good idea to leave it unlocked on the deck anyway."

We spent a couple more days exploring, windsurfing, and reading on a deserted beach—as well as one whole day onboard while it rained continually.

"Now I know what it's like to be a tiger in a zoo," said Lance, watching it rain, and feeling the cabin fever of close confinement.

When Lance and I went ashore to check out of the country, we left the dinghy at the customs dock, declining the services of the local boys who wanted to tie it up and "watch" it for us. When we came out of the immigration office, we saw that they had untied the boat and were attempting to start the outboard engine. Running over, I made it abundantly clear that we were very angry. We had been friendly and given them sunglasses and soft drinks, and that was no way to return our friendship. Several adults were standing by, watching the boys, but had not intervened. We returned to *Grace* with an unsettled feeling. We were glad to be leaving the harbor the following day, but we also wondered about how our actions, despite our good intentions, may have contributed to the problems in this poor area of Honduras.

We talked by radio to four other boats that were anchored across the gulf. We all decided to leave together the following morning for Costa Rica, feeling somewhat anxious about sailing past Nicaragua. Not only was this a rough stretch of sea to navigate, especially when the storms continued, but there was also a tense political situation between Nicaragua and the U.S. We had read and talked with people in this area about the support our government had given to a cruel and oppressive regime in that country, and we were concerned that we might not be welcomed. There had been some problems for cruisers in the past, so we planned not to stop there, nor fly our U.S. flag while we passed. Some of our Canadian friends had stopped, and said they had been well treated.

Nevertheless, we were all excited to get to the cruisers' "Promised Land," as Costa Rica was affectionately called.

The storm continued all night, and we rocked and rolled despite the protected anchorage. The other four boats rolled excessively in the direct ocean swell on the other side of the gulf, even fearing they would capsize when the rail of one boat was thrown underwater during a roll. We all felt sure that conditions would improve once we got out to sea.

Not so. There was little wind to give us forward progress, and the swell created violent rolling. Soon, everyone on all five boats felt seasick. I was surprised, but then realized we had not practiced our "*Seawellness*" tape since arriving in Mexico. The rain continued, and it was stuffy and humid in the cabin with all the hatches and windows closed. This increased our queasy feelings, but the dodger and bimini had begun to leak, so it was wet and cold in the cockpit. Poor *Yobo*. They didn't even have a dodger or bimini, and no inside steering. No one wanted to eat, so we munched on crackers.

Finally the wind arrived and we zipped along under sail, making for a somewhat more comfortable ride. However, as the wind increased, we were busy most of the night taking reefs in the sails or adjusting our direction as currents swept us landward. We tried to take two-hour watches, but no one slept much.

Finally the sun reappeared. The seas continued to be roll-y, but more manageable. I heated up some leftover spaghetti; by then we were all hungry.

"This doesn't taste right," I said after eating a little, even thought the guys had eaten quite a bit.

"I agree. Maybe we'd better not eat any more," Fred said. Oh great! Now we can worry about *food poisoning* in addition to everything else!

Fred had not slept for a couple of nights. Since conditions were calmer, Lance and I urged him to take a seasick pill and go to the aft cabin for some real sleep. The berth there was quiet and had less motion. We seldom used it when offshore because it was too out-of-the-way for the "off-watch" person to be quickly available if needed. We assured Fred that Lance and I could handle the boat by ourselves. Finally, he agreed. He had only just settled in when I saw those darn booby birds trying to land on the boat.

"No! No!" I screamed at the birds. We waved our arms and shooed at them. Suddenly we heard the sound of pounding footsteps as Fred roared out of the aft cabin at full speed to the bottom of the companionway, where he looked up at us in the cockpit like a wild man who was ready to do *whatever* to save the boat. He had heard my screams but had no idea what was happening.

"Oh, no! I'm *so* sorry," I said. "We won't try to scare any more birds. Promise! Go back to sleep." It was a good laugh for Lance and me, but not funny at all for Fred. And sleep he did—for a good six hours!

At daybreak the following morning, while we sailed under cloudy skies, we could see in the distance the huge volcanic mountains of Costa Rica. There, the sun rose gold and pink behind those beautiful jagged shapes under clear skies, and it truly looked like a Promised Land.

RAISING THE "COURTESY FLAG" FOR COSTA RICA.

By eight in the morning, we set anchor in the lovely, *calm,* Salinas Bay. We were ecstatic! On one side of the bay were those mountains towering over us, and a few sleepy little buildings on a strip of white sand. The water was blue and clear and inviting. It was hot, and we quickly put up the awnings and opened a bottle of champagne that Lance had brought us from the Czech Republic a few years before. We had carefully packed it away for this trip, and it was perfect for this well-deserved celebration. We were giddy as we reflected on our journey and its hardships—which were such a contrast to this present, "oh-so-sweet" moment!

After a wonderful nap on a quiet berth, we went ashore. As we attempted to land on the beach, I jumped out and a wave turned the dinghy; I couldn't get my feet beneath me and fell down, getting completely submerged in the surf.

"Oh, Man!" Lance nearly fell over laughing. "Hey, Mom. You look like you're going to cry."

He and Fred continued to laugh, although Fred gave me an affectionate hug. As I stood there dripping salt water, I realized that I had, indeed, felt like crying. Getting dunked was an insult I hadn't needed right then, and it made me mad. But I was relieved there weren't many people around to observe my not-so-graceful landing, and my clothes quickly dried while we enjoyed exploring the beach.

Returning to *Grace* later that day, we began sorting out all the things that were wet from several leaks we had developed over the last few days. Soon we had clothes, food, and gear from storage lockers laid out or hanging from everything in the cabin. All of Lance's clothes and his bed were wet. A bottle of dish soap had broken, and I discovered that trying to clean up liquid soap is something else! The interior of the boat was a disaster. But, afraid of the evening storms, we didn't want to set things outside to dry.

"Hey, we need to stop. It's time for the sunset." Lance motioned us up on deck. He always managed to take a few minutes to watch the gorgeous light show. "Come on! Bring a drink and a chair."

He put some soothing classical music on the stereo, and we hurried to the foredeck to sit and savor the incredible display in the sky and sea. The slight wind felt good on our tired bodies, and the air had begun to cool as the sun sank low on the horizon. The sound of the water bouncing off the hull of the boat felt reassuring as we rocked gently in the bay. And, of course, the sky was painted with an array of orange, yellow, pink, and red as the sun slowly descended through several thin layers of cloud. The finale left us speechless. All of our senses told us that we were incredibly *blucky*.

The following days involved a lot of work getting the boat gear stored again, but also time for play. Lance and Fred did some snorkeling on a reef, while I worked on the boat. *Yobo* had arrived, and one afternoon Lance took Cindy and me ashore so that she could give me a haircut. Ah—that felt better. We shared potluck dinners or happy hours with a couple of other boats that had arrived in the bay. The wind had increased a good deal, creating good conditions for Lance to use his windsurf board.

With 30-knot gusts on the day of a planned shore excursion, Fred and Reed thought they had better stay on the boats. Lance, Cindy, and I went ashore and "hitched" a ride in the back of a pickup up the steep dirt road to town. After the brown, dry landscape of much of Mexico, we were amazed at the verdant green surrounding us in Costa Rica. Plants and trees grew everywhere. Even tree branches stuck into the ground for fence poles grew! The town, perched on top of a hillside, was more modern than many we had seen in Mexico, and we were excited to get some fresh food, which we hadn't had for awhile.

"What a view. This is incredible," Cindy said from the open-air restaurant where we ate lunch.

"The boats in the bay look like little dots, and you can see all the islands and the ocean beyond the bay," I exclaimed.

"Look at this," Lance said, looking into a bush near our table. Just inches from his face were two colorful parrots!

With the wind up, we made our way back to the boats so Lance could do a little more windsurfing before we made the 3-hour sail to Bahia Santa Elena. This port was completely land locked, so it was very calm inside. There was only one other boat at anchor. Lance and Fred did some snorkeling with friends on *Raporiga*, and Lance was jazzed about all the fish he had seen. As night approached it was so quiet we could hear the many sounds from the dense jungle that surrounded the bay. Our cruising notes said there was a national park nearby that had monkeys and jaguars as well as other wildlife. We could hear the monkeys howling—or was that the jaguars? A few fishermen came into the bay and anchored their boats, which looked like large, open rowboats with small outboard engines, and they slept in them overnight. Perhaps they knew what lay waiting ashore in the jungle.

The next day, the guys hauled out all the gear and hooked up our Hooka system to do some diving. I was glad for the chance for some "alone" time. As I repaired a torn sail, I pondered how strange it was to have an adult child back with us. He surely didn't need parenting anymore, but we were often in the role of "teacher" as we explained things about the boat, and sometimes that felt like parenting. We were also keenly aware that he taught us many things—like how to enjoy a sunset or extend compassion without judgment for people different from ourselves. We loved his enthusiasm for new things, his creativity. Best of all, we loved the good times of sitting in the cockpit with him, just talking—rare pearls in this busy world.

We wanted to move on the following day, but we heard that the seas were rough outside the bay. Still, we needed to get to a place where we could call Page, who would soon be coming to spend time with us, for we had a list of things for her to bring. We also needed to check into the country. So about 11:00 in the morning we left with a stiff wind at our back. A wild ride for the next four hours brought us to the Murcielagos Islands, reported to have some of the best snorkeling and diving in Costa Rica. Despite our hope that we'd find some protection from the wind, there was none. We stayed aboard the boat and thought the wind might decrease by morning.

"Wow—the wind has actually *increased*," said Lance the following morning. "We just had a 47-knot gust!"

"We got a call that it was 55-knots at the other island," said Fred. "Someone can't get his anchor up in order to leave."

"They call these winds the *Papagayos*, and they can go on for days in this area," I said as I read the cruising notes. "I vote for getting out and heading to Playa del Coco. It should take us about five hours."

When the wind calmed a little, we took off with *Raporiga*. Another wild ride followed as we flew along at eight knots per hour—just over hull speed. At times Lance had to help me turn the wheel when a gust would throw us off course, but it was kind of fun since we knew we didn't have very far to go. We yelled and whooped it up as we surfed down the waves in the bright sunshine. That kind of sailing was what *Grace* was made for. Lance was really getting a ride on this trip!

In just four hours we anchored in the lovely, calm bay that held a number of sailboats. A large community ringed the shore near the anchorage. There were many goods and services available here, so it was a favorite destination of cruisers.

"Look at all the coconut trees," Lance said. "They're all around the bay. No wonder they call it Playa del Coco."

Going ashore, we found a restaurant that catered to cruisers and was known to have great hamburgers and French fries; we stuffed ourselves after having not eaten much in the last two days.

The next few days were busy ones as we settled in to the country and community. We planned to make it our home base for a few weeks. We checked bus schedules for our trip into the San Jose airport to pick up Page, and also for a side trip to Lake Arenal, where Lance planned to do some windsurfing. This meant leaving *Grace* for a few days, and our friends on *Raporiga* offered to watch it for us. We were given a large bag of fresh shrimp, so I invited Tom and Lydia over for shrimp salad, fresh pineapple soaked in Mexican sherry, garlic bread, and Portugese wine.

"Now *this* is cruising!" Lance laughed. "It sure beats tainted spaghetti!"

Fred had taken special care to make sure the anchor was well set when we came into the bay. Before we left, he gave Tom a list of emergency instructions for the boat.

"It feels like we're leaving one of our children behind," I said. Tom had come to take us ashore in his dinghy when we left for the bus to San Jose.

"It does," replied Fred, "but she'll be fine. Look at that pile of gear Lance is taking. Tom will need to make a separate trip just to get the windsurf board and sails to shore."

It was a five-hour trip to San Jose on the bus, although Lance got off after a couple of hours to make his way to Lake Arenal—a Mecca for windsurfers, with 360 days of wind a year. He had traveled alone throughout Europe when in college, and his Spanish was improving, so he was confident about striking out on his own. Surely he needed some private time by now.

It was hot in the bus, but the lovely scenery and opportunity to be going inland thrilled us. Lush green pasture and ranch land, steep hills, and clean, neat houses in small towns were evident all along the way. The economic standard was certainly much higher than any of the other Central American countries we had seen. We got off the bus at Alajuela, a small town that was closer to the airport than San Jose. Walking around we found a posada/restaurant that had adequate rooms for the right price. The owner was from Peru, and enjoyed talking with us while we ate a delicious meal that was truly *economico* (cheap). Lengthy conversations in Spanish were difficult for me, and at one point our new friend spent many frustrating minutes trying to tell me something about his wife.

"*De roosia, de roosia*," he kept saying. I searched my mind for any word that was similar and finally realized he was saying "from Russia." We all laughed at the struggle and relief in finally understanding.

What a delight to see Page get off the airplane the following morning. She would be with us for two weeks. I couldn't stop smiling and hugging her. She quickly changed from her jeans and sweatshirt to shorts and tank top.

After busing to San Jose, a large metropolitan city, we asked for instructions to the Tileran bus station. Not understanding the reply, we walked a block in the direction the man had pointed. As we stopped to look at our map, three feet in front of us we saw a young man push an older man down, take something from him, and run down the street like an Olympian. We had heard that this area of the city was not safe, and we felt very vulnerable standing there with our luggage. Within a couple of minutes, two different men stopped to warn us to watch our bags, gesturing that this was not a good place for us to be. By then, we were truly concerned. We decided to take a taxi, but, before we could do so, we heard sirens, and three fire engines and an ambulance pulled up to where we stood. Firemen started running all over. A traffic gridlock quickly developed. I looked up and saw black smoke coming from the adjacent building.

"Oh my gosh! What next? How can we get out of here?" I cried.

One of the men who had warned us saw our confusion and offered to walk us a block to where we could catch a taxi. Thank God for kind souls. When we arrived at the bus station, we found that the next bus wouldn't leave for another four hours! Poor Page. She had had little sleep on the overnight flight and was certainly tired, but she didn't complain. Finding a *Sopa* (lunch stand), we decided to eat while waiting—and catch up on Page's news. The woman who owned the small eatery walked us into the kitchen to show us each of the pots on the stove so we would know what we were ordering. Small courtesies make for great hospitality!

We made the bus transfers successfully and arrived at the lodge at Lake Arenal, where we had reservations. We were sure glad to see Lance in the lobby. He also had had an adventure getting there, as he sat in the wrong bus station for four hours before getting to the right place. Unfortunately, despite this lake's reputation for wind, there had been *none* the last two days. Since it was off-season, we were the only guests at the lodge. The owner had taken Lance on a trip into the forest to see the monkeys, as well as an "up close and personal" encounter with ticks.

"It's no big deal, Mom," he assured me.

The lodge served a great breakfast and dinner, and we all felt pampered by the luxury of a nice room, clean sheets, and a bed that didn't rock and roll. The following day brought no wind either, so we hiked the area, enjoying the sound of the howler monkeys—although Page and I thought they sounded more like gorillas. On the road we saw a dead snake with red and black stripes. Costa Rica was known to have many snakes in the bush, but this was the first one we had seen. We knew from a seeing a postcard that it was highly poisonous. That gave me the chills.

When there was still no wind the following day, we disappointedly started back to Playa del Coco. It took four different buses and a van ride to get there, and each time we changed buses we wondered if we would be able to get Lance's gear aboard, but we finally made it.

With the weather being a little more settled, we spent several days sailing to other bays to fish, snorkel, dive, beach-comb, and try Boogie boarding. Lance caught a couple of big fish, one a 44-inch mahi mahi that filled the cockpit and turned those beautiful colors as it died. We were taking life at a slower pace, which seemed to suit Page just fine.

"Page is such a delightful young woman—so gentle and gracious. She will make a wonderful physician, conveying calmness and peace to her patients," I said to Fred one night.

"She sure is a good sport," Fred replied. "She never complains. She and Lance have been chatting a lot. It's obvious they enjoy each other's company."

Sailing back to the Murcielagos Islands, we were able to enjoy the water and sea life. Page and I snorkeled while the guys did some diving with the Hooka system. The vivid blue, yellow, purple, and orange colors of the fish were amazing. There were angel fish that looked like those in aquariums. Big fish moved slowly along, and tiny fish darted back and forth. Other times we saw hundreds of fish traveling in schools. It seemed like we could reach out and touch them, but they always swam aside. One tiny yellow "cleaner" fish swam just an inch or two from the side of my goggles. I didn't like it there and batted it away many times, but it would come right back within seconds.

One afternoon, as we sat in the cockpit just before sunset, we saw a fishing boat approach us. There was only one other boat in the bay, and we felt our anxiety level rise. Two men and a young boy stopped and offered us five freshly-caught fish. They declined taking the money we offered for them, saying the fish were a gift. Finally, after much urging from us, they accepted some soda pop. Again, we were overwhelmed by the generosity and kindness of the people we met.

"Darn. I wish I had asked them how to prepare and cook these fish. They are delicious in the restaurants," I said after they had left.

"Why don't we dinghy over and ask them? The fish camp is right over there on the beach," Lance suggested.

We did just that and, to our delight, two men offered to come show us. They returned with us to the boat and demonstrated the way to cut, salt, and cook the fish. When we asked them to stay for dinner, they smiled shyly but said they would return to their camp to eat. It was "good eating" that night, and *huatchinango* became Lance's favorite fish dish.

When the rain and wind picked up, we were anxious to move back to Playa del Coco; we remembered the *Papagayos* we had experienced here earlier. As we moved out, we heard on the radio that Coco had huge ocean swells coming into the beach, apparently from a storm offshore. No one had slept on the boats at anchor there the previous night, and even the fishing pier had been destroyed by the swells. So we decided to go, instead, to a nearby bay—which also turned out to be roll-y—and I started to feel queasy.

"I must listen to the "*Seawellness*" tape again," I said. "It sure helped before, but I guess we need to keep using it to get the benefits."

We felt an urgency to get back to Coco so we could rent a car and travel inland for two or three days before Page had to return home. The ocean swells had moderated a little so we left for our home base. When we arrived at the anchorage, there were still large swells, and most cruisers there were not willing to go ashore through the huge breaking waves.

"We can do it!" Lance said excitedly. "Let's put on our swimsuits, pack some clothes in the waterproof bag, and give it a go." It was Father's Day and we wanted to celebrate.

Everyone was ready for some shore time, so we got into the dinghy and headed for land. The boats anchored around us called out bets as to how quickly we would "turtle" in the surf, and we started to doubt our decision. Nearing the beach, Fred watched the waves for several minutes, waiting to pick the right one to ride in on. We felt the dinghy rise up five or six feet as it rode over the incoming swells. We shouted encouragement to each other and admonished ourselves to be "ready." We each had our "assignments" and knew that, once we hit the sand, we would have only seconds to get out and pull the dinghy up on the beach before the next swell would submerge us. There would be no second chance. Our mouths were dry in anticipation as we waited for our "assault."

Finally Fred said, "Now!" and gunned the motor as fast as it would go. We surfed in on a huge wave. When we hit the sand, Page, Lance, and I jumped out as quickly as possible while Fred raised the outboard engine, and we grabbed the dinghy to pull it higher up onto the beach. When we realized that we had been successful, Page and I jumped up and down and squealed with delight. What an accomplishment! Was that the sound of applause coming from the boats at anchor, all of whom had been watching?

We walked over to a beach pub that had outdoor showers for the cruisers to use. The water wasn't heated, but it felt very refreshing. Fred and I relished being able to use as much water as we wanted, and took long showers, but Lance and Page decided to pass on the opportunity. Was that perhaps because of that four-inch cockroach in the shower stall?

When it was time to return to the boat, we realized we probably couldn't get the dinghy through the breaking waves and swell. They were still huge. We had seen many boats get flipped attempting to land on or leave the beach. We watched as Mike and Judy from *Melinda Lee* pushed their dinghy into the water to try to return to their boat. Their children, Ben and Annie, were standing nearby on the sand.

"Oh dear! They could probably handle getting flipped, but not the children," I said.

"I think I can help," Lance said, as he stripped to his swimsuit and ran across the sand to the family.

"I'll get in the water and pull on the painter (a line attached to the bow) to weigh down the bow when it starts to crest the wave," Lance said to the parents. "That might keep you from being thrown backward." Of course they were delighted with his offer to help.

It sounded like a good plan for everyone but Lance! He waded out into the surf with the bow-line in hand, while the family got in their dinghy. We all held our breath while we watched from the beach. Normally there is only one set of breaking waves, but after they crossed one line, we could see that there were several more sets to get through. Each time the bow rose at a precipitous angle, threatening to upend the boat, but Lance swam in front, putting all his weight on the painter. He successfully kept their boat from being flipped as it rode up and over each of the huge ocean swells. Finally it was in flat water. We all breathed a collective sigh of relief. As he swam back to shore, several folks congratulated him; he walked over to us with an embarrassed expression and a big grin on his face.

"Hey—the plan worked. Let's go!" he said.

By the time we had anxiously crossed the several sets of breaking waves, with Lance in the water, pulling on the painter, he was exhausted and we helped him climb aboard. Getting back to *Grace,* we decided that it had been a momentous Father's Day celebration after all.

"When you have kids like ours," Fred said with pride, "every day is a father's celebration." Ain't that the truth!

The following morning we again prepared to leave the boat—this time for three days. We packed our things and nervously got into the dinghy. The swell was still large and few were venturing ashore.

"If we get 'turtled' this time, we've got an awful lot of gear and luggage that's going to get wet," I said to Fred. He grimaced in return.

All went well, and we made our way along the dirt streets to the car rental agency to get a car that had *air-conditioning.* Once inside, we started the motor and just sat there enjoying the cool air.

"Man, does this ever feel good," said Lance. "Maybe we should just sit here in the car for the whole three days."

We had no destination in mind as we drove off; we just wanted to see more of inland Costa Rica before leaving Page at the airport to fly home. We laughed at the cows that blocked the road in some of the rural areas, and navigated around the infamous potholes that looked like tunnels to China. We marveled at the miles of picturesque hillsides covered with coffee plants. Arriving in small towns, we looked for "no-frills" hotels and restaurants where the local people stayed and ate. When Page had arrived from the States, she brought news that the renters of our house were still behind in their payments, so our "vacation" budget was limited. But we liked traveling like the locals; it was not only economical but allowed us to experience the country and its people in a very real way.

"Well, the price was right on that hotel," I said one morning, "but it was sure noisy. I counted those church bells ringing every hour."

"So did we!" chimed my three travel-mates.

We especially enjoyed seeing Sarchi, a small town of local artisans, and we were able to watch them work at their crafts. We also toured a butterfly farm and coffee plantation. Unexpectedly, as we traveled about, we found a good number of Americans who were living and working in Costa Rica. Many thought that country would soon become another U.S. state.

Saying good-bye to Page at the airport was difficult. "She looks so little walking away by herself," I cried while Fred hugged me.

"But we'll be seeing her soon when we go home," he replied. "Let's get back to *Grace* and find a safe place to leave her for a few weeks. Our 'vacation' is over. No more riding around in an AC car, stand up showers, flush toilets, and television. It's time to get back to work." He always had a way of making me laugh, and the three of us headed back to Coco.

When we arrived back on the boat, we were delighted to see that *Yobo* had come into the bay; they invited us over for dinner.

"You guys go ahead," said Lance. "I think I'll stay onboard. You 'kids' need a night out by yourselves."

One day, some of the cruisers organized a "Christmas in July" party at the beach pub we all frequented. Similar to many "normal" Christmas dinners, we stuffed ourselves on roast turkey, and, because turkey was not readily available in many Latin countries, we savored each bite. *Unlike* Christmas was the presence of little crabs that scurried around the tables set in sand under the large *palapa* roof, causing an occasional squeal.

CELEBRATING "CHRISTMAS IN JULY" WITH CINDY AND REED.

Lights reflected off the surf and stars shone above us as we made our way back to the dinghy late that night. The surf was really rolling again, but we had changed into our swimsuits, were ready for the challenge, and made our "escape."

The following day we were not so lucky. After crossing the first set of waves in our dinghy, our outboard engine died and two huge waves crashed down, totally soaking us. However, thanks to Lance's effort in the water, we were able to remain upright, get the motor going, and power on.

"Listen to the shouts from shore," Fred said. "This is real entertainment for all those people watching on the beach at the hotel."

"But not *always* funny," I said. "Remember Ben, the two year old on *Melinda Lee*? He was in a boat that flipped, and he was thrown several feet in the air before his dad caught him. His mom said the boy had just laughed, thinking it great fun. I've heard of angels that watch over children and fools. We're not kids, so I guess we know what that makes us!"

One day we were able to get a phone call through to Dawn. She told us the cost of airline tickets to fly home would be 1000 dollars apiece, and we were staggered. It would be a big hit on the cruising budget, but when we thought about our moms we felt we couldn't afford *not* to go.

After painting our boat's logo on the wall of the beach pub, we decided to move on, even though *Yobo* and many of our other cruising friends were going to stay at Coco. We would miss having them around. As we motored out of the anchorage, friends called out their good-byes and encouragement for a good sail. Large, billowy white clouds filled the sky, but soon they turned to dark black ominous threats. We were just about to pass through a very narrow channel between the mainland and a small island when the squall hit. We couldn't even see the bow of our boat through the rain. I hurried to the radar screen, but there was so much water in the air I couldn't detect any land mass on the screen.

"Hurry! Turn 90 degrees to starboard," I yelled to Fred at the helm. "Head out to sea. I can't see anything on the radar. Watch the depth sounder. We could be running right into that island."

A few tense minutes passed until I could believe we were safely past the island. Whew! The adventure's never over. The dream/nightmare continues. The squall passed in about an hour and we made our way into another calm little bay.

"Oh boy. A dock for the dinghy. What a treat!" I said. We went ashore to a community with two luxury hotels. A number of large fishing vessels were in a small marina. We made our way to one of the hotel's

Olympic-size swimming pool, ordered something to drink, and settled into the comfortable chaise lounge chairs.

"Now *this* is the life," Lance laughed.

"Yeah, and look at those folks checking in. They have to go home in a week, and we get to stay," I said, and chuckled.

"You sound pretty smug. How easily we forget the pain of getting here," Fred said wryly.

Our mornings were usually full of chores—repairing a leak in the dinghy, defrosting the fridge, mending some clothes, cleaning the salt off gear, getting more diesel, plotting a course on the charts, etc. Afternoons were time to play. As we worked our way south along the coast of Costa Rica, we stopped in several bays. Many had beaches of dark volcanic sand. Occasionally the beach had beautiful, fine, white sand, creating the image of an artist's canvas showing vivid aquamarine water ringed by an artificial blazing whiteness. The thick strokes of a pallet knife textured the surrounding lush green palm trees and vegetation, and light feather brush stokes captured the clear, azure blue skies—a true masterpiece.

"Let's go snorkeling," Lance suggested. "That bay yesterday was awesome!" We all enjoyed snorkeling and beachcombing. The day before we had been swimming in water about four feet deep when we suddenly found ourselves in water that was 30- to 40-feet deep. As we snorkeled and watched the ocean floor beneath us drop over the cliff, it felt like we were flying! The water was so clear that we could easily see the coral and fish on the bottom. There was much to see, with large numbers of fish of many colors and sizes. I especially liked the purple and neon yellow ones, but I wasn't keen about that coronet fish, which appeared to be about four feet long and only two inches in girth. It looked too much like a snake. The coral also grew in many colors and shapes, from delicate fans to large mounds that looked like human brains. We snorkeled in that underwater paradise until we became chilled.

Going ashore, we discovered a beach that was covered with *millions* of small cone-shaped shells. How had they come to be here? Why were there so many? There were so many mysteries of the deep. We walked into a little town and noticed that the southern sky had changed to an ominous black. Soon we heard a soft roaring sound in the distance.

As we stopped to listen, we could hear the roar becoming louder and closer.

"Could that be the sound of *rain*?" I asked incredulously.

"I've never heard that noise before," said Lance.

"But it *is* rain," said Fred, "and here it comes! Hurry, we are going to get soaked." We ran to a nearby restaurant and waited out the downpour. This was certainly not like Oregon rain. This rain was in a league of its own. Someone had turned on a fire hose!

One day we started for the next anchorage just as a storm came in. With torrential rains, winds of 20- to 25-knots on the nose, and a strong current running against us, it took us three and a half hours to go only *seven* miles. There were several underwater rocks that made our entry into the bay a little tricky, particularly when the rain made it so hard to see. Finally, we were settled and the rain had stopped.

"Why don't you guys go ashore for a Boy's Night Out?" I suggested. I felt a cold coming on and relished the idea of some time to myself. The two of them took off, and it was dark when they returned. Lance was grumpy. The tide had gone out while they were ashore and when they were ready to leave they had found the dinghy "high and dry."

"We had to carry that bugger *five miles* before it would float," Lance said, and plopped on his berth. Another lesson previously learned but forgotten.

We had gone to a hotel pool for a swim and had just settled into the poolside chaise lounge chairs, when I saw something move out of the corner of my eye.

"Yikes!" I squealed. I quickly pulled up my feet as several three-foot-long iguanas ran right under our chairs. Looking around, we heard an occasional "thump" and realized we were sitting under a mango tree where the fruit was dropping. One just missed hitting Fred in the head. It was also the reason the iguanas were sharing our space; they loved to eat mangos. It was time to move to the shade of a different tree!

As we worked our way south along the central Costa Rican Pacific coastline, not all anchorages were pleasant. Fred and I both had nasty colds, making sleep difficult. But trying to sleep in roll-y anchorages was truly impossible.

"Good grief," I said. "The cruising notes say 'A beautiful bay—not to be missed!' Well, it was beautiful all right, but last night even the cupboards rattled when we rolled." We pressed on to get around another of those infamous capes, with their tricky currents, winds, and sea conditions.

"Look at the size of that turtle," Lance yelled. "Its head is the size of a football!" We managed to get pretty close to it before it saw us and dove under the water. A little further on was a pod of dolphins. We never tired of watching them cavort in the bow wake.

Finally, we rounded the cape and entered the large protected waters of the Gulf of Nicoya. Coming into one bay near the gulf entrance, we found calm water, a small pier, and a yacht club (of sorts). It appeared to have a nice restaurant, and the cruising notes said it also had showers. We quickly set up the dinghy to go ashore. We all enjoyed a nice dinner and, after close inspection, reluctantly used the shower facilities, which had no door or curtain on the stalls.

"*Crude* would be generous in describing that shower," Lance said.

"At least it was rather isolated and almost dark," Fred added. "And the water was strong and plentiful." Another C.R.E. (Costa Rican Experience)!

Sailing through the waters of the gulf was wonderful. There were many small islands, and it reminded us of the San Juan Islands of Washington State, except for the many palm trees. Coming into the anchorage at Isla Gitana, we saw another boat.

"Hey—that's *Ossuna*," Fred said excitedly. Sure enough. We had hoped they might still be in the area; what fun it was to get together with them and trade stories. So much had happened since our first meeting in northern California. Our joy in seeing "old" friends was dampened somewhat by Fred's lingering cold and sore throat. He really wasn't feeling well. I had taken his temperature and it was over 102. Lance was still bothered by an ear infection, and we had given him the last of our antibiotics. We had hoped Fred's infection was viral but feared streph throat. Once again, the worry of illness loomed large.

"We're going to Puntarenas tomorrow," said Heidi. "We'll bring you back some antibiotics."

While Fred slept most of the following day, Lance and I went ashore to hike around the island. We quickly discovered that going into the jungle on a narrow, muddy trail, wearing only flip flops, was probably not a good idea. Thinking it was only a short distance, we continued on. Soon we were besieged by bugs—*big* bugs—*little* bugs—*plentiful* bugs! Then, too, there were the spider webs. Neither of us liked breaking the sticky webs across the trail.

"It's your turn to go first," I whined.

"No way! You've only been doing it for two minutes," responded Lance. So much for chivalry.

The humidity was soaring as we slipped and slid up and down the trail, dripping with sweat. It was not my idea of great fun. True, it was lush and beautiful, with gorgeous plants that grew huge leaves and exotic flowers reminiscent of a florist shop. But we were always watching where we stepped, fearful of snakes. Thankfully, we didn't see any, but we did see an anteater, a wild boar, lots of birds, butterflies, and many "leaf-cutter" ants. They were easy to spot, for it looked like a parade of small leaves walking across the path. Each ant carried a piece on its back, and the column wound its way to and up a large tree.

Before going back to the boat, we visited with some folks on the beach. I loved to watch Lance interact with others. He was a good listener—friendly in manner, and able to talk with just about anyone. It was fun to see him with his dad, as well. They obviously had a good deal of respect for each other, but they also loved to play. Lance was good for me, too, trying to teach me to run the dinghy motor, or not to get so upset when things went badly. Good advice. Where did he learn all that good stuff? We would miss him when he returned to the States.

A great delight in those waters was watching the phosphorescence at night. Just splashing a hand through the water created thousands of diamond-like twinkles. It was more intense than any other place we had been. We discovered that we could even see tiny fish swimming at night. All we had to do was stomp our feet on the deck, and they would all scurry at once, lighting up the water around our boat just as if there were underwater flashlights. Fascinating!

A not so fascinating part of Costa Rica was worrying about the critters there—particularly snakes. We were aboard the boat one evening when we heard a cruiser's voice on the VHF radio. Her husband was a much older man and not in the best of health, so she and her 17-year-old son handled the boat.

"Does anyone in the anchorage know how to get a snake off the boat?" she asked in a shaky voice.

Several people anchored near her answered her call. In the discussion, we learned that, when she had reached for a potato in a hanging basket in the bow cabin, she had discovered a large, coiled, hissing snake. From her description, it sounded like a poisonous one and had likely climbed up the anchor chain and followed the chain into the boat. Several men headed over to help find a way to get rid of it. We all waited tensely.

"*Freedom, Freedom,*" came the radio call. We recognized the anxious voice of one of the men who had gone to help. He was calling his wife. "Go up on the deck. We got the snake off, but it's in the water heading right towards our boat! Make sure it doesn't come up our anchor chain!"

Everyone in the anchorage ran up to their decks and anxiously searched the water for snakes. Fortunately, none were found, and the harried snake had likely headed for shore. Ahhh! The cruising life! Fred found some rags, soaked them in diesel, and wrapped them around our chain. We didn't know if it would stop a snake, but we wanted to do *something.*

Finally, Fred's temperature was down and we sailed another 10 miles with the incoming tide. We stopped at Playa Naranja, about two hours away from Puntarenas, the town where we hoped to safely leave our beautiful *Amazing Grace* when we went back home. We were the only boat anchored off a lovely resort, with a nice pool, palapas on the beach with hammocks, a restaurant, and a laundry bodega. The bodega was basically a thatch-roofed area on the lawn, with huge laundry tubs, a large table, and running water. When exploring the resort, Fred tried to pick up a parrot and got bitten by it.

"Another war wound, Dad," laughed Lance. Fred had previously tried to pick up a little crab that was in a restaurant and causing children to scream. He thought he could handle it like the Dungeness crabs of the Northwest, and picked it up from behind. But it reached around and bit him hard.

That night, I awoke thinking I heard some whistling sounds. I decided it was just my imagination. But since I was awake, I got up to look out the aft cabin window. To my utter surprise, five feet away from me was a man, sitting in his boat in the dark, with his hands on our dinghy. I was *outraged* and yelled out the window, "What do you want?"

My voice sounded so low and gruff! I turned and saw that Fred was still sleeping, courtesy of those darn earplugs, so I reached over to shake him. Then I remembered to press our panic button on the cabin wall. By then, Fred was yelling at the man, who said something about needing oil. But when the alarm started, he motored off at full throttle. Lance was up by then, and we were all dazed. I was mainly mad, however. How *dare* he try to take our dinghy? We knew there would be little sleep the rest of the night because, by then, the adrenalin was really flowing.

"Well, we were told not to anchor in a bay by ourselves," Fred said. "We know there are lots of dinghy and motor thefts around here."

"I'm sure glad we can lock ours onto the boat," Lance said, "although that cable could probably be cut by wire cutters."

"We don't need to worry," Fred said, nodding at me and laughing at my capering about. "We have our *little warrior* to keep us safe." We didn't fear personal violence, something almost unheard of in this country, but there was a great deal of theft. Finally, we got back to sleep, but later Fred woke me, saying I was yelling "Stop!" In my dream, I had seen a guy taking off with our dinghy!

We were up early the next morning, went ashore, and walked about a half mile to catch the ferry to Puntarenas. It was about an hour-and-a-half ferry ride, and we stood up most of the way so we could be in the shade; it was very hot. After completing our paperwork with the Port Captain, we explored the town and went to find the Costa Rica Yacht Club. Taking a bus, we found it about five miles from the city center on a river that emptied into the gulf. Most of the boats there were tied to mooring buoys in the river. We walked around the grounds, pool, and clubhouse and talked with the manager.

"This is really nice," I said. "When could we get in here?"

"A mooring buoy won't open up for about three weeks," Fred replied, "but it's pretty expensive."

"Hey—after last night, you guys need the security and peace of mind, even if it does cost more," Lance added.

In order to leave the boat for a month, we needed to get legal papers to extend the vessel's visa, and then hire someone to look after it while we were gone. This usually meant having someone sleep in the cockpit overnight, even in the yacht club—although night guards would also be patrolling around the moored boats. The club manager introduced us to Mario, who could manage everything for us. Mario spoke no English but was pleasant and helpful, and we arranged to meet him at a lawyer's office that afternoon to draw up the necessary papers.

"How much longer do you think this will take?" Lance asked, while we sat in the attorney's small, crowded waiting room. Mario and his 10-year-old son were with us, and we had been trying to converse with the children there.

"I don't know," I said. "I sure hope we get in pretty soon. The last ferry back to our island leaves in about an hour, and the dock is on the other side of town. I sure don't want to be stuck here overnight."

We continued to apologize to Mario and his boy for taking so much of their time. He would smile amiably and assure us that it was *no problemo*. When we finally had the legal papers, it was *pouring* outside, and we had only minutes to get to the ferry dock. A woman, who had also been sitting in the waiting room, came up and asked us if we'd like a ride. An angel unaware! While driving to the dock, I told her how much we enjoyed the people of her country; they were so helpful and kind. I also found out that she was not going on the ferry.

"I'm so sorry to impose on you," I tried to say in my halting Spanish. "Thank you *so* much. Why are you doing this?"

"*La sonrisa de la Señora*," (the smile of the lady) she replied and pointed at me. We were touched by her kindness. I had forgotten how others observe us in our interactions and behaviors. Hopefully, we were succeeding in our goal to be "good will ambassadors" for the U.S. We squeezed into the ferry office just in time. The ferry took about 150 passengers, but there was room under cover and seating for only about 40, so everyone pushed to get on first. We laughed as we stood under a doorway trying to keep from getting soaked by the rain—until some kind locals made room for us on a bench. We finally disembarked at our island and slid through mud all the way back to the resort.

"It's definitely 'Miller Time,'" said Lance.

We were all tired when we returned to *Grace* after a busy, long day and little sleep the night before. We heated a can of soup and went to bed, but Fred and I slept with one ear open. We each got up at least 10 times during the night to check the dinghy whenever we thought we heard something, and we decided that, from then on, we'd remove its motor each night and pull the dinghy onto the bow deck. It was extra bother, but worth a good night's sleep.

With a couple of "recovery" days at the pool, for reading and naps, we were ready to move on. We sailed *Grace* across the gulf to Puntarenas and took a mooring buoy right near the center of town for the last few days before Lance returned to the States; he preferred to stay in this area rather than go sightseeing in San Jose. Being in Puntarenas, a good-sized town, was different for us, and we enjoyed the hustle and bustle ashore. When we were ready for some relaxing time, we would ride the bus out to the Yacht Club and swim and talk with other cruisers around the pool. Gringos were definitely not an oddity in this place, and we met a number from countries other than the States. Some of the younger folks led a rather vagabond life—skiing in the winter, wind-surfing in the summer, and planting trees for an income to finance their travels. Lance was ready to sign on! While the town provided some night-life, something we seldom did, we were told that it was not wise to leave the boat unattended on the mooring buoys after dark, so we would return for an early bedtime.

"It's cool, Mom," Lance said. "I get *lots* of night-life at home."

I could only imagine. At least he got in lots of reading on his trip with us; the count was 22 books and climbing. Thank goodness there were many places where we could exchange used, English paperbacks.

"What would you like for your last dinner on *Grace?*" I asked Lance.

"Easy—*huatchinango* fish like we had in the Murcielagos!" he replied.

We had saved a couple of bottles of fine wine, and I pulled out all the stops for an enjoyable dinner. Thankfully, an earlier rain shower had cooled the evening air. As we sat in the cockpit watching an incredible sunset over the gulf waters, we reflected on all that had happened in his two-and-a-half months with us. The *huge* golden globe of the sun slid away and the sky changed into a brilliant red-orange, silhouetting sailboats, palm trees, and mountains. It was a poignant symbol of the blessings of this dream and its adventures that the three of us had shared. We were so *blucky.* How we would miss him!

Awesome!

"Oh my goodness, these bags are heavy," I exclaimed. We were unable to find a taxi that could carry all Lance's gear, so we were walking the half-mile to the bus station the following day on our way to the airport.

"That's because of all your old charts that you packed in them," Lance reminded me.

We found the same hotel in Allajuela that we had used before, and walked to the little Peruvian restaurant, where the owner remembered us and was so glad to see us. That felt nice. The following morning, Lance was excited to be going home—but he also knew he would be missing our ongoing adventures as well. We said our goodbyes, which were not so difficult since we knew we would be seeing him in a couple of weeks, and got on a bus for San Jose.

Traveling is definitely stressful at times, and that day proved to be one of those times. We finally found the Customs Office in San Jose, and stood in line for two hours to get our boat visa extension. At last it was our turn.

"I'm sorry," the woman said. "You need another 'new' form from the Yacht Club in order to complete the extension."

"*Another* form," I said, wanting to cry. "That will mean another whole trip here, *before* we come in again to leave. I can't believe this!"

On another level, we were not terribly surprised, because there was always a concern about what we were hearing in the translation process, and the government bureaucracy in many countries was such that procedures were never the same twice in a row.

Another three-hour bus ride and we arrived back at the Yacht Club—only to learn that one of the cruising boats anchored in a bay across the gulf was robbed when the owners were gone for a week. There were a number of other boats anchored around it, so everyone thought they would be safe, but still the thieves managed to strip the interior of *everything*—dishes, photo albums, clothes, and all the electronics. The couple had no insurance, so they were searching pawn shops and putting out fliers because they believed the police were ineffective in any recovery process. The cruising community was collecting donations to help them out.

"Oh dear!" I said. "Let's get out of here and go check on *Grace.*" On the morning cruisers' radio net two days before, several had asked about us taking Lance to the airport, for he was carrying mail for everyone. That meant that anyone listening would know we would be gone overnight. I had purposely said, twice, that we had hired a guard to sleep on the boat, even though we hadn't. I also mentioned that our alarm system would sound if anyone were to come aboard. We hoped that would be enough to deter anyone planning theft.

"Everything looks fine," Fred said with relief, after friends took us back to the boat. Looking around, we gave another prayer of thanks.

Because there are many shoals and a very strong current in the river going to the Yacht Club, we wanted to take the boat there on a high water, slack tide. This would not occur during the daytime for another eight days, so we made arrangements with the club to enter at that time, and then left to explore some of the other islands in this huge gulf. It was a relaxing time after all the activity with Lance aboard, and we took a leisurely pace. We tried to do things before it got too hot. Actually, *hot* depended on whether there was any breeze, not on the time of day, because it was hot as soon as the sun came up. Only breeze and shade made the heat bearable, and putting up awnings was the first job after dropping the hook.

We used the tides and currents to help travel to several anchorages when there was little wind. We were the only boat in one little, protected bay when in came *Ossuna*. We got together, either on our boat or theirs, and enjoyed visiting. Together we visited an "ex-pat" that lived ashore with his Costa Rican wife. We spent some time at their home, high on a hill overlooking the gulf waters. The view was stupendous.

"Did you hear how they kept "no-see-um" bugs out of their home?" I asked Fred later. "They sprayed their screens with diesel, which collects in the corners of the mesh and catches the bugs."

"*That* was what I kept smelling," he said. "I guess it worked, but it sure stunk."

One night we were watching videos on *Ossuna*. It had started to rain when we went to their boat, anchored about 50 yards from ours. As the evening progressed, we realized that the rain had become a major storm, and the deluge pounded so hard on the deck that we could hardly hear each other in the cabin. Finally, knowing it wouldn't let up, we bailed out several inches of water in the dinghy and made a dash for our boat. We were soaked, and as we slowly made our way in the strong winds and rough water, we were cold. We were freezing! By the time we were in our cockpit, my hands were shaking so badly that I couldn't get the key in the lock.

"I can't believe we are so cold in a country that is so hot," I said. It felt *wonderful* to finally get inside—although we had to go back out again to take the motor off the dinghy. All that rain could swamp it during the night. No rest for the weary!

Besides all of the routine tasks of daily living on the boat, much of our time was now spent getting ready to go home. It always felt strange to say "home," because we wouldn't be going to our house, and it truly felt as if *Grace* was now our home.

"This list of things to get the boat ready to leave seems to be never ending," I complained.

I was going through all the lockers and food to check for bugs, putting out mothballs to retard the growth of mildew, and boric acid to kill the bugs. Fred had the water-maker all disassembled, biociding the filters. The boat was in total disarray.

"Well that's what happens when you get ready to go on *vacation*," he said.

We laughed to think that being home would be our vacation, while others wanted to be here in Costa Rica (or on a sailboat) for theirs.

On cloudy days we finished waxing the deck and hull after Lance had started the project. The wax helped protect the boat from the damaging UV rays of the sun. There was so much bending, stooping, and crawling around in living and working on a boat, that our bodies often paid a price.

"I feel like a human *pretzel* sometimes," Fred sighed.

"I know. My hands and fingers ache. I'm so glad we didn't wait until we were older to do this. I don't think my body could've handled it," I said.

Finally, the list got down to the worst job of all—cleaning the hull. It was the one we kept putting off, for the waters in the gulf were not very clean for swimming, but we knew it had to be done. Fred used the Hooka to dive under and clean the bottom, while I used a snorkel to swim around the waterline and clean as far under as I could reach. All of the gunk we scrubbed off the bottom and sides floated in the water around us.

"Yuk!" I said with disgust. "This junk gets all over you."

"Let's just hope that one of these tiny crabs doesn't crawl in our ears," Fred said. Several hours after completing the same job, another cruiser had felt something in his ear. Out crawled one of the little crabs that attach themselves to the hull.

I tried not to think about it, mentally went to my "Happy Place," and hurried to get the job done. It took about two hours to complete the task, and we quickly showered to get off the little worm-like bugs and green slime of the seaweed. It was only noon, but it was definitely "Miller Time!"

"You know, I think we get along easier now than when we first left," I said one evening.

"Were we not getting along?" Fred asked with a grin. "Okay, okay—I guess I know what you mean. Maybe as we've come to adjust to this kind of lifestyle and its stresses, we're a little gentler with each other."

"Yeah, but not just that. I think we have more appreciation of each other's strengths, and can better use our interdependence on each other. I think I resented so much of that at first. I wanted something that could be my 'own,' one little thing I didn't have to run by you."

"Well, in such a small space and being together so much, it sometimes feels like we're 'joined at the hip,'" he said with a laugh. "But we both said that no adventure was worth it if it damaged our relationship."

We agreed that this cruising dream had definitely made our relationship better, but it had not been without some "growing pains."

One day, in the midst of our preparations, we hiked to a nearby pool to cool off and practice the "vacation" lifestyle. While there, we enjoyed playing with Ben and Annie from *Melinda Lee*. We missed having small children around. Coming back on the trail through the jungle, we watched for the howler monkeys. We saw them in the trees above us, but hurried by because they are known to spit and throw feces at people underneath them. We saw their "calling cards" on the trail. Not very hospitable! In contrast, we loved watching the butterflies. There were so many different kinds, each looking like some exquisite painting. They were plentiful in the verdant foliage, and they reminded me of dancing fairies as they floated through the air.

It was time to take *Grace* the five miles up river to the Yacht Club. Pulling up anchor, we found it covered with sticky black mud, and it took a long time to clean it off before we could leave. We hurried, because we didn't want to miss the slack water tide. All went well, and we arrived at the club without incident.

"I don't like the position of this mooring buoy," Fred said, when we settled on the buoy we had been assigned. "It's isolated from most of the others. They are all on the other side of the river, close to the clubhouse."

"Not only that, but it's closer to shore and those darn Mangroves. That means more bugs," I said. "But I guess we are lucky to get a spot. Most of the boats moored here are local."

Riding the bus later that day, we talked with a friendly man who we learned worked at the club. He kept trying to tell us what he did. "Wah-chee-mahn," he kept saying. Finally we got it—*watchman*. His name was Randolpho, and he was a night guard who came by each evening in his rounds of checking the boats. He liked to help us practice Spanish, but spoke no English. Fred was tickled with the way he pronounced the word "watchman," and since I was the one who heard most things at night, he began to call me his very own "wah-chee-mahn." It was a name that stuck.

Randolpho picked us up at 5:30 the following morning so we could take the early bus back into San Jose to complete our visa paperwork.

"I sure didn't sleep much last night. Did you hear all those noises on the river?" I asked.

"I did. It sounded like we were in the middle of the jungle," Fred replied. "What kept me awake was worrying about that Customs Office. They are still on strike, and even though they said they would be open when we called yesterday, I don't trust that they will be."

After our three-hour bus trip and making our way to the Customs Office, we were greatly relieved to find it open, but we were then told that the manager needed to sign the papers, and the staff didn't know if he was coming in that day. *Oh no! This couldn't be happening!*

Fortunately, he showed up a few minutes later, we received our necessary papers, and we had a whole day to spend in San Jose. It was fun seeing the downtown area and buying souvenirs to take home to family and friends. We were tired by the time we got back to the boat that evening and turned in early. At midnight, we were startled awake by a knocking on the hull.

"It's Randolpho," Fred said. "Come on. He says it's not safe to leave the motor on the dinghy, so we need to take it off."

"Good grief," I exclaimed, and climbed out of bed. "Why couldn't he have told us that earlier?" No rest for . . . .

During the night we heard the sounds of gunfire. What now? In the morning we learned that the night guards would occasionally fire a gun just to let potential thieves know that the guards had weapons and were ready to use them—rather like a scarecrow that protects the field. I didn't like the constant need to be concerned about theft, but it seemed to be the way of life in this country, and we adjusted to it. In most of Mexico and Central America, broken glass glued on the tops of walls that enclosed property was a barrier to climbing over them. Bars often covered windows. Even when people bought property, as several cruising friends had, they needed to hire a watchman to make certain that "squatters" didn't start living on it, as they could then claim ownership. One couple told us that they then needed to hire someone to watch the watchman! It was definitely not our idea of a desirable investment.

In the early morning, and again at evening, we would see many locals on the river in large, log dugout boats, going to or returning from work. We made a point to speak or wave, and they would always return the gesture in a friendly way. Some began to call out to us. They especially liked seeing me play the guitar in the cockpit. We wondered what they must have thought as they passed us. Likely, we seemed like millionaires in that large, beautiful sailboat. Did they think that all Americans were rich? As we thought of our blessings, we realized we certainly *were* rich in many ways.

One of the joys of being in a city was worshiping in a church on Sunday mornings. So much of our cruising time we had been anchored in isolated bays where there were no churches nearby. Certainly we could worship in the great outdoors we were experiencing, but we missed the opportunity to rub shoulders with "family" and have a collective, supportive experience. We were always welcomed sincerely in the Spanish-speaking congregations, regardless of the denomination, and we looked forward to seeing our own church family back home.

We continued getting the boat ready to leave. That meant washing everything we could think of, knowing that anything dirty or sweaty would mildew when the boat was closed up and had little air circulation. Mario would come to open up the boat occasionally, but we didn't know how often that would be. We lugged our big wool mattress cover to the dock and washed it, mainly with our feet, as it was too heavy to scrub and wring by hand. At least we had unlimited water from the hose there. The dock boys could only smile and shake their heads as they watched us "dancing" over the wooly cover. I also carried many things to the women's shower to hand wash, and we again had unique, colorful "flags" hanging all over the boat to dry. A sudden thunderstorm meant quickly grabbing things to take below, and I even ducked as one clap of thunder sounded *way* too close.

It seemed there was never a dull moment, and we actually would've liked some. We continually faced new experiences and challenges, and often we would laugh and ask ourselves why we were doing this.

"I think the adventure aspect of this journey becomes rather addictive," I said one day to Fred. We were reflecting about going home. "It's wondering what lies ahead, and how we'll handle it."

"Right now all I can think ahead to is non-moving beds, flush toilets, cars, and feeling clean all day," he replied with a laugh. "Oh yeah, and washing machines, peanut butter, and television." Even more, we looked forward to seeing the people we missed so much. I think we had come to value those relationships even more than we did before we left.

Mario came to the boat and, in our improving Spanish and with many hand gestures, we showed him all of the emergency procedures we thought he might possibly need. We had disconnected all of our electronics, brought everything possible from the deck into the cabin, added new chafing gear to the mooring lines, opened all the storage lockers for air circulation, and packed our things to take home. We were *ready.* We were going *home!*

Nine

On To The Canal Between The Seas

It was nearly eight weeks before we returned to our beautiful *Amazing Grace*. How strange, yet familiar, it seemed to be back onboard. It was a long time to be away—and in the midst of an incredibly different lifestyle and experience. We had been so busy with business and medical appointments, getting more gear for the boat, and seeing everyone possible, that the time went quickly. Our renters had moved out after being unable to make their payments, which necessitated finding new renters. Of course, cleaning and getting the property back in shape took a lot of time and effort, but the good news was that the empty house provided us a place to stay. It felt like we were camping, though, as we had no furniture, slept on a mattress on the floor, and pulled out only the bare necessities from storage.

"Whew, this carpet really stinks," Fred had said, one warm afternoon. Apparently the renters' dogs were not housebroken.

"The carpet-cleaning service said that we'll need to replace all of this carpeting," I said angrily. "That's really going to cost a lot."

"True, but that rent check helps pay the cruising budget," Fred said. "And it's good for us, now, not to have to stay with someone else. Besides that, we are close to the kids."

We frequently mused about how nice it was to have adult kids, and I especially liked being able to go see them and take all *our* dirty laundry! After so many years of them coming home from college with huge piles of dirty clothes, it was "turnabout is fair play." Each of the kids was doing well, although struggling at times with different issues. I had to remind myself that struggles produce character, confidence, and growth, and they were capable of handling things without our being there.

We had been especially fortunate to drive back to Nebraska by delivering a car for a friend. It was made-to-order for us in getting to see Fred's mom. Both our moms were doing well, for which we were very grateful. They were such good models for us for our senior years. When the time came for us to say goodbye to our loved ones, I wondered again, "Why are we *doing* this?" It was so hard to leave them.

Because we wanted to paint the bottom when we returned to the boat, and preferred to use a superior American product not available in Costa Rica, we had made numerous inquiries in Oregon to see if we could take the paint back with us on the airplane. The final word (at that time) was that we could bring it as "carry on" luggage. Bottom paint is *extremely* heavy. Two gallons of it meant torture if carrying it any distance. In that trip back to the boat—from home to airport, to connecting flights, to customs, to taxi, to hotel, to taxi, to bus station, to Yacht Club, and finally to *Grace*—Fred's arms lengthened by at least four inches! We had so much other luggage and gear that it took many minutes of shuttling back and forth in each place to load it all. Some of our baggage contained heavy stainless steel bars that were custom-made for two of our hatches. These would allow us to leave the hatches open at night, or when we were off the boat, while securing it from someone gaining entry. They would be especially helpful in the dry season. For the present, we were just glad to be back on *Grace*. And it felt so *right!*

"She looks pretty good," Fred said. "The head's not working, though. It probably has crud over the seacocks."

"There's some mildew, too," I responded. "Mario said it wasn't opened up a lot due to the rain."

Mario had also told us that a large barge upriver from us had broken its mooring lines in a storm and had come down, hitting us. Thank goodness, there was only a little damage to the fiberglass of the hull. We were fortunate that it was not worse, and I was grateful for Fred's efforts to protect our mooring lines from breaking.

"It's strange not to see more familiar faces," Fred said. "So many of our friends have gone on to Panama."

"Yeah," I responded. "There are lots of reports of bad things happening for cruisers in Golfito, so most folks are skipping it and going directly to Panama. I think we should do the same. Everyone raves about its pristine anchorages—the warm unpolluted water and the majestic mountains around protected bays. It's what Costa Rica was many years ago."

We had been able to talk to *Yobo* on the ham radio, and hoped to catch up to them eventually. We were getting "itchy feet" and anxious to be "on the road again." In order to be able to leave, we worked long, hard days to get *Grace* back in shape. I always felt frazzled when things were out of place and the boat was a mess. The refrigeration had gone out just before we left for the States, and we arranged for someone to come to the boat to work on it. His name was Marcell, and he was a big man. When we went to the dock to pick him up, his eyes grew large and he looked worried.

"*Es plastico!*" he said, when he looked down at our dinghy. He was apparently fearful that it would not support him. When he climbed aboard, the vinyl hull flexed a little, as it normally does, and Marcel was then truly frightened. We laughed and reassured him; although it was plastic and not rigid, it would indeed hold him. We hoped! He and his friend who came to help were really nice folks, and as we waited to see if the compressor would work correctly, we talked (and even told and heard some jokes) in Spanish. Because it is subtler, humor is difficult to translate, but we had great fun trying.

After spending many hours trying to fix both heads, Fred wanted to dive in the river and clean the bottom by the through-hulls. Many people had told us this river water was too polluted to do that. So we argued. I wanted to pay someone to do it—it wasn't worth getting sick—and I eventually won. Fred was also struggling to fix half of our electronics, which wouldn't work. He spent many hours troubleshooting and was completely frustrated. Finally, they all popped on.

"Terrific," I said. "What did you do?"

"I have absolutely no idea," he responded, and shook his head.

We were quickly longing for the cool of Oregon as we adjusted once again to the heat and humidity of the tropics. A shower felt *so* good, but almost immediately we would again feel sweaty and sticky. Clean sheets and pillows would also feel sticky after only a few hours, but they were such a pain to wash. We laughed as we remembered one of Lance's last comments to us before leaving Oregon: "Aren't you going to miss the . . . *conveniences*?" He well knew what it was like!

We needed to take one more trip to San Jose to go to the Customs Office. We dreaded the time it would likely take. After arriving in the city, we completed the necessary paperwork.

"Wonder of wonders," I said to Fred. "That was simple and quick."

"That was truly amazing in this land that thrives on bureaucracy," Fred responded.

Getting back to the boat, we looked for the club manager; our haul-out into the boatyard was scheduled for the following day. When we found him, we learned that the lift was broken and there would be no haul-out until it was fixed. Oh my! But we had lots of other tasks to do, so we kept working and tried to "go with the flow," like so many people in these Central American countries seemed to do. It certainly added less stress to your life. Maybe we should do more of that at home as well.

When the lift was finally repaired, a couple of days later, the dockmaster announced, "*Mañana* for *Amazing Grace*." The following day we realized that *mañana* does not always mean "tomorrow," but sometimes means "soon." So we raised the mainsail to clean out all the bugs and spider webs, scrubbed and deep-cleaned the teak decks, and washed the mooring lines that had been in the water for a couple of months. Yuk. So much scrubbing!

"Remember," I said to Fred. "We're living everyone's dream."

"Covered with gunk and sweat," Fred laughed. "If only they could see us now."

We planned pool time for breaks during the hottest part of the day, and occasionally took the bus into town for groceries or fun. The bus cost only fourteen cents, and the people on it were friendly and helpful. Since we were the only gringos to ride the bus, we were pretty easy to spot. People would smile warmly and sometimes offer us a seat when we got on, and wave when we got off. The custom for notifying the driver that you wanted the next stop was to whistle. Since we didn't know how to make that piercing whistle sound, folks would whistle for us when they saw us preparing to get off. They all knew we were going to the Yacht Club on our returns. One time we had decided to get off about two stops before the club to go to a little restaurant.

"Oh my goodness," I laughed, walking away from the bus. "Was that ever funny!"

As we had prepared to leave the bus, several folks kept shaking their heads and encouraging us to sit back down. Soon others joined in, trying to make us understand that we were at the wrong stop, and, before we knew it, the whole bus was involved. They were determined not to let us get off too soon, and wanted to make sure we got to the Yacht Club. We finally convinced them that we knew where we were, and that we were going to a restaurant first. It sure felt nice to have people taking good care of us.

One morning I woke up grumpy. It had been especially hot; yet, if we didn't stay under a sheet during the night, mosquitoes bit us. We were using a mosquito coil, fans, and repellant at night. But if, in applying the lotion, we missed a tiny spot on our skin—like an ear lobe, or between our fingers—those nasty little buggers would find it, and we'd wake up with bites. Besides the heat and mosquitoes, I had also not slept well because of jumping up to look out the window whenever I heard a noise. The final time I had been *sure* that I heard something, and I was right. There was a huge bird sitting calmly as you please, right on the dinghy motor! I had to laugh.

The dockworkers got quite a kick out of the two of us. They weren't used to seeing boat owners (and especially women) working on their own boats. Most of the local owners hired work done. The dockworkers would smile and wave when they saw us exerting such effort and getting so dirty in the process. One time an old man on the dock had watched me wash a bucket of clothes. When Fred came over, the man said, "*Comer*" (to eat) and pointed at me, saying "*Mucho trabaja*" (much work). He apparently thought Fred should feed me, after working so hard. We enjoyed the men's camaraderie and conversations. When we took the cockpit floorboards to the dock to clean, the manager came over to say that a haul-out was *possible* the following day.

"Save some of that energy," he said with a laugh.

His advice was appropriate. We needed energy—*lots* of it—for the next three days.

It is always a little scary to haul a large sailboat out of the water and watch it dangle in the air in a canvas sling, with the back stay removed and the mast so vulnerable. In addition, this time we knew that the weight of our boat approached the maximum for the lift, and we were not sure how knowledgeable the yard staff was. There was also the fact that we couldn't communicate very well with them. It made for anxious moments.

"Look. Mario just dove in the water. I guess he's going to make certain that the sling isn't over the prop," I said to Fred.

"He didn't even hesitate. These guys really do know what they're doing," he responded.

We had arranged for a young man to help us once the boat was settled in the boatyard, but when the time came, he was nowhere to be seen, so we started the dirty process of cleaning the hull ourselves. Along came Geronimo, who offered to help. He turned out to be the best deal in town. He worked like a beaver, eagerly did the most disagreeable jobs, knew what he was doing, and was pleasant, too. Fred had many specific projects he wanted to do, such as cleaning the seacocks, retro fitting the rudder, replacing the stuffing box, etc., so Geronimo and I did the cleaning and painting preparation. Fred and I wearily left the yard at dark to go to the club motel.

"Boy, does it feel good to shower off all this yukky stuff," I said. "We're covered with it."

"Clean sheets and a 'real' bed feel mighty good, too," Fred responded, "but it is definitely *Advil* time."

We were up at five the following morning, wanting to start work while it was still somewhat cool. It was a long day, and we worked until dark to get the painting done.

"Doggone it. These no-see-ums are eating us alive!" Fred yelled in frustration.

"It must be the sweat, all those mangroves over there, and no wind," I added. "I hate these bites. The itching lasts for days and days." We hurried to the motel.

"One more day in the coal mines," Fred said the next morning. It was another long one, but finally *Grace* was ready to be put back in the water.

"She looks so pretty," I said with satisfaction.

"But take a look below," Fred said. The cabin was an absolute *disaster* area. Locker contents were thrown all over as we had searched for replacement parts, tools, or supplies. We couldn't even walk through the boat. Tired as we were, we were almost obsessed with getting it all picked up and back to "ship-shape."

"You are a workin' fool," I said to Fred, when he just wouldn't stop.

Where did he get all that energy? I was so impressed and proud that he had been able to tackle, struggle with, and fix just about every system on the boat. He had the patience of Job, and he never hesitated to do the worst of jobs. With the big job done, we were almost ready to move on, and we felt satisfied that we had taken care of *Grace* just as she was taking care of us.

Several tasks remained before we could leave, though. One day was a perfect example for a response to the oft-heard question from folks back home: "What do you *do* all day?" We started by waiting to get on the ham radio net and make a phone patch to Dawn to wish her a happy birthday. After making contact with her, we hurried to the Port Captain's office, because we were told to come at ten to get our *zarpe* for checking out of the country. Since he also had our passports, we sat and waited. It was after twelve when he finally arrived. I needed a haircut, but they took no appointments, and there were five people in front of me when we arrived. We waited another two hours. We also needed to load up on groceries since there would be no place to do so for the next few weeks. The market was crowded, and there was more waiting at each stall. We waited another half hour for a taxi to get back to the club, because we had too many provisions to take the bus. Getting our groceries loaded into the dinghy and then onto the boat and out of boxes into plastic containers and putting everything away took another couple of hours. We had planned to go out for a "final" dinner and to the disco nearby, but when the time came, we fixed a salami sandwich instead—and fell into bed, exhausted. A typical day in the cruising dream!

As we said our goodbyes to the Yacht Club staff, we realized, again, how much we had come to care about many of them and that we would miss them. It was about three in the afternoon when the dockhands helped turn the boat around in the narrow river, and we headed for the gulf and San Lucas island, about eight miles away.

Ahhhh. Yes, yes, YES! We were "on the road again!" It felt almost as exciting as it did more than a year previously, and it seemed as if it was just as much work in getting ready for it.

"Boy, does it ever feel good to be moving again," Fred said.

"I can't believe it was three months ago when we came here," I replied. "I have to actually stop and think about how to run the boat now that we're underway."

"Me too. But it comes back quickly."

We were filled with satisfaction, joy, and not a little pride in the work accomplished and how beautiful *Grace* was, both inside and out. It wasn't just a physical beauty, but all the things she stood for. And we were greatly touched and awed by the Grace of God that gave us the opportunity and blessing of the dream. There were more than a few tears shed by both of us that afternoon.

As we motored across the waters of the great gulf in light wind the following morning, we were very grateful that we had listened again to the *"SeaWellness"* tape. The rolling swells coming in from the ocean made for lots of motion, and we knew we'd have to gain our sea legs once more.

"I keep hearing a phrase from the tape in my mind," I said to Fred. "The boat is doing what it needs to do, and your body is doing what *it* needs to do to adjust to the motion of the boat."

"It's funny how certain phrases stick with you," he replied. "The one I like is, 'All is well!'"

By afternoon, we anchored in a calm bay where we were going to wait for friends to join us. We were looking forward to having *Traveller* as company on our trip to Panama. We went ashore, landing the dinghy in gentle surf on a soft sand beach, and explored the area, including a large luxury hotel resort. We looked for a phone to call Lance, and were glad to hear that he was happy being back with his friends in the ski resort of Vail, Colorado.

"When Lance described the roaring fire, and watching it snow outside, I realized how much I miss the changing seasons," I said to Fred later.

"Yeah. It feels like summer all the time here. When he said he had a job hanging Christmas lights, I had to laugh," he responded.

"It soon will be November. I don't think I'm going to like the holidays without the kids this year," I said, and began feeling sorry for myself.

We eased the pang of homesickness by going for a swim and lounging around the beautiful resort pool. Later we went in for a lovely dinner, changing into our good clothes after getting ashore.

One of the simple pleasures for me during this cruising adventure was keeping a daily log on the computer. It was rather like a diary, describing what we had been doing, but also our goals, inner reflections, frustrations, and joys. I knew that, for me, it was almost like having a personal therapist aboard, and some days I could hardly wait to get typing. It was also something I occasionally made copies of and sent to the kids and our moms, so they could share the experiences we were having. I knew that the value of my writing it was much greater than their reading it, however. It also spared Fred from having to listen to me babble quite so much.

While waiting for Vickie and Bill to arrive, we continued to explore the area. One day we saw hundreds of hermit crabs, in all sizes, scurrying across the beach after apparently eating some fallen peaches. The shells they carried covered the sand. It looked like the floor of the beach was moving! There was also a loud buzzing noise coming from the jungle that ringed the beach. We were told it was some kind of beetle. From the intense sound, there must have been thousands of them. I hoped that they would stay in the jungle.

One afternoon a swim in the bay turned frightening. "Fred," I yelled. "Help! I can't move my arm, and it really hurts!"

Not knowing what had happened, I feared that I would not be able to swim and keep afloat. Fred immediately swam over to me. Large angry welts had appeared on my arm. We got back to the boat, assuming I had probably encountered a jellyfish, and in 15 minutes the pain began to subside. Thank goodness! I was ready to try the remedy suggested in our medical book, but hadn't relished the idea of urinating on my arm.

We spent one more day in the area after *Traveller* arrived, and then we got ready to depart for Bahia Drake, about 100 miles south. We had been reading about Sir Francis Drake's exploration of this area and were always amazed to imagine what the old-time mariners accomplished without having all the electronic gear we used. As we prepared for the overnight passage, we discussed how much safer all the equipment made sailing, even though there were still risks.

"My dad used to say to me, 'Think!' when I was going to do something different or risky. I had to laugh when Lance said that to *us.* I sure said it to him often enough," I mused. "Do you think he worries more about us now, after having been with us and knowing what we experience?"

"Could be," he replied. "I don't know that when I was 24 I would have wanted my parents to be doing something like this."

And that night there *were* risks. We sailed south in choppy seas with a strong current set against us. About midnight our GPS failed. We got out our backup, but it ran on batteries, so we only turned it on occasionally when we needed to check our course. With the ocean current push, I felt anxious, not knowing at a glance, exactly where we were. Then our running lights stopped functioning.

"It's likely due to corrosion from not being used for so long," said Bill, via the VHF radio. "Why don't you follow us?"

They were sailing slower than us, but we did not want to arrive before daylight; so we fell in behind them and were glad that we were buddy-boating. After enjoying a beautiful sunrise that showcased the sky in glorious colors, we arrived in Drake's Bay and threw down the hook. A big breakfast and a nap helped, and Fred began to troubleshoot the electronic problem. Rain prevented our going ashore later, and we turned in early.

The next morning, Vickie looked over at us and yelled from their boat, "Some people will do anything on a Sunday morning."

We had forgotten what day it was! I ran down to turn on our Sandi Patti tape and then continued winching Fred up to the top of the mast in the Bosun's chair to check out the wiring, hoping it would help our electronic problem. It was a tough, hot job, and we had waited until the sun went behind a cloud to avoid some of the piercing rays and heat.

"I'm sure glad you put in those mast steps up to the spreaders," I said. "I'd hate to think of trying to winch you all the way to the top without them."

"Now I'll just call you my little 'winch-ee-mahn,'" he laughed. "But we got the job done. Everything's working! Let's go ashore."

After visiting with some locals and seeing *all* the school papers of a little girl, we met an American, Canadian, and German who had a wilderness camp nearby. It was off-season, so they invited us to hike with them through the jungle to their lodge, where we'd all make a shrimp dinner. Entering the trail from the beach, we quickly noticed the light dim to a shadowy haze as the sun's rays filtered through the compact overhead canopy of branches and vegetation. The narrow winding path was muddy due to the rainy season, and we slid along in our flip-flops. Abundant trees and plant life surrounded us as we worked our way up one steep hill and down another. The huge size of many of the plant leaves made them look almost artificial. Crossing a suspension footbridge made of rope, while a river raged below us, I felt I was in a jungle adventure movie, complete with hanging vines and all. The men warned us not to put our hands on the trees for support as we climbed, due to the possibility of snakes. They were very knowledgeable about the ecology of the area, and we learned a good deal from them as we walked along. It was a great CRE.

After dinner, as late afternoon approached, we began to feel nervous. We certainly did not want to make that jungle hike in the dark, and we even were apprehensive about finding our way back in daylight. Would we be able to get back while we could still see? We hurried along and successfully made our way back to the beach. Darkness descended quickly, and it was pitch black by the time we got to the boat. But what a fun day!

It rained hard during the night, and the hoses that led from our awnings into our water tanks had filled them completely. Some buckets left on the deck were also full of water, so I used that for laundry. Chores done, we saw Bill and Vickie heading towards us in their dinghy.

"Want to go on a dinghy ride up the river into the jungle?" Vickie asked.

Despite our desire to move on to Panama, we couldn't pass on one more CRE. Once again we were awed by the lushness of the jungle. Sliding along the quiet water at the edge of the river, we nervously looked up as we went under overhanging trees. We had seen no snakes yet, and we wanted to get out of Costa Rica without having had the pleasure of doing so. We did see lots of birds and lizards, although not as many flowers as we would have expected. We were thrilled to see four colorful macaw birds, with their four-foot-long tails. They could only stand on branches (rather than the ground) due to those enormous tail feathers. Their vivid red, yellow, and blue markings looked just like the pictures we had seen. I kept pointing out plants that were the type I had at home as houseplants—only these were super-giant size. We stopped at Drake's Wilderness Camp and saw a memorial stone for Sir Francis Drake. Some cute little squirrel monkeys played outside a coffee shop there, wrestling with each other like real pros. They reminded us of the kids.

EXPLORING THE JUNGLE BY DINGHY.

Upon our return, after stowing the dinghy aboard and readying everything for another ocean passage, I pulled out my guitar and sang well into the evening. Fred kept calling out names of songs. When we got down to ski songs, and thought of Lance in the mountains, we knew it must be time to quit. At quiet times like that, we tended to start talking about the kids or our moms, and that would usually lead to homesickness. Best not to go there.

We took off shortly after dawn the following morning. It was about 500 miles to the Panama Canal, and, since we could not get diesel before then, we were anxious to sail rather than motor. The winds were light at first but became quite strong in the night, and we zinged along, making up time we had lost during the day. By the following morning, we could see the outline of the islands of Panama and we raised our Panamanian flag. It was noon when we dropped anchor off Isla Parida and Isla Gomez. There were no other boats there, nor could we see any signs of civilization. It was hot, and, after quickly putting up our awnings, we dove into the calm and inviting water. Ahhhh. The aquamarine color of the water turned to a light turquoise next to the soft, white sand beach, where palm trees waved gently in the breeze. I never tired of this amazing picture. It was truly an island oasis. The water was not as clear as we would have liked for snorkeling, due to the rainy season, but it sure felt good for a swim. After our nap, *Traveller* arrived, and we all went ashore to meet Jose and his family. Other cruisers had told us about them. They were the only ones who lived on the island, were extremely friendly, and asked if we wanted limes or lobster. Back at the boat, we barbequed the 36-inch sierra fish we had caught on the trip down and talked late into the night, feeling very content in that lovely, serene place.

We were glad to talk with *Yobo* the following morning on the ham radio. They were at Balboa, the western end of the Panama Canal, and we were hoping to transit the canal with them. We also wanted to get over to Cartagena, Columbia, before the winter winds began in mid-December, for they made it a very rough trip. Consequently, we would not have as long as we would like in the beautiful northern Panama islands.

"Look, here comes someone paddling a dugout canoe," I said to Fred, shortly after talking with *Yobo*. The man identified himself as Filo,

Jose's father. When Fred introduced himself, Filo's face brightened as he pointed at me and said, "Katrina?" He then told us that he had been waiting for us; he had a letter for us from Cindy. He was heading off to dive for lobster and asked if we wanted some. Sure enough, he and Jose returned in a couple of hours with four lobsters for each boat. We traded flour, oil, pencils, and powdered milk for them, and arranged to go to his home in the afternoon to retrieve our letter.

As Bill, Vickie, Fred, and I arrived by dinghy at the neighboring island, we approached the 12-by-12-foot structure a short ways from the beach. It had a dirt floor, bamboo stick walls, and a thatch roof. We were greeted warmly by Filo and his family, and invited inside. In one corner stood an elevated firebox containing sand and a number of stones on which to set pots for cooking over a wood fire. Four adults and two children lived in the confined space that had a sleeping loft at one end. Despite the lack of electricity, running water, or plumbing, all were clean and neatly dressed. They were gracious in their hospitality and offered us a cold juice drink, complete with ice from their fishing boat, and then proudly showed us around the home and yard with its various fruit trees. Filo said the island was a quiet and peaceful place to raise a family, and he had no desire to go to the city. They worked long days growing rice, fishing, and cutting wood, but life was good. His son, Jose, lived on the island where we were anchored, about a half-mile away. The children shyly gave us plastic bags of shells that they and the women had collected on the beach, and they loved the candy we gave in return. We had brought a message from Jose to his mom, who said that his son had an infected wound on his leg and needed medicine. When we told her this, she went down toward the beach and pulled some leaves off a tree, packed them in a sack, and asked us to give them to Jose.

Later that night, after eating our delicious lobster, we talked about our experience.

"What kind of leaves do you think she gave us for the boy's wound?" I asked Fred.

"Who knows, but I bet they were effective. They also appreciated your leaving the antibiotic cream for them."

"It makes me wonder who is the wiser," I said. "Their children are terrific, and all seem so content with what they have. They certainly seem happier than many families back home who tend to always want more."

"And they're certainly rich in hospitality, really gracious and giving," Fred added.

Although we really enjoyed traveling with Vickie and Bill, they wanted to stay in those relaxing islands for several more weeks, and we reluctantly decided to move on the following day. We would miss their company and the safety of being with another boat.

Our day started much earlier than we had planned. About three in the morning, I awoke thinking that the sound made by the dinghy floating beside us in the water wasn't right. I got up to look, and was instantly awake when I was not able to see our dinghy. Going on deck, I saw its cable, but the boat itself was totally submerged! It had rained so hard, and the waves were so rough, the dinghy had filled with water and sunk. Only the cable locking it to the boat held it from sinking to the ocean floor. Waking Fred, we assessed the task at hand and put on our full body Lycra snorkeling suits; it was cold in the heavy rain and wind.

"Hey—you look like Superman in your suit," I said.

"And you, Superwoman," he added. "We'll need to be to get this job done."

We set about trying to raise our drowned dinghy. Every time Fred stepped into it, though, it sank further, and it took about two hours of working in the dark to finally raise the boat. Our chief concern was for the motor.

"We've got to get the salt water out of the engine," Fred said. "If we don't, it will seize up, rust, and be useless."

Over and over, we poured fresh water and oil into the motor and then lowered it onto the dinghy, but each time it failed to start. It was now Sunday morning, and we stopped for breakfast, frustrated and worried about whether we could save the engine. Finally, after five hours of work, I heard the motor start.

"Yahoo!" Fred yelled. I ran to the cockpit from the cabin and saw him sitting in the dinghy, grinning from ear to ear.

"Listen!" I said. I had been playing our favorite Sunday Sandi Patti tapes, and just when the engine had started, she had begun to sing "Amazing Grace." "Do you think that's coincidence?" I asked with a grin. We could only shake our heads in wonder.

Soon we were on our way. We waved to *Traveller* under a beautiful sunny sky and left our island oasis. There were some clouds further south, but our joy of the moment could not be contained. We felt like we had already done a whole day's work. Little did we know! We motor-sailed for a while, for there were many large rocks and light winds. It wasn't long, however, before the wind picked up, hitting us on the beam; we began flying. *Big* swells were coming in.

"Time to reduce sails," we said in tandem. Even with reefed sails, we zinged along, flying through the water. It was too rough for the autopilot to hold the course, so we took turns hand-steering.

"Wow! I'm not going to look over at those approaching seas anymore," I yelled to Fred. "That's scary."

"Just keep your eyes on the sails and compass," he yelled back.

In a few hours we were at Isla Cavada, where we had planned to anchor. Two shrimp boats were in the small anchorage, taking refuge from the storm. After searching around, we found that there were no other good places to drop our hook; it was either too deep or too shallow, not enough shelter, or too much seaweed. Besides, those shrimp boats were known to drag anchor in a storm, for they used only a homemade rebar anchor. So we looked in an adjacent bay. Finally, we found a place, but Fred thought we were on the rocks, so we worried about whether we could successfully pull anchor when it was time to leave. Oh the joys of cruising!

We tuned into the ham radio net and attempted another phone patch to the kids, connecting with Dawn. We again savored the "all's well" reports—and heard about the latest in a long list of boyfriends. Later we talked with *Traveller* on a prearranged ham schedule.

"You know you're getting older when your daughter goes out with a basketball *referee*," Bill said. They sheepishly admitted listening to our phone call to Dawn, and we all laughed.

"Wonder of wonders," I said the next day, after Fred hauled up the anchor. "It came up easily."

"Well, that's if you don't count pulling up the 250 feet of chain I had down," Fred replied.

"True, but I kept reminding you to use your legs, not your back," I laughed. I was glad our anchoring technique required me to be at the wheel, a definite "pink" job.

Again the wind built as we sailed, but the seas remained flat, so it was much easier to handle the boat. It was exhilarating to fly along at seven knots with reefed sails. Shortly before coming to our destination's entrance passage, we were hit with a heavy squall that totally blocked our vision. Even the radar was blocked. In those conditions of poor visibility and powerful winds, we knew that it would be tough to drop the sails, so we talked through our procedure beforehand. We got the job done and all went smoothly, if not easily—although we were both completely soaked. Then I went to the cabin to navigate us through the entrance; we still could see nothing beyond the bow of the boat. With the radar, GPS, depth sounder, and charts, we slowly worked our way to the bay where we hoped to anchor. Shortly after we entered, however, we heard the VHF radio blast an alarming message.

"Incoming sailboat, incoming sailboat. *Stop your forward progress!* I repeat, stop your forward progress. There are pinnacle rocks right where you are! You must back out exactly the way you came in, and go to the east side of the bay to anchor."

We frantically looked around. The message must have been for us; we were the only boat in sight. Nervously we did as we were instructed. Only later did the caller identify himself as Ingo, a German who had been a cruiser and had settled in the bay, planning to build a yacht club there eventually. He was in a cabin on the hillside overlooking the anchorage.

When we were finally settled and enjoying our "Miller Time," we sat in the cabin and thought about all we had been through the last two days. Once again, we shared a great sense of accomplishment and gratitude.

"Really, we *do* make a good team," I said.

"That we do," Fred agreed, "and we've really learned a lot, not only about sailing, but about us."

We had, indeed, become more aware of a number of things in regard to our relationship. We had found that a little humor could salve a myriad of potential irritations or small problems. We knew that sometimes we needed to have a little space and time to ourselves, particularly when we were upset with something. We also knew that we had to talk through small disagreements when they occurred, as well as big ones: The boat was too small to have something "festering" between us. One of the most important realizations was that of the ongoing need to share our appreciation of each other. I recalled the night we worked to raise our sunken dinghy. Fred had patted me on the hand at one point and said, "You're a real trooper!" It had made me feel so good. I continued to be awed by Fred's stamina, patience, hard work, and determination, and I tried to let him know that as well.

"I'd be squeamish about jumping into dark, cold water in the night, but you'd do it in a flash if it needed to be done," I had said to him.

We sometimes reflected on our wish that our children have partners whom they respected and cared about as much as we did for each other. We felt very *blucky!*

That's not to say we didn't have occasional problems. Sometimes, when I became upset, I would go to the aft cabin to pout. Thank goodness for aft cabins. It was either that, or, as Fred sometimes threatened, he'd put me in the dinghy and pull me along behind!

The following day we met Ingo. He had been told by *Ossuna* and *Yobo* to watch for us, so we got a warm welcome. He said he could get us some fuel, and later brought 15 gallons to the boat. That eased our anxiety about running out of diesel as we approached the busy Panama Canal shipping lanes. As we chatted with Ingo, we were intrigued by a shriveled and bent old couple that paddled to our boat in a dugout canoe, beaming with toothless smiles as they proudly pointed to a large dead turtle lying between them. Ingo explained that this was a great catch for them and would provide a feast for the entire village. They likely had no concept of "endangered species," only knowing that they were extremely fortunate to have caught the huge creature.

Shortly after Ingo left, the local police came by, asking if they could use our ham radio. They had found a dead body and needed to get a message to the nearest town, 12 hours away by boat. We helped them make the call, but they were not successful in making contact. We had not realized how isolated this area was.

Despite a cordial offer to have dinner with Ingo the following day, we continued to affirm to each other our desire to take advantage of this small "weather window" in the Caribbean to get to Cartagena. Feeling a sense of urgency, we pulled anchor in the morning.

"You know, we could easily have stayed a month in this beautiful part of Panama," Fred said.

"Just look at this bay ringed by lovely mountains, with numerous waterfalls, jumping fish, and friendly people," I replied. "It's really a tough choice to move on. We are trading the paradise of Panama for that of the Caribbean."

After another day's hop, we stopped at an island and prepared for a three-day passage to Balboa, at the Pacific end of the great Panama Canal. To get there, we needed to go around Cape Mala (Bad Cape).

"It sure doesn't give me warm fuzzies to see the name of that big cape on the chart," I said.

"Hey, we've been around lots of capes, we can do this one," Fred said reassuringly.

Our passage was often tough. The first night was nice, with a beautiful moon and stars. We hadn't seen that for a while due to the rainy season. Since it was dark from six in the evening until six in the morning, the nights seemed long. The second day we had strong winds and very strong currents, both "on the nose." We were very grateful for our "*SeaWellness*" tape; there was lots of motion. At one point we were motor sailing at full cruising throttle because we could make little headway against the current. However, in doing so we worried about using up our fuel—and we still only managed about two knots per hour headway. The boat was pounding up and down, and salt water dumped over the bow and sometimes into the cockpit.

"This could be a *very long* night," I groused to Fred. "When I went into the cabin, I actually felt *airborne* one time."

"I know. It seems like the waves are so close together that we bounce up and down over about three of them, and then slam into the fourth one."

Poor *Grace*. I kept reminding myself that she was well built as she groaned and shuddered in the violent motion. Finally, the seas smoothed out a bit, and we were able to catch a fish and talk with *Yobo* and *Ossuna* on the ham radio. We were getting excited about seeing them. We noticed many large freighters in the distance, coming and going from the canal, and remembered that *Grace* had already been through it one time—on the deck of a freighter coming to Oregon from England. *We* were the neophytes. As we got closer, we knew we had to make our way to the south side of the canal shipping lanes, thus crossing all the busy vessel traffic.

"Wow. Am I ever thankful that we were able to get that extra fuel from Ingo," I said.

"Me too. This is no place to run out of diesel!"

We darted across the lanes, dodging ships. At last we picked up a mooring buoy at the Balboa Yacht Club, which was close to the gigantic "Bridge of the Americas." Towering over us, the bridge linked the North American continent to the South American continent. How special was that! It was tall enough to allow the huge freighters entering or leaving the canal to pass underneath it. It felt simply overwhelming when looking up at this unique structure. We also felt pretty small as the monstrous vessels slid silently by us in a continual parade, making their way to the ocean or the canal. They were only about 80 yards from us, and we knew they would be passing all day and all night.

"Look. There must be 50 boats on the buoys here," I said with delight. "There are flags from all over the world. This is incredible!"

"It looks like most of them are cruising sailboats," Fred added. "It will be fun to talk with them."

To go ashore, we called for a launch to come get us by giving a short blast on our air horn. No more messing with dinghies. We were going ashore in style! The club was on a U.S. military base, which made it very secure in a city that was known for an extremely high level of theft and muggings. As we walked up to the large old funky clubhouse, we saw Reed and Cindy along with Heidi and Harvey. I squealed with delight, dropped my bag, and ran to them for hugs and kisses. We had not seen them for four or five months, and they were our favorite cruising friends. It was like "old home" week! Everyone talked at once, and there was lots of laughing while I was jumping up and down. As we later sat around the clubhouse catching up on all the happenings, I couldn't help but think about our relationship with these people. Again I was struck by how the sharing of so many dilemmas, frustrations, joys, fears, and even life-threatening situations had made for such strong bonds between us. It was far different from the good friendships back home. These people felt more like "family" than friends.

"We made reservations for all of us to go to the Officer's Club at Fort Amador tomorrow," Cindy said.

"Isn't that the place with the legendary Sunday morning champagne brunch?" Fred asked.

"It sure is," said Reed.

"Man," I said. "Are we ever ready for that." We talked late into the night, and fell into bed, still giddy with excitement.

The following morning, we decided to go to church before meeting our friends for the brunch. We met some local people heading the same direction and they took us to a large non-denominational church about a half-mile away from the club. We joined a Sunday school class of about 10 (both American and Panamanian), and had a meaningful time.

One of the local couples invited us to meet them a couple of days later. They said they would show us around the city, take us for lunch, and point out the good places to buy *molas*. *Molas* were the unique reverse-appliqué fabric pieces of the Kuna Indian women who lived in the San Blas Islands on the eastern side of Panama. Their culture and lifestyle remained much the same as it was 100 years ago. The *molas* were beautiful in design and color, and took great time and effort to make. We looked forward to seeing the city with these new friends and buying some *molas* for ourselves and for gifts.

Leaving church, we made our way to the Officer's Club to meet our friends. The brunch, complete with ice sculptures, was lovely—as nice as any we had ever experienced. We stuffed ourselves with the good food and champagne. We spoke with several of the cruisers that we had met who were from other countries.

"This truly is the 'Crossroads of the World,'" I said to Fred. "I love the international flavor."

"Did you notice that most of the French folks do not socialize much with others?" Fred said. "They don't have a very good reputation amongst the cruising community, particularly with those from other European countries."

We were tired when we got back to our boat, but we wanted to continue reading a wonderful book about the construction of the canal. We didn't get very far, though; the peepers just wouldn't stay open.

Lots to do the next day, as Fred, Reed, and Harvey went to the various offices to complete the necessary paperwork to transit the canal, and we gals went *shopping*. We had all been warned that it was not safe to walk or bus to many parts of the city. One cruiser had been thrown up against a wall and had his wallet stolen just recently—in broad daylight. Repeatedly we were told not to be off the base at night. So, after looking in some stores on the base, we took a taxi to a large, modern shopping mall. It was fun to do something so "normal," and I was thrilled to find replacement strings for my guitar. Later we met the guys for lunch.

"Did you see the armed guard just outside the restaurant?" Fred said to me.

"I did, and there's another one here inside," I replied. "How difficult it must be to live in a place where there is constant fear. I'm not sure I could do it."

Following our lunch, the guys left us gals at the supermarket where we would get groceries while they went to some marine stores. An armed guard at the market came over to speak to us. He was quite concerned after seeing the men leave. He warned us that it was not safe, and urged us to take a taxi back to the base when we were done with our shopping. That had been our plan, but the constant warnings certainly created anxiety.

Early the following morning, Fred and I were at the gas dock when we saw a French boat that had just come through the canal. We hurried over to it and talked with a very nice family; they completely negated the stereotype regarding French cruisers we'd heard about earlier. We arranged to take seven automobile tires they had hanging on the side of their boat. The tires were covered with plastic bags, and acted as fenders to prevent the boat from scraping along the walls of the canal when in transit. The tires were passed from cruiser to cruiser and went back and forth through the canal. We felt fortunate to get some.

"Hooray! It's one more thing off of our 'to do' list," I said.

"We still need to find one more person to be a line handler," Fred reminded me.

We had heard of a Panamanian man named Harper, who was recommended by other cruisers, and hoped he would be available. We needed to pay him, as well as the Canal Commission Pilot who must ride along with us during transit. There was also the fee to the Commission for the transit itself. Heidi and Harvey had agreed to be our other two line handlers, for they had decided not to take their boat through the canal, but to go on to Hawaii. We needed a total of four line handlers besides the captain of the boat. We were expected to provide food and drink for all the crew, plus bus tickets back to Balboa for Heidi, Harvey, and Harper. Most transits took two days for sailboats, with an overnight stay in Lake Gatun.

We hurried to meet our new Panamanian friends who were to show us around the city that day. We spent the whole day sightseeing and benefiting from their knowledge of the Panamanian culture. We traveled by local buses or collectives to different areas, tried some typical local foods for lunch, and shopped for *molas*. We deeply appreciated their kindness in spending the day with us.

That "fire hose" rain had begun just as we approached the clubhouse, and we ran inside where we were pleased to see Andre and Maggie from *Volovent III*. We had heard on the radio that they would be at the canal and were asking for us. They were a French couple that lived in Vancouver, B.C., and we enjoyed being with them. We visited until the rain stopped.

"We were hoping we might transit the canal with you and then sail with you over to Cartagena," they said. "We read that it is often a very rough passage, and thought that, with a name like *Amazing Grace*, you may get some 'extra' protection we could benefit from if we tagged along." We laughed, and welcomed their company.

Back on the boat we had dinner and prepared for *Yobo* to come over to look at charts and listen to the Gore/Perot presidential debate on the radio. The armed forces had their own radio station for the area, and it was great to hear things in English.

On the cruisers' radio net the next morning, the community was stunned to hear tragic news. The sailing vessel, *Clambake*, had been hit by a freighter off the Mexican coast and sunk in a very short time. Fortunately, the crew had been able to send a Mayday call, and the freighter had picked up the three people who had been onboard. We had not met these folks but had heard the boat name on the radio many times.

"That is so frightening. What an ordeal!" I said.

"At least they were able to use the freighter's radio to let their families know they were okay," Fred replied. "Sure makes you think about our nighttime watches. They apparently didn't see it coming." It was an event that caused great concern and much discussion amongst all the cruisers for many days.

We spent nine days at the Balboa Yacht Club in a whirlwind of activities getting ready to make our canal transit. Exhausted by nighttime, we would collapse into bed.

"You know how we worried about being three or four months in Cartagena due to the weather window and the winter winds?" I said to Fred one night. "That we wouldn't know what to do with all that time in one place?"

"I know where you're going with this," he said with a laugh. "Right now that sounds terrific—to have some quiet time to relax and do nothing."

Fred left at seven the next morning to meet the *admeasurer* for our boat. Payment for the transit depended on the size of the boat, and an official person needed to measure *Grace*. Then we traveled all over the city to get more paperwork completed. We taxied to one commission office only to find out that it was the wrong one, then walked in the oppressive heat to the right office but couldn't pay the fees because it was lunchtime. When we returned, we had to wait forever. When we tried to mail our Christmas presents, we couldn't find the UPS office. We wanted to make a phone call to Mom, but, due to the time difference, we needed to wait until afternoon, and then we could barely hear; the only phone was in the club bar, where music was blaring. We were longing for those wonderful, "life is simple" Panamanian islands.

One day we took the boat over to the fuel dock to fill our tanks. We wanted to get there early in the morning, but it was pouring rain. When we arrived, at nine o'clock, the dock was already full and we had to return two hours later. When we eventually got in and tied up, we filled our tanks with water and started on the diesel. Fred had estimated that we would need about 25 to 30 gallons. When the fuel pump registered 40 gallons we were concerned.

"Boy, I didn't think we needed *that* much. Maybe we should check that it's not flooding the engine room," Fred said, thinking he was being funny. *Not* funny! The fill hose had come off the deck fitting and filled the hatch with diesel, which then filled the bilge. We were floating in 10 to 20 gallons of smelly, greasy *diesel*. What an incredible mess! All of our dive gear, plus everything in the hatch, was swimming in diesel! It took us the rest of the day at the gas dock to clean it up. Heidi invited us to spend the night on *Ossuna* to avoid the fumes, but by that time we were so used to the smell we were numb to it. It was surely *not* a memorable day in cruising.

Sometimes it was a real frustration just to get to shore. We could call for a launch but not take our dinghy. This was great *if* the launch came in a timely manner. Occasionally we waited up to an hour, and they were non-existent if it rained. Rain in Panama is not like rain in the Northwest. One became soaked in only a matter of seconds, and everything seemed to stop when it rained—which was frequently during the "rainy" season.

Slowly we got everything done. Fred hauled out four heavy 100-foot long lines from somewhere deep in the lockers. I managed to get all the groceries aboard and laundry done. Harper, our new Panamanian friend, was hired as a line handler, even though we both had a hard time understanding the 60-year-old man, and Harvey and Heidi were ready to leave with us. We had invited them to sail with us to the old city of Portobelo on the Caribbean side after the transit, so we needed additional supplies for four people aboard.

The Canal Inspector was to arrive at our boat at noon, to check to see if *Grace* was ready for transit.

"Oh no," I said. "Cindy just told me that she heard it was much easier to get your '*zarpe*' and check out of the country here than in Colon."

"Boy, that doesn't give us much time to get the job done. Let's go!" replied Fred.

It was Saturday, and others told us that it was impossible to check out since the Port Captain's office would be closed. But we were undaunted. We scurried around, paid an additional 20 dollars for a "weekend" fee, and got the job done. We still needed to stop at the supermarket for supplies to feed the transit crew. We threw things in our basket and hurried back to the boat, getting there just as the inspector arrived.

"That's the same young man I talked to in the Canal Commission office," Fred said afterwards. "After he saw our boat, he said he had the day off on Monday and he could be our Pilot."

"Oh, I hope so," I added. "It would be nice to have another Panamanian aboard. He's really nice and speaks English well, too."

I spent the remainder of the day cooking pasta salad, my famous caramel brownies, and getting everything ready for our Monday departure. Normally, even the blare of the disco music from the club didn't keep us awake, but that night I slept fitfully. Too much excitement.

I awoke to see a beautiful bouquet of roses from Fred, and a new *mola* T-shirt. It was my birthday, and what a happy day it was! We got ready and attended the same church as last week; the people were friendly and glad to see us back.

"I came out to see you at the Yacht Club on Monday," said the lady pastor, "but you weren't there."

"Harper gave us your card," I replied. "It's so nice to have 'family' so far from home. Thank you."

Afterwards we again hurried to the champagne brunch, where a table of 10 had saved a place for us. There were lots of warm wishes, and the jazz combo played "Happy Birthday" with everyone singing. Fun!

We had one more task to do before returning to the boat. I had wanted to serve fried chicken for lunch during the transit, and Fred had suggested we buy it already cooked, to spare me the effort of making it. It was late afternoon when we hurried to the small restaurant to buy it.

"Oh no. It's closed," I said. We had not known it was closed on Sundays.

"Where else can we get some?" Fred said.

"We'll have to go to the 'Colonel Sanders,' but that's *off base*," I said, "and it'll be dark soon. We're not supposed to go off base after dark."

But we were stuck, and I wanted that chicken, so we started walking quickly. By the time we got the chicken it was, indeed, dark, and we began our return to the base. I decided that I was *not* going to look like an easy "victim," so I took my small umbrella in hand and began striding down the sidewalk, "rubbernecking" my head to watch for anyone around me, and wildly swinging the umbrella as if it was a weapon.

"By gosh, nobody better mess with me!" I growled with false bravado.

"I don't think you need to worry," laughed Fred as he hurried to keep up. "I'm even afraid to walk with you." We were relieved to make it back to the base unscathed.

Back at the boat Cindy and Reed came over. "One of the cruisers engraves these little brass plaques," Reed said. "We thought you might like one to remember this birthday." On it was engraved, "Amazing Grace, Panama Canal Transit, November 15, 1993."

"And you can wear this mola sun visor," Cindy suggested. She had taken fabric paint and added "P.C.T. 11/15/93" to the brim. What sweeties. We quickly put up the plaque in the most prominent position in the cabin.

Our transit day started early when Harper arrived at six o'clock. *Yobo* had been scheduled to enter the first lock at 6:15 a.m., but our time was not until 7:30 a.m. We were disappointed about the schedule and sure we would not be able to make it through in one day with the later departure time.

"What's for lunch?" our Pilot/Advisor asked with a smile, shortly after he arrived. I told him my planned menu and asked if he was hungry.

"Not yet," he replied, "but I'm so glad to hear it's not tuna sandwiches. That's all you ever get on the French boats."

We got to the first lock and, at the Pilots' directions, rafted together with *Volovent*. It was an exciting time adjusting spring lines so that both masts would not collide if we got swinging. There were six people on each boat, so there was lots of commotion. We tied the long lines to our starboard side, and *Volovent* tied theirs to their port side, which allowed us to tie up to the walls but stay in the center of the chamber. We entered the lock immediately after a huge freighter and were told by our pilot to move our raft up *very* close to the freighter's stern.

"Heads up," yelled Harper, "here comes the monkey fist from the lock men."

Men atop the high lock wall threw down a small ball with a thin line attached. We tied our lines onto it, and then they pulled it all back up to the top.

"We saw a big bull's eye target that we were told the men use for target practice," Harvey said. "They even have competitions to improve their accuracy in throwing that monkey fist."

The lines were secured and the chamber began to fill. We constantly had to adjust the tension on the lines to keep them taut and keep the raft in the center. Slowly all the vessels rose until the lock gates were open and we could move our raft into the next lock. There were three locks going up, and three locks going down, so there would be lots to do. The currents caused by the incoming water, as well as the wash from the freighter ahead of us, made some tense work for Fred at the motor, especially since we were rafted to another boat. All went well through each of the three locks upward. We then untied our raft to motor across the narrow Gaillard Cut into Lake Gatun.

"This is just incredible," Fred said in awe. "We are crossing a mountain."

As we observed the Cut, we thought about the engineering needed to carve a path for vessels through the mountain of rock. So many people had died of malaria in the process. Even the lake was man-made, and had small islands sticking out of the water, which were really mountaintops. Harper told us that many of the Panamanians did not want the canal to be turned over by the U.S. to Panama in 1999. They feared that their country would not maintain it well, having observed this process happening with other structures. That was surprising to hear.

As we entered the lake, we were hit with a ferocious thunder and lightning storm.

"Wow. I can't see anything in this rain," Fred said. "I'm glad we have our friendly Pilot/Advisor aboard."

"Holy Cow! That lightning strike was so close it made the hair on the back of my neck stand up!" I squealed.

"I felt it 'snap,'" said Heidi. "I've never felt that before."

"And smell that ozone," yelled Harvey. "That had to be incredibly close!" The thunder was deafening. We were all shaken by the closeness of the bolt, and Heidi and I actually trembled for several minutes.

Soon we learned that the huge freighter in front of us had run aground in the storm. It took some time for them to get it freed and underway, but that meant we had time to catch up to it. Our Advisor told us that we would now be able to "lock down" with the freighter that afternoon. They wouldn't keep a freighter in the lake overnight, like they did the sailboats. What good fortune for us. The storm soon abated and we moved on.

When we got to the locks for descending into the Caribbean, *Yobo* and *Volovent* were both there! We were thrilled, and we all rafted together at the Advisors' directions. Moving a raft of three sailboats was trickier, but Fred and the other skippers did just fine.

"Now we have a *real* party," I yelled over to Cindy.

"This is as much fun as when we first started making these trips many years ago," agreed Harper.

When we reached the final lock, there was a mixture of fresh and salt water, which created a great deal of turbulence. As we untied the raft and moved out of the chamber, the skippers all had their engines at full throttle trying to control the boats until the water smoothed out.

"We are in the *Caribbean*," I yelled over to Cindy and Reed.

"*Now* we have a real party," yelled Reed, and the champagne popped on each of the boats with lots of whoops and hollers. Our Advisor laughed as Heidi poured champagne over Fred's head. As I joined the laughter, Harvey came and poured it over my head too! In a few minutes, the Pilot boat came alongside and our Advisor got off. I think he had enjoyed this trip.

A CHAMPAGNE SHOWER FOR A BENCHMARK EVENT.

It was dark by the time we tied to the dock at the Panama Yacht Club in Colon, and we were very happy campers. We waved goodbye to Harper, who headed back to Balboa on the bus, celebrated a little in the club, had dinner on the boat with Heidi and Harvey, and truly *fell* into bed that night. What a P.E.!

Ten

South American Sojourn

We quickly learned that cruisers at the Panama Yacht Club considered it something of a "fort." There was a high level of security in and around the premises. Extra precautions were taken when leaving the club. Due to the very high level of crime on the streets of Colon, it was necessary to take a taxi from the door of the club to your destination, and the taxi driver would then escort you inside. Even Harper said he wouldn't walk the streets of Colon. There also seemed to be a sort of generalized anxiety in many of the cruisers about trying to sail on to other ports, with many believing the winter winds had started a month earlier than usual. Strong east winds had recently turned a number of boats back to Colon who had tried to reach the San Blas Islands of Panama.

"Oh great," I moaned. "Here we hurried to get here before the winter winds started, and they have already begun."

"I doubt that. I bet it's that 'harboritis' we've read about. I think we should go on to Portobelo tomorrow," Fred replied. "One or two stories of rough conditions get blown up and everybody is afraid to leave."

So early the next morning, after two days in Colon, we took off along with *Yobo* and *Volovent* and had a wonderful day of sailing under sunny skies, with good wind and fairly smooth seas. Heidi and Harvey were pleased to be able to take the trip with us and see the wonderful old port, where there was such a rich and colorful history of trading, battles, and pirates. Centuries ago, huge amounts of gold and treasure from Peru, other South American countries, and the Orient had been carried overland by mules to this area from the Pacific. Spanish vessels then delivered the riches to Europe. Many perished trying to claim some of that wealth. When we saw the old fort ruins with the rounded turrets keeping watch over the harbor from high on the hill, and the crumbling stone walls about the village, my imagination went into "overdrive." I was sure I saw a swashbucklin' sailor with sword in hand, hiding behind the huge iron cannons pointed out at the harbor. There were five boats in the anchorage near the old fort, and, after setting our hook, Heidi and I quickly decided to cool off with a swim. Just after diving in, some local fishermen passed us in their dugout canoe.

"*Hay tiberones aqui en esta agua?*" (Are their sharks in this water?) I asked them.

"*Si, si,*" they replied seriously, and nodded their heads.

"*Por cierto?*" (for sure?) I said incredulously, more than a little alarmed. They reluctantly smiled while shaking their heads back and forth, enjoying the joke on us.

The next morning, all four couples went into the town nestled near the harbor and hiked up the steep hillside to examine the ruins of three different levels of the fort. We were amazed to find that the walls and fort were made of large blocks of dried coral, and that it had endured all these many years. Some restoration had taken place, using the same process.

Amazing Grace at anchor in Portobelo's quiet harbor.

"What an incredible view," Cindy said, puffing from the climb. "The waters of the Caribbean are much more colorful than the Pacific. Look at those beautiful shades of turquoise."

"They are not nearly as deep," replied Reed. "Maybe that accounts for the difference. Since we've made it to the top, I think this occasion calls for something special." He proceeded to climb a small coconut tree for some *pipas* (young coconuts), and we all enjoyed a refreshing drink.

The next day, after a swim and a chance to clean *Grace's* waterline, we went back into the village to visit the large, old church in the town square. We wanted to see its popular "Black Christ," which has been associated with many healing miracles. We had not gone inside the day before because we were all wearing shorts. We tried to be careful to show respect for the things that were valued by the local people in each place we visited, so we had changed to wearing dresses and walking shorts for the guys.

In walking about the town, we observed that the people who lived in this community were much poorer than those in the city and had a laid-back lifestyle. They apparently never threw anything away, either, but found some other use for broken possessions. We laughed to see children playing in an abandoned old car that was not much more than a frame and steering wheel.

I appreciated the opportunity to stop in a restaurant for lunch, because fixing food for four people in a small, hot galley was more work. Heidi and Harvey would be going back to Colon the next morning with *Yobo*, and then taking a bus back to their boat. It would be hard to say goodbye, although we hoped we might see them again if they flew over to Cartagena. We planned to move on to the San Blas Islands, along with Andre and Maggie on *Volovent.*

It felt nice to have the boat back to ourselves. We made a short hop to the next anchorage in light winds and sunny skies.

"It seems strange to be heading east when we've been going south for almost a year and a half," Fred said.

"I'll say. I sure am glad for no rain, too. It seems I was always opening or closing the hatches with all the showers."

With such nice conditions, it was hard to stop sailing, but the next good anchorage was a considerable distance, and I was just plain tired.

We spent the afternoon getting the boat back into shape after our six days of having company, baked some banana bread from the ever-ripening bananas, and turned in, planning an early morning departure.

We were up at 5:15 a.m., but Fred discovered a problem. Many of our electronics, including the refrigerator and GPS, were not working. After some troubleshooting, I heard the refrigeration motor start.

"Terrific," I said. "What was the problem?"

"I was just taking out the screws on the electrical panel board when everything started working," he replied, shaking his head in wonder.

"Must be gremlins!" I observed. Humidity and salt air did strange things to electronics.

We took off, along with *Volovent,* planning to stop at the first anchorage in the San Blas Islands, off southeastern Panama. The seas were flat with little wind, but it was coming from the west, which was quite unusual. We had a nice current that also pushed us along in the right direction. As we approached our destination, we saw that many of the *islas,* as they were called, were small, sometimes with only one or two palm trees on them. They were all flat as pancakes, with white sand beaches that showed in sharp contrast to the turquoise water sparkling in the sunlight. Some of the *islas* appeared to be uninhabited while others had small huts. Since there was no significant tidal difference in the Caribbean, the huts, with their thatch roofs and bamboo walls, were built just a few feet from the water's edge. The underwater coral reefs that surrounded the *islas* also protected the beaches from the damaging waves of storms.

One of many *islas* in Panama.

About three in the afternoon we arrived at Chichime Cays. "This is the first time we've gone through a reef to reach an anchorage," I said. "I'm sure glad the sun is behind us." It was possible to see through the water in order to find the entrance cut when not looking directly into the sun.

"Why don't you go to the bow and watch the water for coral heads and rocks?" Fred suggested. "I'll handle the engine."

We carefully picked our way through the narrow opening. Once inside, it was difficult to keep my eyes on the path of the boat. Everywhere around us, it looked like some kind of fantasy tropical island in the south seas. There were three other boats at anchor, and we prepared to drop our hook. We swung *Grace* around to check for depths, then Fred dropped the anchor and I prepared to motor backwards to lay out the chain. As I looked behind me, I saw four or five dugout canoes, each holding several Kuna women, clustered behind our boat.

"I can't go in reverse. I'll run right into them," I yelled to Fred. "Please move," I yelled to the women, but got no response.

Finally, I began waving my arms to tell them to get out of the way. It was only after several minutes of my protestations that they reluctantly moved their dugouts, but then they stood up and held on to the sides of our boat. For a moment, I thought they were going to climb aboard. Each was shouting, looking into the boat, and trying to get me to buy their *molas*.

"Later. Later," I cried. "Come back later!"

"Just go slowly backwards," Fred yelled from the bow. I did, and we finally got the anchor set. By then I was angry and refused to talk more with those determined saleswomen. Only after much persuasion and insistence did they finally leave.

"Good grief," I said. "We heard that the Kunas were a friendly, curious people, but no one said they were so aggressive in their sales techniques!"

"They sure weren't going to take 'No' for an answer," Fred laughed. "They speak their own language, too, so trying to talk with them in Spanish didn't seem to work."

"I think I'll call it the Mola Monsters' Invasion," I said, and laughed too.

The women were fascinating to look at in their colorful attire. They were small in stature, averaging about four and a half feet in height. Each was dressed with intricately decorated *mola* blouses, printed wrap-around skirts, and yellow and red print scarves on their heads. Most of them wore a gold ring in their nose. Each of the older women had a black line that went from her hairline down to the tip of her nose. Around their wrists and ankles they wore about six inches of beadwork that we were told they do not remove unless it needs to be replaced. Many of the men now worked on the mainland and have adopted western dress. They occasionally came by the boat to sell fish or conch and wore regular T-shirts and shorts.

The setting sun in that island paradise simply has to be seen to be believed. Astonishing colors burst throughout the sky and were reflected again in the sea through the silhouettes of waving palm trees. As we watched this visual miracle explode before us, we realized again, what an incredible artist was our Creator.

The following morning, when the Mola Monsters approached, we insisted that we would come ashore to buy our *molas*, and they pretty much left us alone. The water was so inviting that we were anxious to go snorkeling.

Swimming in those crystal clear waters was like swimming in an aquarium. Fish were everywhere! I had not always felt relaxed when snorkeling, and often had trouble with water in my mask and nose. I also worried about stepping on one of the sharp pointed spines of the many sea urchins. They could create very painful wounds. But here I was so absorbed by the underwater scenery that unfolded before me that I felt quite calm. We made our way over to the reef that surrounded the island and were amazed at the many types of coral that grew there. Lacey spine-like coral waved in the ocean currents with little brightly colored fish darting amongst the fronds. Huge mounds of the brain-like coral had larger fish hiding in the shadows. The water was surprisingly cool, and after 30 minutes we began to feel chilled. Exhilarated from the experience, we returned to the boat and got ready to go ashore.

There were only about four or five homes on the two islands where we were anchored. The people were friendly and anxious to show us their *molas*, but they wouldn't bargain in their prices. Refusal to

236

negotiate was apparently a sign of pride in their craftsmanship and culture—contrary to other ethnic groups we had encountered where extended bargaining was expected. Some did speak Spanish, and they showed a good sense of humor, enjoying a joke as much as we did. The women giggled and laughed as they dressed me up in their traditional costume for a picture.

The unusual west/southwest wind continued the next day, and we began to get "itchy feet;" it was the perfect wind to get to Cartagena. Usually, the trade winds blew from the east or southeast, which was exactly the direction we needed to go, thus creating a difficult, wet, and rough trip. Many cruisers admitted it was the worst segment of their travels. So we decided to move on to Hollandese Cays, which could be a starting place for the passage to Columbia. Again, the entrance there was a tricky one. The sun was in front of us as we tried to enter the cut in the coral.

"Oh, I don't like this," I yelled to Fred from the bow. "The sun reflects off the water and it's impossible to see what's underneath."

"I know. Just do what you can. I'll go slowly," said Fred. "If we need to, I'll climb up to the spreaders. I can see better from there."

We inched our way forward a little farther and suddenly felt a bump. We had run aground. Fortunately, it was not the hard sound of rock or coral, but a soft thud, and we knew we had hit sand. I ran to pump up the keel while Fred gently put the engine in reverse. My heart was pounding from both the exertion of pumping and the adrenalin that was pouring into my blood. In a short time I heard Fred say, "That's enough. We're off." Thank goodness for that wonderful swing keel.

I ran back to the bow, we tried again, and this time we were successful in guiding *Grace* into the calm waters of the lagoon. I was dripping with sweat but so relieved to have the hook down. We anchored in a protected area close to shore, but soon realized that the location blocked any wind flow, making it *very* hot there. With the absence of wind, we found ourselves in the midst of a massive swarm of "no-see-ums." We quickly pulled up our anchor and moved out away from the islands, but the "no-see-ums" moved right along with us! We sprayed ourselves with repellant like crazy, lit bug coils, and put up the screens on the hatches, but the darn little things just seemed to thrive despite all we were doing. We finally jumped into the water.

"I thought going for a swim would help us get away from the bugs," I said, back aboard, "but then I saw that shark. I'm not staying in the water with that thing swimming around, even if it is only a small one!"

"It was just a nurse shark," Fred responded. "It wouldn't have hurt you. It was the barracuda that made me nervous. It had to be at least four feet long. I tried to hide my wedding ring."

"Why?" I asked. "You think it prefers married men?"

"They're attracted to anything shiny."

Andre and Maggie agreed that, if the wind were to hold, we should take advantage of it and sneak across to Columbia, leaving the next day. That meant a lot of work on the deck, putting on our storm trysail and storm jib to be ready for the expected strong winds and rough seas. That also meant fighting the bugs. Making it more difficult to use my hands was a bad burn on my thumb, which had developed into a big open sore. I had also pinched my knuckles on some line, causing more scrapes on my fingers, and I was sure that I had at least 100 bug bites. So when I got hit in the face by the rigging and cut my lip while trying to "hank on" (attach) the storm sail, I exploded.

"That does it," I said. "I've just about had it! I can take night watches, scrubbing hulls, and fighting storms, but, when my body gets physically beat up, I draw the line!"

Fred was sympathetic and caring, and sent me down below to close up the boat. We had paid two dollars for a bunch of *langostinos*, or small lobsters, so I cooked them for a yummy meal while we tried for about two and a half hours on the ham radio to get listed on *Southbound II* for a weather report of our area. Finally we were able to talk with him, and he told us that the unusual west wind would continue for 36 to 48 hours. Hooray! We had heard so many stories of horrendous crossings . . . we felt truly blucky, once again. Anticipating the passage, we tried to go to sleep early, but tossed about much of the night.

"Stop scratching," I heard Fred whisper quietly, sometime in the middle of the night.

We took off at eight in the morning, figuring it would take two days and two nights to reach Cartagena.

"This is terrific," I said. "That wind is coming directly behind us. And the seas aren't too choppy either."

"I don't know if this will last, but I'm sure enjoying it now," Fred replied. "We're going six or seven knots with only a poled-out jib."

"But I don't care for the 'washing machine' motion of the short choppy waves here in the Caribbean," I added. "They're coming at us from every which way. I prefer the big rolling swells of the Pacific."

"I don't mind it at all," Fred chuckled, "there's no bugs out here."

The winds continued to be favorable, and *Volovent* was flying a great big Genoa sail that made them faster than us. They slowed down to wait for us to catch up since we had agreed to buddy-boat, and they did not have entrance charts to the Cartagena harbor. By the second day we realized that we would be arriving much earlier than we had planned. We usually chose not to enter a new harbor at night, but we didn't want to stand off for 10 to 12 hours, either. Fred used the ham radio to call a boat that was in Cartagena, and they said that entering the harbor at night was do-able. So we "threw caution to the wind" and decided to go for it.

"This is awful," I said, after spending a considerable amount of time trying to plot routes from our charts. "Different charts have different lat/longs for the entrance. Even the buoy numbers and positions are different. I don't know what to trust." All the work definitely didn't create a secure feeling for the navigator.

The harbor of Cartagena is very large, and, after going through a very narrow entrance, it would be about nine more miles up to the cruising anchorage. It was possible to stop earlier, but we had heard many reports of theft in those areas. We knew from our cruising notes that the whole area was heavily populated and the shoreline packed with commerce. It would be difficult to find our way at night.

As we approached the harbor, more and more boats appeared and it seemed like we were on a crowded Los Angeles freeway. Night came quickly in this part of the world, and by six o'clock it was dark. Our anxiety increased. We weren't certain about the position of the buoys, the entrance, or the depths of the channel. We could see the glow of city lights in the sky. In the heavy blackness that surrounded us, we timidly approached what we thought was the harbor entrance about seven at night and frantically searched for the first navigational buoy.

"There are so many lights from the city in the background, I can't find the green buoy light," Fred said.

"It's the same way on the radar," I replied. "There are blips all over the screen. I can't tell which of them are buoys." We were overwhelmed with vessel traffic, lights, and confusion, and beginning to regret our decision to enter at night.

"Oh, my gosh," yelled Fred. "We just passed Buoy One. We almost ran into it!" I looked back to see the shadowy outline of the buoy pass only a few feet from our stern and shuddered to think how close we had come to it. The anxiety increased, and every muscle in my body was tense. *Volovent* followed a short way behind us, trusting that we would lead them in safely.

We continued to slowly move forward and look for the green flashing lights that marked the harbor entrance in the congested waterway. We saw one green light, but it wasn't flashing, and we gasped when we discovered that it was a warship coming our way! We went aground at one point, and nearly so another time. We quickly radioed *Volovent,* telling them not to follow us until we got into deeper water. Again, we were grateful for the marvelous swing keel.

"They have it easy," I said. "All they have to do is stay behind us. This is nerve-wracking, to say the least."

Finally, after three and a half hours, we saw the anchored sailboats of the cruising community, and, with a sigh of relief, threw out our hook.

"Look around," I exclaimed. "It feels like we are in the middle of Paris or New York."

"You're right," Fred replied. "Well, the city has a million people. Look at all the skyscrapers around the bay. What an incredible change from the San Blas Islands."

"I'm sorry we weren't able to get a phone patch through to Lance today to wish him a happy birthday," I said. "I think he'd have loved this downwind sail and exciting entrance to Cartagena."

"I bet he would have," Fred replied. "He'd definitely agree that it's a real 'Miller Time!'"

We awoke the next morning to realize that it was Thanksgiving Day. It was also raining and the wind had shifted from the west to the east. The weather window had closed, and we had caught the break just by the skin of our teeth. Did we ever have a lot for which to be thankful! We heard on the cruisers' net that many folks would be going to a nice restaurant for dinner, and we decided to go, too. Taking the dinghy to shore, we met Norm, an American and former cruiser. He was married to a Columbian woman and they had a small marina and bar/restaurant called Club Nautico, which catered to cruisers. There was no space for us at the dock, which held about 40 boats, so we anchored nearby, along with 30 other boats.

Norm gave us a good introduction to the city and services. It was strange to see so many cruisers and not recognize any of them. Some were from the eastern and southern U.S., but many were from Europe, and there were a number of French racing boats that had just completed a non-stop race. This was definitely an international community. Since we planned to be in Cartagena for several months while we waited out the hurricane season before continuing on into the Caribbean, we had hoped to be at a dock rather than staying at anchor. We learned of a nearby marina and walked a few blocks to the Club de Pesca. It was a private Columbian yacht club. We had been told that it seldom accepted cruisers, and there were only two cruising boats currently moored there. We decided to inquire about the possibility of dock space anyway, put our "best foot forward," and said we'd continue to check with them when told there was nothing available.

Enjoying the feeling of being on land and having the worrisome voyage from Panama completed, we walked another few blocks to a huge modern supermarket. There, it felt like we had entered something from the space-age. All around us were bright lights, glass, and stainless steel, arranged in contemporary displays for food and flowers. What a contrast to the markets we had been seeing! Service people were everywhere, offering demonstrations and samples. Even the shopping carts had small calculators built into the handles.

"Can you believe this?" I said.

"We don't have anything like this at home," Andre replied.

"I think I'm really going to like it here," Maggie added. "It's definitely not 'roughing it,' and I'm sure ready for that."

"Me too," I giggled. "I've heard that many boaters said they came here for a week and ended up staying months or even years. I'm beginning to see why."

Our dinner that night was nice, but it sure didn't feel like the Thanksgivings we were used to celebrating. Luckily, we had been able to phone the kids and our moms, and they all were going to be with other families for the day. Oh, how we missed them!

We slept soundly that night, and awoke just in time for the morning cruisers' net on the VHF radio. When we introduced ourselves, one woman offered to show us the way to the closest bank in order to exchange our money for some local currency.

The short walk into the "old" city was an architectural treat to the eyes. Old Spanish style buildings were everywhere along the narrow winding streets, with wonderfully carved wooden balconies on the second floor that extended out over the sidewalks. The balconies were covered with small tiled roofs and pots of flowers, and plants draped from the railings. Bricked or stone archways covered the doorways, and cobblestones lined the streets. Friendly people smiled and greeted us warmly.

"This is absolutely charming," I exclaimed. "I can just imagine 'Carmen' dancing down the street with her castanets, singing her arias."

WE WERE CAPTIVATED BY THE BUILDINGS OF OLD CARTAGENA.

When we saw the wall surrounding the ancient inner city, we were amazed that it was in such good condition. Large elevated round turrets appeared at intervals and had provided additional protection from attacking forces. A narrow arched tunnel under a clock tower provided access through the wall. Before entering, we had to cross a wide busy street that had numerous cars zipping about in chaotic fashion. Most of the cars were taxis, and they sped by only inches from the curb. Car horns blared a raucous and enthusiastic symphony. Making our way across seemed a rather daunting task without the aid of stoplights or crosswalks. We watched the locals, and when they crossed so did we. Cars didn't slow down for pedestrians—it was every man, woman, and child for themselves! No one seemed concerned, although we thought it life-threatening.

"Oh my goodness," I exclaimed, when we walked through the entrance arch into the Plaza del Aduanas. "Look at this."

"Man, this is like stepping back in time!" Fred said.

"This was where the old slave market was held," said our new friend. "Cartagena was the largest slave port in the New World."

The large cobblestone courtyard was surrounded by impressive colonial buildings, all with red tiled roofs. Graceful stone arches stood in front of the buildings that encircled the courtyard and provided a shaded walkway around the perimeter. Protected from the piercing sun, vendors sold coffee, coconuts, jewelry, and souvenirs on tables or blankets spread on the cobblestones. Colorfully dressed women walked along, balancing large baskets of fruit on their heads, enticing us to buy some. In my mind, I could see a raised platform in the center of the square, holding the arriving slaves who were being auctioned to the highest bidder, and crowds of men, horses, and carriages. My imagination was going wild!

Arriving at the bank, we found that doing business there took a good deal of time and patience, and there was no air-conditioning inside. I was beginning to wilt.

"It's much hotter here than I had imagined it would be," Fred said, wiping the sweat from his face.

"It's definitely cooler down by the harbor," I added. "Every little exertion makes me sweat, and that makes those darn bug bites itch—my souvenirs from the San Blas Islands."

After finally receiving our money, we cautiously made our way to a quiet corner of the bank. Fred turned to the wall, and I stood in front of his back, watching the people inside the bank while he placed the bills in his money belt that was secured under his shorts. We knew that, in any large city, tourists are vulnerable to theft when coming out of a bank. We tried to use good "street sense" to protect ourselves. Keeping our actions casual and "normal-appearing," we walked outside using our "rubber neck" routine and hurried away from the bank, making sure we were not being followed.

We continued our tour by taking a bus over to Bocagrande and the beach, which was the tourist-oriented area of the city—a place that reminded us a good deal of Waikiki, Hawaii. There were strips of large, modern hotels and many upscale restaurants and shops, but the beaches left much to be desired. We had seen so many lovely ones—these were rocky, small, and dirty. Crowds of people in beachwear strolled along the busy streets.

"There sure are lots of tourists here," I observed, "but they all seem to be Columbian. I don't see many gringos."

We knew that Cartagena was a major vacation spot for the Columbian and South American people. Because there were U.S. State Department warnings cautioning people about traveling in the country, there were very few American tourists. We assumed the warnings were because of the large amount of drug trafficking. While drug cartels and political rebel groups were very active throughout the country, it appeared to the cruising community that Cartagena was an "off limits" area for those groups. Perhaps they all needed a safe place to take their families for vacations.

Walking back to the boat, we stopped at a tourist office near the harbor of old town to get a map. There we met Carmen and Rodrigo, who worked for the tourist department. They were surprised to hear that we came here by sailboat and were anxious to talk. They spoke a little English, and, after a short time, Rodrigo asked us to join them at Carmen's place for dancing, food, and drink on Christmas Eve.

"Talk about friendly people!" I exclaimed, after leaving the office. "I'm glad we invited them to the boat next Sunday for a drink. Carmen especially wanted to see a sailboat."

"I liked hearing them say what the cruisers have said—that it's safe to walk about the city day or night. That feels good after all the warnings in Panama," Fred said. "But it may not be true in other areas of Columbia."

Settling in to Cartagena and getting familiar with the area around us became our goal that first week. We were enjoying the task. Everywhere we went, people were smiling and friendly, and usually assumed we were from Argentina. They were always surprised when we said we were from the States.

High on a hill overlooking the harbor was the massive and formidable San Felipe Fort, and we were anxious to explore it. It had been an important part of the defense of Cartagena long ago. We needed to tour it with a guide because it was so large and honeycombed with tunnels; people had actually been lost inside, unable to find their way out. Unfortunately, all the guides spoke only Spanish, but, with Andre translating for us, we got to go deep into this labyrinth of old. There were miles of tunnels, and the dungeon gave me the chills. I was glad to make it outside safely and breathe the fresh air.

When we wanted to make an international phone call, we learned from Norm that lightning had knocked out his phone lines the previous week and that it might take months to repair them. We were told the location of the TeleCom office in old town, and started walking there.

"Where did he say it was?" Fred asked, after I stopped a third pedestrian for help, receiving different directions every time.

"I'm not sure," I groaned. "I don't think he knew. This is so frustrating."

We decided to ask one more person. This man was so determined to help that he spent 20 minutes studying our map, asking questions, and finally walking behind us after he had told us where to go. But he was *right*. We were so glad to reach Page, but learned that, *again*, the renters were three months behind in payments. What is it with renters? Now I had something more to worry about.

Back on the boat, we had to run the engine to charge the batteries. It had been cloudy a good deal since we arrived here, and our solar panels weren't keeping up with the electrical demand. The dry season would start soon, which would be nice, although we dreaded the thought that it would also be hotter without the clouds. Another hassle of anchoring was that we also had to take the engine off the dinghy and pull it aboard every night because there was considerable theft. Anything left on the deck would be gone by morning. We again walked over to Club de Pesca, hoping that if we were persistent in our inquiries we could get into their marina. Wonder of wonders: They had room for us!

The Columbian club was in an amazing facility. It and a restaurant were built around a well-preserved old Spanish fort. To arrive by land, we walked through a narrow, low stone arch and entered a cobblestone parade ground, now used as a parking lot. Fort walls and turrets surrounded the area, and all were handsomely lit up at night. Many tourist pamphlets featured this picturesque setting on the harbor. Occasionally the restaurant was closed to the public for private parties, and musicians played atop the fort walls that were illuminated by colored lights. Sometimes helicopters hovered overhead, and we were told that the president of Columbia was dining there. Many military guards and police patrolled the area at such times. And this was to be our new home!

After 10 days at anchor, we eagerly moved *Grace* into the club.

"Look at all the dinghies and equipment left out here on the dock," I said, after we were securely tied up in our slip. "There apparently isn't a problem with theft in here."

"The locals may steal from the 'yachties,' but they sure aren't going to mess with the Columbian owners," Fred laughed. "They likely want to stay alive."

What a joy to be able to get on and off the boat any time we wanted without having to go ashore in the dinghy. We also had shore power and quickly bought a large oscillating fan for the aft cabin at night. There were showers available and lots of security, with night and day watchmen and locked gates. We could even leave all the hatches open at night!

We quickly became acquainted with the club's staff, as well as Humberto, the owner of a sailboat next to ours. He also owned the prestigious and expensive restaurant in the marina. We were soon good friends with Saul (pronounced Saw-ule), a 20-year-old who worked on the large power vessel on the other side of us. His father was the skipper when the owners used the boat. They owned a large corporation that produced soft drinks. We were amidst some serious money here!

One day I became alarmed when I was at the supermarket, and hurried back to the boat to tell Fred. "Everyone was talking and appeared excited," I said, still puffing from my fast walk home. "They kept trying to get me to understand, and saying the name Pablo Escabarra. One guy pantomimed shooting a machine gun, and I heard several talking about dead people. What's happening?"

"The dock boys were doing the same thing here," Fred said. "They kept talking about mafia, cocaine, and killing."

In discussions at Norm's, we learned that a top mafia and drug cartel boss was killed in a drug-bust along with a number of other people. Apparently, there was U.S. help in the take-down. The people of Columbia were delighted that he was dead, but also worried about who would take his place. There were extra guards around the marina that night. Other cruisers said that boats were sometimes a front for drug money, or that others in the cartel may be trying to escape the country using a boat. We didn't know what to believe, but it was definitely exciting.

After asking on the morning net, we connected with a cruiser who was a retired Episcopal priest, and he and his wife took us to an Episcopalian church one Sunday morning. It was a surprise to learn there was a protestant church here. The service was all in Spanish, but very familiar to our Lutheran background. People were so delighted to have us there. They ushered us to seats up in the front, had one man give us a special welcome in English during the service, and even asked us to carry the communion elements at the offering time—something they considered an honor. The four of us were the only gringos there.

"What an experience," I said as we left the church. "Those people were so caring that it brought tears to my eyes."

"When we first sat down and they moved that large fan that normally blows on the priest so that it would blow on us, I was shocked," Fred replied.

"And we were invited to that couple's home for Christmas." There was no doubt—these people excelled in making us feel welcome and loved. We could learn from that!

One morning, I looked at the calendar. "It's only three weeks until

Christmas," I said, "but it sure doesn't feel like it. I think I'll see if I can get a cruisers' caroling group started."

After spreading the word on the net, I had a small group that practiced on our boat several times a week. When we found there wasn't enough space on the boat for two guitar players and numerous singers, we asked if we could use the bar at the club and were enthusiastically welcomed. Since the walls of the bar were open lattice, we were heard throughout the marina, and several folks clapped or told us that they liked hearing the singing. The music of the holidays meant so much to me, and brought a small feeling of something familiar into a celebration that, up until then, had felt so strange. Snow scenes in shop windows also evoked familiar feelings, although I had to laugh when I realized that most of the people here had never seen real snow and it was 90 degrees.

There were so many fun things to do in Cartagena—and always people who wanted to do them—that our days and evenings were full. We took a 15-mile trip, along with 12 other cruisers, in Norm's large open boat to the Rosario Islands. We attended a choral concert by the University of Cartagena, a ballet at the convention center, and a 3-day international jazz festival. At these events, it was strange to have our bags searched, walk through a metal detector, and have our tickets examined to see if they were counterfeit. One time they even frisked the men before we could enter the theater. It reminded us that this was a country used to sudden upheaval or conflicts, and killings from either the drug cartels or the extremist political groups that fought with the government. When we remembered the violence created by gang wars back home, it didn't seem all that much different.

We continued our friendship with Carmen, and she took us to her home one afternoon. We loved playing with her 2-year-old, although at first he was wary of us, saying, "*Le no habla!*" (Don't talk to me!) Carmen and her husband had a very modest home in an impoverished neighborhood, but they obviously had spent a good deal of effort and money to entertain us. After admiring their 7-month-old daughter, I admitted that I was eager to become a grandmother.

"*Aqui, un regalo,*" (here, a gift) she said, and handed me the baby. We all laughed.

It was informative to spend time in a Columbian home, although it was also a lot of work for me and sometimes awkward, as Carmen spoke only a few words of English and her husband none at all. Again, we marveled at the hospitality of so many of the people we were meeting.

When I went to find a hair salon one day to get a permanent, I met Marta, the hairdresser.

"Wow—*curly!*" Fred said when I returned to the boat.

"I told Marta that my hair curled easily, but I guess they just aren't used to fine, blond hair here," I said. My hair was *fried!* "Oh well, it will grow out eventually."

Marta, too, became a friend, and we had her and her family to the boat on several occasions. She lived just a few blocks from the marina, so we visited in her home a few times as well. One day I asked her how old her mother was and learned that she and I were the same age. Marta quickly said that her mother was not as young as Fred and me—that her mother was very "*tranquil*" and never got excited about anything. When I said that I, also, was "*tranquil*," she, Fred, and I all laughed heartily. Despite the language problem, I guess she had me figured out. She spoke no English, and sometimes Fred was not so involved in the conversations. Other times, we had Andre or someone else to translate for us, and at those times the conversation certainly flowed easier. We began taking Spanish lessons from Sylvia, a young local woman who came to the boat each day for an hour. We mostly talked and tried to listen to the spoken word and did some study on our own, but the practice definitely helped.

Sometimes it was a plus to speak English. One of the artisan souvenir shops employed several of the English-speaking cruising women to come to their shop to be saleswomen when the big cruise ships came to port. I tried it for a while, and it was fun to do something so different.

"I don't think I'll continue to help at the souvenir shop," I said one evening. "It's starting to feel like *work,* and, besides that, I spend all the money I earn on things from the shop and going out for lunch with the girls!" So much for my sales career.

Getting to know the locals was one of the best parts of this adventurous dream we were experiencing, and Cartagena provided many opportunities for this. We learned a bit about the relationships between men and women from our discussions with Josephe, Humberto's 25-year-old son who lived in Bogata, and Henrique, a store manager whom we had met and invited to our boat. Both spoke excellent English. While we knew that Josephe was engaged and Henrique married (admitting that he loved his wife very much), in separate conversations they both mentioned their "*novia*," "best *novia*," or "other wife." I thought *novia* meant fiancé, and expressed surprise. When I asked them about this, they each became quiet, and I learned later that *novia* also meant "lover." Apparently, for the men, having a mistress is an acceptable part of their culture, and they talked about it freely (other than with older *gringas*). It was not so acceptable for many of the women. Marta said she would never marry another Columbian man for this reason. Sylvia said the same, calling it "*machismo*." Henrique also admitted that the men in his economic level felt burdened with maintaining a certain lifestyle. It was expected that they hire people to do all of their cooking, cleaning, and childcare, even when that was financially troublesome. He and his wife both worked in order to keep this standard, even though they would prefer something different. We were grateful for these opportunities to gain insight into our host country and its customs, and I was grateful for my American husband!

"Hey—we got *mail*," I squealed. We found that the Columbian mail was much more reliable than in other Latin countries and could hardly wait to open the packets sent by Page. On those days we got nothing done on the boat, and we read every letter several times. Sometimes the news stirred up some anxiety, like when Lance said he wanted to talk with us about something "important." What did that mean? Was it something good or bad? We tried several times to reach him by phone without success. When we finally connected, we woke him up early in the morning, and he was almost comatose. He was so sleepy that he would hardly speak, and we learned nothing except that he was okay.

"I'm still worried," I said to Fred. "What's he not telling us?"

"Hey—we know we can't shelter the kids from tough times now or in the future. We've just got to hope that we've given them the skills and foundation to deal with them when they come, as they surely will," Fred said. I knew that in my head, but how difficult it was to believe when we were so far away. We also were concerned to hear that the renter's check had bounced and she was now four months in arrears.

We were taking advantage of being in the marina and had begun to set our alarm clock and get up early enough in the morning to go for a 45-minute exercise run before the sun rose.

"I can't believe we are doing this," I said, as we stretched and gulped a cup of coffee in the darkness.

"It does seem a little bizarre," Fred chuckled, "but if we're going to do it, it has to be now. It's just too hot once the sun comes up."

It took a while to get back in shape, but after the daily struggle to get out of bed, we began to enjoy this predawn venture. We explored different parts of the city as it came to life, and arrived back at the marina security gate puffing and dripping with sweat. The guards would smile as they let us in and shake their heads in disbelief. Crazy gringos!

Saul didn't think we were crazy. We had developed quite a friendship with this delightful young man, and he was so helpful to us. He was very bright, had a terrific sense of humor, and eyes that sparkled when he talked. It was always uplifting to engage with him. He spoke a little English, wanted to learn more, and always tried to help us learn Spanish. He often asked the meaning of a word that one of us had used.

"Don't teach him that!" Fred insisted one day. I had just responded to Saul, saying "Okey dokey." Fred was sure Saul would sound like some "nut case" if he tried to use the old-fashioned phrase, but—too late—the damage was done. Later that day we heard him reply to us with a broad smile and a proud, "Okey dokey!"

We often thought Saul would make a great Charades player. "I can't believe that you and Saul can sit and talk for such a long time," I said once.

"Well, he uses as much hand and body language as you do," Fred had replied. "You two are from the same mold!"

The Sunday before Christmas, we gasped when we entered the little Episcopal church we so enjoyed attending. "Oh my," I said. "Look what they did to the front of the church."

The altar had been moved aside and the entire space was a three dimensional scene of the manager and countryside surrounding Bethlehem. It had a backdrop of sky, with stars hanging from the ceiling, a village in the foreground, meadows with sheep grazing, paper mache mountains and rivers, and hundreds of twinkling lights. We went forward to just admire it for several minutes. As with the crèches we had seen pop up on many street corners, the baby Jesus figure was nowhere to be seen. But of course! He would arrive on Christmas morning! The whole congregation was proud of the wonderful display. It was "beginning to feel a lot like Christmas!"

Finally, it was time to go caroling. One night the eight of us who had been practicing met at Norm's. He took us out in the harbor in his big skiff, and we motored around the anchorage, singing for three and a half hours. We had three guitar players to accompany us, and as we stopped to sing at the second anchored boat, a Polish man on a sailboat from Finland ran into his cabin, came back with his violin, and jumped into the skiff to join us. He was a professional musician and did he ever make us sound great! He could really sing as well. Soon another dinghy with four people in it had joined us, and Norm pulled them behind us. Many of the boats provided us with a drink or something to eat, but that wasn't too surprising, as I had explained on the cruisers' net that morning that this was the custom when carolers called on you. Actually, I think I had said, "If you want the carolers to move on, you need to give them a little Christmas cheer to speed them on their way." People all seemed to enjoy it, and one man told us that his wife was in tears a couple of times when we sang. I think that meant she liked it. Often, Norm was a rather gruff and grumpy guy, but that night he and his wife were lovin' it and didn't want to stop. We grinned all the way back to the boat!

Christmas Eve day arrived and we had decided that, despite some invitations to join local families in their homes, we would join our cruising family at Norm's for dinner and celebration. We had made small plates of goodies that we delivered that morning to the various club staff members, both on the docks and in the office. They were all so pleased and were very gracious. Then we hurried to deliver some toys to Carmen and a small gift to Marta. These people had welcomed us so warmly that it felt good to make some small gesture of caring in return. We had a special gift for our neighbor, Saul. He was our most cherished Columbian friend.

Norm supplied the meat for 80 to 100 folks who came that Christmas Eve. Each of us brought a side dish to add to the table. It was a nice dinner, but there were too many people for us. A Yankee Swap followed, with good-natured joshing and silly gifts. Although there was to be music later, the electricity went out and everyone headed home. It was a nice evening, but it sure didn't feel like Christmas Eve. *Grace* looked festive, though, as we walked down the dock towards her. We had some large inflatable ball decorations hanging from the boom, large snowflakes scattered about the windows, and the lights on our little Christmas tree twinkling from the cabin. We sat in the cockpit and enjoyed the cool night air, reflecting on the reason for the season rather than the ache created by missing family.

"Feliz Navidad," I said the next morning. "Papa Noel came during the night and left us new rugs for the boat."

"Well, I think he also left this little poem for you," Fred chuckled.

As I read the poem describing the hiding place of my gift, I nearly lost it. For so many years I had written poems for the children, and now Fred had attempted one for me. We had even honored the tradition last year on the boat in Cabo, when the kids had joined us for Christmas. Now it was just the two of us. We were glad that we had invited the other six cruisers who were moored in the club for a brunch, as there was a lot to do to get ready. When they came, we all enjoyed the relaxed gathering and good food—a nice way to spend Christmas morning. Later in the afternoon we went to our Episcopal church, where we and another couple had organized a non-denominational Christmas worship in English. There were only 15 of us attending, along with a few local folks, but it was special. We had lots of singing, which I accompanied on my electric keyboard. The church had kindly let us use their facilities, and we were all grateful for this Christmas celebration in our own language. Coming back to the boat, we talked about dinner.

"I've got lots of leftovers from the brunch," I said.

"Why not our traditional Christmas turkey dinner?" Fred asked. "I bet we have some canned turkey."

"Yeah, we do." Seeing the grin on his face, I began to share in his delight at the idea. We dug through the food lockers and the two of us whipped up a savory taste of home, with canned turkey, canned gravy, and canned corn. We even found some instant mashed potatoes—all served in the cockpit where we sat in the moonlight of that warm Columbian night.

"Oh no!" I cried. "Not the children!"

Once again, tragic news had struck the cruising community and had been relayed from ham radios to the local morning radio net. We were stunned to hear that *Melinda Lee* had been hit and sunk by a freighter as they sailed to New Zealand. Judy was the only survivor—Mike, Ben, and Annie had all been lost at sea. The shock was overwhelming as we slowly absorbed the reality of such a catastrophe. We ached for Judy, so badly injured, as we thought of her grief in losing her whole family. We prayed for healing for both her body and soul. Life would surely never be the same for her. The image of a laughing 2-year-old, Ben, kept appearing in my mind, along with the memory of Lance helping the family through that wild surf. As we met with others who knew these good folks, as well as those who had not known them but were simply a part of the cruising community and staggered by the news, we all shared our own grief and tears. At such times, it was good to feel the support of "family." We were reminded once again of the fragility of life, the risks of the dream we were following, the bond with loved ones, and the enormity of shared pain and suffering. We were drawn to a small plaque on our bulkhead: "A ship in a harbor is safe; but that is not what ships are built for." Throughout the years, we had reflected on that metaphor for life, even as we sailed on our own bona fide ship. Was the adventure worth the risks? Were there not risks in all of life? Were we doing the "right" thing? There were many more questions than answers.

It seemed that someone had flipped a switch somewhere, and suddenly the rainy season was gone and the dry season had begun. We wanted to look spiffy in the sun and decided to hire someone to wash and wax the boat, something we previously had always done ourselves. Saul helped us contract with one of the men who worked on the dock. The second day he came to work for us he made it clear that his price was double what we had understood from Saul.

"You know we're getting taken here," I said to Fred. I was angry.

"Probably so," he said, "but we want there to be a good feeling with the men on the dock. Even at double, it's still not very much for a whole day's work. I think we should just pay it."

"OK, but next time we need to get it in writing so there will be no 'misunderstanding.'"

We had learned that lesson before, but had forgotten to apply it. We knew that, for many, the perception was that all cruisers were rich—just look at their boats! And compared to the standard of living of the working class folks, we were. Perhaps this perception also justified the frequent theft in the anchorage—rather like Robin Hood taking from the rich to give to the poor. As it was in many countries, tourists were often targets for some form of cheating. Other (more affluent) residents of Cartagena were very surprised to hear of the occurrence of theft in the harbor and the ill feelings it created. They wanted people to come to their country, particularly Americans, and couldn't understand why Columbia was considered unsafe. The police had not been helpful in protecting the cruisers, so I decided to organize a letter-writing campaign to the Tourism Bureau, saying the image of this lovely city was being damaged by the problem. Perhaps it wouldn't help, but at least it felt better to try *something*.

It was New Year's Eve day and we were excited. Cindy and Reed, from *Yobo,* were flying over to Cartagena from Panama to spend some time with us, and then meeting Reed's folks here for a week. After they arrived, we took them to old town to show them the sights. It felt so good to have them with us again. We decided to be *real* tourists and took the horse-drawn carriage through the city while sharing a bottle of champagne. We spilled more than we drank as we bounced along the bumpy cobblestone streets. Everywhere we went Fred inquired if anyone had cable television; he *so* hoped to be able to see the Nebraska college championship football game later that day. Fred was more than a fan of Nebraska football—he was a *fanatic!* Of course, football in South America meant soccer, and we couldn't find any place to see the game. Such disappointment—we all worked hard to cheer him up. He decided he would check in on the ham radio the following day to find out the game's results. Later, we gussied up for the evening, received many good-natured compliments from the club guards and workers, and all went to Norm's for a special buffet dinner. Sitting in the cockpit later that night, we watched the display of fireworks in the harbor.

"Wow, Columbia really knows how to do fireworks," Cindy cried.

"Yeah, these are *wild*," agreed Reed. "Look at those flares with parachutes."

"We've seen those before," said Fred. "The cruisers in the harbor don't like them, for sometimes they land on the boats and do damage."

We continued observing the festivities while people on the *malecon* (seawalk) between Norm's Club Nautico and Club de Pesca were also shooting off fireworks of their own. Many were little paper lanterns with a candle which, when lit, would float up into the air. Some would catch on fire and crash to the ground while everyone groaned with dismay. Perhaps people all over the world celebrated the hope of the coming year, and, as we shared a toast with good friends and wondered what this year would bring, we knew we were *blucky*!

Cindy and Reed were busy with Reed's parents and we had tickets to the day's *Los Corridos de Toros*—the bullfight. We arrived an hour early so that we could watch the people. The stadium was a huge round structure with pointed spires ringing the top edge. Colorful flags flew from every spire. There were a number of bands, and the excitement in the air was palpable.

"I'm sure glad we paid the extra money to get *sombre* (shaded) seats," I said, as we waited with the throng of spectators to get our bags searched before going inside. "I can't imagine sitting all afternoon on the sunny side."

"I'm not sure we will want to stay for all of this," Fred said. "I've heard that it can be pretty bloody."

"I know, but I'm trying to keep an open mind. This is an important part of this country's culture."

THE *PLAZA DE TOROS* AND THE PRESIDENTIAL BOX.

With a little uncertainty, mixed with curiosity and anticipation, we entered the bullring. It was definitely a "people-watching" event. Trumpets blared, and with much pomp, pageantry, and music the opening parade began. The crowd went wild when the 12 matadors marched in, with their colorful capes draped over their shoulders. Three of them were featured fighters, and the noise was deafening every time they appeared. The fights began quickly and we tried to understand the process and goals of each of the different phases. I worried about the thickly padded and blindfolded horses, particularly when one fell down. Certainly the bull wasn't having a good day either! When a matador was through making his passes with his cape and ready to make his kill, the crowd obviously wanted it done quickly and began to boo if it was not. Twice, a matador received the wave of a white handkerchief from a V.I.P. sitting in a special box above us. Thousands of people in the stands were doing the same and roared approval when the triumphant fighter was awarded the ear of the dead bull.

"If I focused my attention on the participants and what they were doing, it wasn't so bad," I said to Fred as we were leaving the stadium. "I sure didn't like looking at the poor bull, though."

"I know. I'm glad we came. I enjoyed the experience as a whole, but I don't know if I'd ever go again."

"You know, some people here think American football is a violent game. James Michener and Ernest Hemingway pointed out that many more young men in the prime of life are killed and maimed every year in that sport than in bullfights," I said.

"Point well taken," he agreed.

The following day was a real "zoo" at Norm's: The Queen Elizabeth II had anchored in the harbor, too big to use the regular cruise ship dock. All of the boats on one of Club Nautico's docks had been removed to allow for the ship's tenders to bring 1400 passengers ashore. Outside the club, there were buses lined up for half a mile, and taxis galore. Tourist agents crowded along the sidewalks, all wanting to get inside the locked doors of the club. There were souvenir stands set up in the restaurant, as well as out on the lawn, and cruisers helped with the crush of people coming from the ship. The price of drinks had doubled in the bar, reminding us that we had been told, "Never buy anything on a day that a cruise ship is in port." It was exciting to watch all the activity, and Fred didn't want to leave.

"I can't believe you have become such a 'people-watcher,'" I laughed.

I had also noticed how much more comfortable he was now in introducing ourselves and talking with people we didn't know. He was becoming a regular "social butterfly!"

We were awakened shortly after midnight by several loud blasts and the glare of sudden bright lights. We got up to see a spectacular display of fireworks in the harbor, just yards from our boat. We went out to the cockpit and watched for about 20 minutes. When it was over, we heard the sound of clapping from a large party boat close to us in the bay, and a band began to play "Happy Birthday." What a coincidence! I turned to Fred and gave him a big hug.

"I hope you enjoyed the birthday surprise that I arranged for you," I said and grinned.

Walking along the hotel beach at Bocagrande that afternoon, we watched the college kids on their spring vacation cavorting in the sand. Whether playing volleyball, dancing wildly to loud music, doing the "wave," or laughing while spraying folks with bottled water, it wasn't difficult to imagine two of our three doing the same.

At a cruisers' swap meet, we bought a small TV with VCR. We hadn't missed having one, but the price was right. We were thrilled to be able to watch VCR movies many evenings, and felt like kids in a candy store with our new "toy." Cruisers traded movie tapes as well as paperback books, so there was always a good supply.

One day we noticed six very serious-looking men with dark glasses and two-way radios, each carrying a small shoulder bag. They accompanied a group who boarded the boat that Saul worked on and it left the marina.

"I don't think you want to mess with those guys," Fred observed.

Upon their return, we talked with Saul and learned that the group was the owner's daughter and family. When they went on the boat, they also brought along a cook and a nurse, as well as Saul, the deckhand, and Saul's dad, the skipper. The men we had observed were bodyguards, and the shoulder bags did, indeed, carry weapons. Kidnapping for ransom was a constant threat for the wealthy in Columbia, and the boat's owner had 25 bodyguards, although they were not all in one place. It didn't sound like a lifestyle I'd enjoy.

We continued to appreciate our opportunities to worship at the little Episcopalian church. The priest was such a caring man with great good humor. We were invited and went to his birthday party, as well as dinner at a home of one of the members. One Sunday was especially meaningful. As several men brought the offering plates up the center aisle, a mother with an infant came forward as well. The priest took the tiny baby in his arms, turned, and raised the child up towards the cross that hung over the altar while the congregation sang a familiar hymn – "Praise God From Whom All Blessings Flow." Although sung in Spanish, we knew the meaning of the words, and I reached for Fred's hand.

"That gave me *goose-bumps,*" I whispered to him, with tears in my eyes.

"Have you ever seen that before?" he whispered back, incredulous. "That was really powerful." We were *blucky* to have been a part of it that morning.

We began preparations for an inland trip that would last several weeks. We had met Sara, a young woman who lived in Bogotá, and she had invited us to visit her, so we accepted. Our general plan was to fly to Bogotá to visit Sara, and then fly on to southern Columbia, where we would proceed by bus into Ecuador. By doing this, we hoped to avoid the areas of violence involving the government rebels and drug cartels in Columbia.

As usual, there was much to do to ready the boat. Saul said he would keep a keen eye on *Grace* while we were gone, and another cruiser would have keys to the cabin and engine, should it need to be moved. We also raided the lockers for the warmest clothes we had on board; we knew we would often be at high elevations where it would be much cooler.

Finally, we were ready to leave and called for a taxi. A group of our Columbian friends had "coached" me on how to ask the driver for the cost of the ride to the airport.

"Are you ready to use your 'best' Spanish?" Fred asked me as we approached the taxi. "Fabio doesn't want us to be taken for tourists and overcharged."

"I'm ready—but remember—he also said for you just to keep your mouth shut."

What a rich assortment of experiences we had for the next four weeks. Traveling through Columbia, Ecuador, and Peru, we saw breathtaking panoramas, beautiful buildings, and historic landmarks. But the interactions with the people were the best. Again and again we were awed by the hospitality and friendliness shown by the diverse groups we encountered.

When we arrived in Bogotá, Sara was there to meet us. It was much cooler in this large metropolitan city at an elevation of 8300 feet, and there was virtually no humidity—so different from the coastal communities to which we were accustomed. When we stopped at a large modern shopping mall for coffee, I looked around and began to feel self-conscious. My simple sundress and Birkenstock sandals were entirely out-of-place in this cosmopolitan city, where the women wore stylish wool suits, classy dresses, and high heels. Sara assured me that it didn't matter, but I still felt like a "country bumpkin."

After exploring Bogota for a couple of days, we flew south in a small propeller plane to Pasto, a city in the foothills of the Andes and close to the Ecuadorian border. This flight afforded an "up close and personal" opportunity to view the incredible Andes scenery. Jagged snow-covered mountain peaks and rolling green valleys extended as far as we could see. It reminded us of Switzerland. In Pasto, after finding a hotel, we were again surprised at how cold it was, and the rooms had no heat. When walking about the town, we were often followed by uniformed, giggling school children, wanting to talk with us. We saw no other *gringos*.

"What luck," I said. "Tomorrow's the big market day. They only have it once a week."

"This town is known for its leather products," Fred said. "I hope you can find a warmer jacket."

We explored all the stalls in the marketplace, and bought not only a leather jacket but a warm wool sweater for me with Mom's birthday gift money. I lived in that sweater, jeans, and jacket for much of the next few weeks. Taking a small "collective" bus to Ipiales, we asked a woman if she could recommend a hotel. She eagerly walked us to *three* before we found one with the right price. There, we met Martin, a very helpful young manager. "*Si, si*," he responded after we asked several times, thinking we had misunderstood, that it cost only 12 dollars a night. Like many, he assumed that we were German, and was eager to talk when he learned that we were from the States, sailed to Columbia on a sailboat, and that Fred was a ham operator—for Martin was also a ham. He excitedly took us to meet his friend and to use the ham radio at his house. The next day he walked us a half-mile to catch a *collectivo*, or van, to go to the beautiful Las Lapes—a huge stone gothic church built long ago.

"Wow—that is breathtaking," I said when we first saw the imposing structure, deep in the narrow canyon below us.

"Look how it creates a bridge between those rock walls on either side of the canyon," Fred added. "You can see the river far below the church." We couldn't imagine how people had brought building materials in to such a remote place.

We joined others walking down the winding path. There had been many reports of miraculous healings here. Inside, the entire altar space was the natural stone face of the canyon wall. It extended high up to the vaulted ceiling and exuded strength, ruggedness, and a striking beauty in its simplicity and grandeur.

"That was certainly unique," I said, as I puffed along the steep path back to the area entrance, "both the church and the setting."

"It sure was," Fred replied. "Come on, walk a little faster."

"Whatever for? I'm winded now!"

"Hey—we don't want those local folks behind us to pass—they'll think *gringos* are soft," he laughed. Good grief. Now we had to compete with the climbing ability of Inca descendents? Maybe the altitude was getting to him!

To get into Ecuador, we took a bus to the border, got out, went through customs, walked across the border, went through immigration, and got on another packed local bus. I was fascinated to observe the many indigenous folks in their distinctive dress who also were riding the bus. Different tribes had their own styles. All wore hats. They were a *very* short people, and many were barefoot. Most of the women had a baby on their back, wrapped in a shawl, or were nursing a child, sometimes up to the age of four. Some were not clean, and some had clothes that looked old and tattered. The women also wore gold plastic beads around their necks and three inches of small red bead bracelets. Men usually wore white pants, a shirt and poncho, and were often seen shuffling along the road, stooped over, with large, heavy bundles on their backs.

"What is that strange smell?" Fred said shortly after getting on the bus.

"I was told that comes from the *Achoyete* spice that the Indians eat so much of," I replied.

Just then, we heard the sound of laughter that soon spread throughout the bus. A small guinea pig-like animal had gotten loose and was darting about under the seats. This bus even provided entertainment. We later learned that this little critter was a highly prized dinner food!

When we got off the bus to Ibarra, we found ourselves in a remote area and wondered where the city was. An older man came walking by, and, after asking him, he said we could ride into *el centro* with him on another bus. Accompanying us, he showed us his attorney office and then took us to a hotel where he invited us for coffee. We were glad to finally find some place to stay and deeply appreciated his kindness. Coming out of our room a short time later, we met a woman who said she was the hotel owner.

"What did she say?" Fred asked.

"I'm not really sure," I said. "She spoke so fast. I *think* she invited us to be her guests tonight at a dinner and fiesta in a neighboring town. It might be something to do with tourism."

With many unanswered questions, I put on a skirt, my only nice outfit, and we met her in the lobby at eight. Still wondering about what we had gotten ourselves into, we proceeded to a large gathering of tourist agents, where, as American tourists, we were V.I.P.s!

Because it was a cold night, we had assumed the dinner would be indoors in this town at 10,000 feet elevation, but the tables for 75 people were set in a lovely outdoor courtyard. We sat where we were told, and waiters started serving a warm drink, which they poured into small ceramic cups that we wore on a ribbon around our necks. We had hardly finished it when they were there to pour another cup.

"Hey—this stuff, whatever it is—it's not bad," Fred grinned.

"I know. After two or three of them, I don't even feel cold anymore!"

A wonderful dinner of many new tastes was served, and more drinks. Live music played throughout, and folklore dancers performed. A few people spoke English, and our quirky hotel owner fussed about, but seemed to relish showing off her hotel guests. It was late when we returned to the hotel and laughed about the evening's unforeseen events.

One day we took a taxi to a village famous for its woodcarvings. We had planned to stay for a couple of hours, but ended up staying the entire day. Every house on almost every street had a small shop that sold exquisite carvings. Families had been handing down the skills for this incredible craftsmanship for generations, and we saw many small children and their parents at work. We had planned to continue our bus trip the following day, but when we returned to our hotel, we saw crowds running in the streets and police using tear gas to disperse them.

"What's going on?" we asked with alarm.

"No problemo," was the reply. It was only the students and locals, striking the recent rise of gasoline prices—apparently not an unusual occurrence. The protest, however, would block all the roads out of the city for two more days. Thankfully, we were flexible.

In one little village, we met two Irishmen. That charming Irish brogue lulled me into forgetting where we were. They were having a drink with ice cubes and assured me that the water and ice were "safe," so I tried one too. Ahhh . . . I did not have the "luck of the Irish," and soon regretted that decision. Hadn't we already learned our lesson about ice cubes?

As we bused about the country we marveled at the scenery. Cobblestone roads alternated with narrow paved roads through green valleys, and always those incredible mountains towered over us. We were definitely in the Andes. Roads wound in serpentine, up and down the valleys and hillsides, and all those curves occasionally created a problem for the children. When one young boy in front of us vomited all over his mother, I handed her some Kleenex, for which she was grateful.

One sight and smell that was especially disturbing to me, though, was that of men urinating on outdoor walls throughout the towns, even on the walls of churches. This seemed to be an acceptable practice in many of the Latin countries, but the odor it caused was nauseating. Sometimes garbage left in the street also created a rotten smell. These behaviors were such a contrast to the sight of women sweeping the sidewalks and streets outside their shops and homes every morning, sometimes wetting the dirt with buckets of water in order to minimize the dust. We wondered—was the contrast gender-related? Encountering different cultures often seemed to raise more questions than answers.

Throughout Ecuador we saw many folks begging. It was painful for us to see, because frequently they were older people, often infirm, with sores on their hands and feet and wearing dirty old clothes. There were so many that it was impossible to help them all. Apparently there was no system of pensions or Social Security in this country. Occasionally we saw local folks giving them something, but we wondered about how they all survived.

In Otabalo, we were anxious to see a Saturday market that was famous throughout Ecuador. Once again the little hotel room had no heat. These people were tough!

"We'll never get these socks and underwear dry," I said to Fred after doing some hand wash. "It's too cold in here."

"Here," he said, and draped the items on top of the lamps and over the warm TV set. "That ought to do it." We also routinely left the lights and TV on when we weren't in the room, hoping they would provide a little warmth by the time we returned.

The huge market did not disappoint us. It was held in three different sites and took an entire day to see. Hundreds of animals filled huge fields in the early dawn, and men negotiated the buying and selling process. This was followed by a food market, as well as another that lined every street in town with stalls selling every imaginable item, including beautiful artisan articles. We shopped carefully for gifts, decorations for our home, and two brightly colored duffle bags that were made in the traditional indigenous weaving patterns. We needed them to carry back all the souvenirs we were getting.

"Hey—at least we won't have any trouble spotting these bags on the airport luggage carousel," Fred said. "They are one of a kind!"

Since it was "Carnival" time, we were hoping to find a place that had some kind of celebration similar to those of Brazil or Trinidad. We decided to look in Baños, a small city deep down in a protected valley, where there was an entrance to the Amazon jungle. On the way there, the bus broke down. After Fred and a number of the men tried unsuccessfully to fix the old vehicle, we had to get off and wait for the next bus. Sitting by the road, we heard a thud, felt water splash on our backs, and heard the sound of laughing children.

"Hey—what's going on?" I asked a man sitting near me.

"This is the way we celebrate 'Carnival,'" he said. "The kids throw water balloons." Oh no! We dashed for cover behind the stalled bus to the kids' great delight.

It was warm and humid when we finally arrived in Baños, where we had hoped to hike into the jungle. But I still wasn't feeling well after losing my gamble with the ice cubes; so, from the safety of our second floor balcony, we watched the antics of young folks running about the streets throwing buckets of water. The hotel clerk suggested that it would be better if we didn't go outside until evening.

Disappointed in our search for a Carnival celebration, we decided to give it one more shot and jumped on a bus to Ambato, the "City of Flowers." At last! The parade that night didn't compare with Portland's Rose Festival, but we had fun letting eight children stand in front of us to watch, even holding up the smaller ones so they could see. The moms were appreciative, but the kids seemed more fascinated with us than with the parade. There were many street dances following the parade, and we joined in, enjoying the lively music.

"I haven't seen any other *gringos*," I said. "Everybody keeps looking at us."

"Yeah, but they seem pleased that we are dancing, too," Fred said. "Maybe we're showing them some new steps." The "Freddy" had come to Ecuador!

We waited outside one cold dark night to make a call from the Telecom office of a small town nestled high in the foothills of the Andes. Two men in the line in front of us kept turning around, stealing shy glances our way, and then look at papers they held in their hands. Finally, I said, "Can we help you?"

That became our introduction to Peter, an Ecuadorian Methodist minister, and his son, Samuel, a third year seminary student. They spoke no English and were hoping for help translating a call to the States. They needed to talk with someone there regarding a possible grant for Peter's missionary work with the indigenous on the Amazon. While we felt very inadequate in translating, we could find no one else who spoke English. We made the call for them, but had to leave a message because no one was home. Frustrated, Peter showed us his papers, written in English. As we looked them over, we suddenly realized that Peter was being asked for a financial statement.

"What does that mean?" Peter asked.

"Fred used to be a banker, before retirement!" I said excitedly. "He can tell you exactly what is needed."

We all went back to the hostel where we were staying to get our Spanish dictionary, and for a couple of hours we all worked to complete the necessary paperwork. They were friendly, good humored folk and really appreciated our help. We suggested they fax the information and gladly offered to pay the cost, as that was prohibitive for them. Coming back from the Telecom office, we told them how we came to be in their village. When Peter heard the name of our sailboat, he stepped into the middle of the dark street, threw his arms out wide, and in a rich, deep baritone voice belted out a melodious, "Amazing Grace, how sweet the sound." It was the first time since leaving Mexico we had encountered any local person who knew this song! His beautiful singing echoed off the stone buildings of the deserted street that cold night and warmed our hearts.

"Can you believe it?" I said, as we got ready for bed later that night. "Do you think that was *coincidence*? They needed a translator and financial information, and—*hello*—we just happened to be there with a little knowledge of Spanish and a lot of knowledge about loans and grants!"

"It does seem incredible, doesn't it?" Fred grinned. "We sure were in the right place at the right time." It was a long time before we could calm down and finally drift off to sleep.

In Quito we found a newly refurbished hostel that had only two or three other guests. This was to become our home base, where we would leave some of our luggage while taking three different side trips. Quito was a large, modern city with many tourists, partly due to the large number of Spanish language schools that attracted young European students. It also had incredible old churches and palaces, and we made the circuit to see the biggest and best.

"I don't think I can take in another ornately decorated church," I said. "So much gold gilt! It's starting to seem commonplace. I think I'm saturated with sightseeing."

"Me too. I'm ready for a sports 'fix'," said Fred.

The Winter Olympics were taking place in Norway at this time. So we diligently searched until we found a large expensive hotel with a lounge and TV that received the Olympics broadcast; we nursed a beer there nightly. On the final night, the place was filled with Norwegian students, rooting excitedly for their homeland. It was a fun break in our traveling. We were still worried, however, about our renter, and contacted Page.

"Fantastic!" I heard Fred exclaim on the phone. "The renter has paid all her back rent!" "Yippee Skippee," I squealed, as I jumped up and down on the sidewalk. "Let's go to Machu Picchu!"

The plane trip from Quito, Ecuador, to Cuzco, Peru, was a welcome change from travel by local bus. The flight took us along a narrow corridor between two mountain ranges in the Andes. We could see the city below when we made a tight 180-degree turn and began a breathtakingly steep descent. I was petrified as I looked out the window, watching the ground race toward us.

"Look!" said Fred. "There are *cows* grazing on that grass right by the runway. There isn't even a fence around them!"

"Oh my gosh!" I gasped. "There are *kids* playing soccer there, too! What's to keep them off the tarmac?" Welcome to Peru!

Repeatedly we were cautioned on our arrival in the city that first day to rest and move slowly, because the altitude was more than two miles high. But we were anxious to see this ancient city of the Incas, and it was a treat to behold. When the Spaniards took over the city, they tore down everything but the Incas' building foundations, and on these the conquerors built their lavish colonial churches and palaces. Walking around the cobblestone streets, we felt dismayed as we encountered many small children begging. We had been told by several tourist officials not to give them money; doing so encouraged the practice and taught them that they don't need to work. Some of the older boys were quite aggressive and would get angry when we didn't give them anything. One small boy, likely two or three years old, ran alongside us, hardly able to keep up with our steps. He extended his hand, saying, "*Por favor, por favor*." He was barefoot and wearing only a sweater and typical Peruvian helmet hat for warmth, even though it was 11 o'clock at night and very cold.

"Oh—this just breaks my heart," I said.

"I know. Why don't we get a bunch of bread rolls, and give those?" Fred suggested. We did that, and sometimes the children simply *wolfed* them down, they were so hungry. So much tourism, yet so many hungry and needy people!

While we seldom went on organized tours, there was so much to learn about this fascinating culture and its history that we decided to take two group tours. One was an 11-hour trip to the Sacred Valley of the Incas. Vast numbers of terraces climbed like giant stair steps all the way up the steep mountainsides. At one place we hiked up a portion of the famous Inca Trail, where a precarious and rocky two-foot wide path dropped off to the valley far below.

"This trail is *so* dangerous," I said to Fred, as we flattened ourselves against the hillside when someone passed from the other direction. "They'd never allow tourists to climb something so unsafe in the States. I wonder if anybody has ever fallen?"

"Well, imagine the Incas carrying all these rocks up here for these terraces," said Fred. "Those people had to be all muscle."

Examining the ruins of an Inca temple, we could see the precise architectural skills used in the construction of their buildings. Stones were cut with such accuracy that we couldn't pass even a single piece of paper between them, and there was absolutely no mortar used. The ancients' knowledge of engineering and their use of the stars—along with time and distance in the precise placement of their temples—simply staggered our imaginations.

We stopped at a marketplace in an indigenous village where people lived much as they had more than 100 years before. Often we saw the adults chewing the leaves of the cocoa plant, and selling it openly in large quantities.

"They chew it for the effect," said our guide. "It's illegal, but the government makes no effort to stop it, for they know that it dulls the feeling of hunger."

Some of the locals, dressed in their traditional costumes, wanted to be paid when their pictures were taken. Our guide said that the real Indians would not do this, for they had great pride. While having lunch at a restaurant, two children in their native dress danced to Peruvian music with its unique and haunting sound of wood pipes, and then passed amongst the tourists for donations.

"At least these children are earning their money," I said. "That sure beats begging."

Often, in discussing the history of his people, our college-educated guide, who was an Inca descendent, revealed his bitterness toward the conquering Spanish.

"They did not *conquer* our civilization," he said. "They *decimated* it!"

Back in Cuzco, we were able to recognize the distinct construction of the old colonial buildings. The foundations built by Incas were neat and precise, with no mortar, while the upper structures of the Spanish were rough and crude by comparison. It made us wonder: Which was the more advanced civilization?

Our tour of Machu Picchu took two days and began with a train trip. Initially, the rickety old train made eight to ten switchbacks, crisscrossing the mountainside as it worked its way up and out of the valley of Cuzco. It then wobbled for four hours along the Urubamba River, the longest tributary of the Amazon, with rugged mountains rising abruptly just beyond the river and train tracks. We then boarded a minibus for a 20-minute ride, with many more switchbacks, up to the top of a mountain. We followed the guide down a path, turned a corner, and gasped when we saw the panorama unfold before us. There was the Lost City of the Incas! Steep terraced mountainsides fell away to the valley far below. Two forbidding mountain peaks soared over us, and the well-preserved ruins of the city fanned out before us.

"No wonder Frommer says this is the number one tourist destination!" I cried.

There were eight in our tour group, and for several hours we learned about the restoration of the city, along with the history, architecture, and religion of the Incas. Temples were prominent, and the worship of their gods was a central part of daily life. Agriculture was highly developed, even to carrying up different types of soils from the river and valley below to the terraces. We finally just sat and absorbed the wonder of this incredible place.

Simply amazing!

When it was time to return, we boarded the minibus for our descent into the valley.

"I think I saw that kid before," I said to Fred, as we passed a smiling and waving 10-year-old boy in a bright yellow shirt.

"Hellooooo!" he yelled as the bus went by.

At the next switchback, I saw him again. Several other passengers were commenting on him as well.

"Here he is *again!*" Fred laughed on the next switchback. At each pass the boy would yell his hello and wave at the bus. Soon the whole busload was watching for the yellow shirt to appear on the roadside. The boy was apparently running straight down through the forest and waiting for the bus to come along the road. There had to have been ten or more switchbacks on the steep mountain road. At the bottom, the driver opened the bus door, and the boy, dripping with sweat and gasping for breath, climbed aboard.

"Anybody who works that hard to entertain certainly deserves a reward," said Fred, as he reached for his wallet. This kid was a true entrepreneur.

We spent the night at a hostel in Aqua Calientes, a small town with hot springs at the base of Machu Picchu, and returned to Cuzco the following day on the train. We were tired when we finally reached the city, and I was disappointed that it was so late at night; we were to fly back to Quito early the next morning. I had really wanted to buy some unique candlestick holders we had seen in a shop in the plaza. On our way back to the hotel, we walked by the shop and were delighted to find it still open. *Let's go shopping!*

Back in Quito, we made a side trip to the "Mita del Mundo"—the middle of the earth. We did the typical "tourist" ritual and stood with one foot on either side of the Equator, taking pictures of the monument and ourselves.

"I always thought the Equator would be *hot*," I laughed.

"Not at 10,000 feet elevation," Fred added. The wind was blowing fiercely, and we shivered and ran for the museum.

One night we walked about a half-mile in the rain to call Dawn. It had been a tough few weeks for her, and I nearly lost it when I heard her tearful voice say, "I need you." Oh my! What were we doing so far away? We didn't want to solve problems for her; she was capable of doing that herself. But it was difficult to be supportive via the telephone. We firmed up our plans to see her in Cartagena. Walking back to the hostel, we were worried, and my stomach was again bothering me. I was afraid I had picked up an amoebic infection. To make matters worse, we kept slipping on the slick, wet cobblestones, nearly falling down. Worn sandals aren't great in the rain, so we tried to hold each other up while we hobbled and slid along the dark streets, slowly becoming soaked and cold. We were beginning to feel saturated with this "tourist" role, and ready to head for home.

"Let's fly to the border instead of taking the bus," Fred suggested.

I was ready in a heartbeat. Our return trip to Cartagena was quick and easy compared to our initial journey—although we cherished the sights and experiences we had shared in all the small towns, traveling by local buses. Apparently, this wasn't something many Americans did.

While waiting in the airport for our flight, we heard security warnings broadcast which caused a few anxious moments. But, other than delayed flights, we got home without incident.

"I'm *so* ready to sleep in our own bed," I said on that last leg of our trip. "I'm even ready to cook our own food instead of eating out. I can't believe I actually *said* that."

"Yeah—a month is long enough to live out of a suitcase," Fred said.

Getting out of the taxi at Club de Pesca, it felt good to be greeted warmly with lots of smiles and "welcome homes." Then we saw *Grace*. She sparkled and shone in the sunlight—as clean as a whistle—even cleaner than when we had left her!

"Saul washed her every single day," said our friends in the marina. "He didn't want you to come home to a dirty boat."

What a *sweetie!* He would take no money for his efforts, but was pleased with the T-shirt we had brought for him from Machu Picchu. We talked on the phone again with Dawn, and she had her ticket to Cartagena. All right. It was wonderful to be home.

"Ahoy. Amazing Grace. Anybody home?" came the voice from outside the boat. I hurried up to the cockpit from the cabin.

"Are you Kay Koudele?" asked a woman, standing on the dock with a man and another couple. "I'm your cousin, Mary Evelyn."

What a surprise! I had not seen any of my cousins who lived in eastern Canada since I was 13. My mom had told her sister-in-law that we were sailing and in Cartagena. Mary Evelyn and her husband had joined a number of Canadians who escaped the winter snow by coming to Columbia, and my cousin decided to track us down. It had taken a good deal of effort on their part, and we welcomed them aboard and tried to catch up on 40-plus years.

When Election Day arrived, we found that it was taken very seriously by the Columbians. All businesses were closed for the day, and even church services were delayed until six in the evening. Police guards stood around the parks where polling places had been set up. Perhaps the people of this country valued the opportunity and responsibility of casting their vote more than did folks in the States. We could learn from that.

"Hurry up! We don't want to be late," I said, as I waited for Fred on the dock.

"You think a Columbian plane would be *on time*?" Fred laughed.

After waiting two hours at the airport, we finally saw Dawn. I squealed and hollered and jumped up and down, ignoring the looks of those around me. We all talked and hugged at once, excitedly making our way back to the boat. When we arrived outside the club, guards with weapons were all around and prevented us from entering. After many patient explanations, they finally let us in.

"Wow—is it always like that?" Dawn asked.

"Nah, just when there's some important officials at the restaurant," Fred assured her.

We helped her unpack, talking until our throats were dry, and examined all the "goodies" she had brought from the "Things to Bring" list we had sent her. We soon noticed a couple of the armed guards standing on the dock by the stern of our boat. One blew a kiss to Dawn and said, *"Muy linda"* (very beautiful). It appeared we would have extra good security that night!

We delighted in showing Dawn many of the sights of Cartagena the following day. While at Bocagrande, it suddenly started to rain—something it had not done for four months. It was not just an introductory sprinkling, either. It was a *deluge*! We immediately thought of all the open hatches on our boat, and hailed a taxi to try to get back to the marina quickly. No such luck. Within minutes the streets were like lakes, and traffic snarled its way to a crawl. We jumped out in the club parking lot and tried to run across what was now a lake with six inches of water. In just a few seconds we were *drenched*! What would the boat be like?

"Thank goodness," I said, when I saw little water damage. A carpenter had been aboard making a stand for our new TV, and, with Saul's help, he had been able to close some of the hatches in time.

"Saul really saved us," Fred gasped. Because we had steel security bars on two of our main hatches, they could not be closed to the downpour. Quick thinking Saul had run for his rubber mats to place over the top of the bars. Again, we were touched and grateful for this remarkable young man. When we went to thank him, he simply smiled and said, "Boaters help other boaters."

Our friend, Fabio, a local physician, and the roommate of Sara's husband, had invited us to come with three of his friends to the *Musica del Caribe* festival the following night. Fabio spoke no English but talked very slowly and distinctly, which helped us understand him. The group picked us up and we all went to the bullring where the event was held. After having our bags inspected and bodies frisked, we made our way inside the dirt floor arena to a place about 15 feet from the huge stage. Several thousand people stood with us, all in a party mood. Bands from many of the Caribbean countries took turns playing lively Latin music, and everyone danced in place, clapping and singing. Not a little rum was consumed as well. As the night went on, it became wilder and wilder. When Fred and I danced together, there were lots of smiles and "thumbs up." But Dawn was the one who really attracted attention.

"You simply can't stand still with this music," I yelled to Dawn, as we bounced around like all the others.

"And everybody is so *friendly*," she yelled back. "They all seem happy to see us here. I just wish I knew what they were saying."

"That guy just said, 'Thank you for sharing with us.' Since we're the only gringos around, we're rather noticeable." And a beautiful young *gringa* at that! Fabio and his friends took great care of us, both protective and anxious that we all have a good time.

The three of us finally sat in the stands for a break, and after four-plus hours of music and dancing, we decided to head home by ourselves. Where did these people get such stamina? We learned later that the festival went on until five in the morning—these folks really knew how to party!

Besides the fun events, we also had lots of time to sit and talk with Dawn. We caught up with what was happening in her life, the struggles she was facing, and helped her look at options for the future. She had not found a job that was satisfying and wanted something different. It was strange how sitting in a cockpit under a star-filled sky was conducive to those kinds of discussions. We hoped that she would go home with more hope than she had when she arrived.

One day, at a nearby fishing village, we sat around a pool and *palapa* restaurant and talked too long. Dawn ended up with a painful sunburn on her legs. She also had quite a few bug bites, some swelling from the heat, and, to top it off, a recurring sore throat. Fabio wrote a request to the airlines that allowed her to change her ticket and stay another five days. Yippee!

I tried hard not to cry at the airport when we said goodbye, knowing that would make it harder for her. When the plane lifted off, we made our way back to Norm's.

"Why are we doing this?" I said once again. "It keeps us so far from the people we love."

"It won't be forever," Fred said reassuringly, and for the first time we began to think of when and where our dream adventure might end. Many of the other cruisers were supportive when we returned to the club. They, too, knew the pain of departing family. *Grace* seemed suddenly big and empty that night.

One day we were going down to Norm's when we witnessed a major commotion. Several men were running around the outside of the building and climbing a ladder to the *palapa* roof.

"What's happening?" we both asked.

"There are boa constrictors in the roof," one man said. "They built a nest and had babies in the drain pipe, and it's stopped up all the plumbing." None of us knew that Norm had placed the snakes up in the thatch some years before, as a way to eliminate the problem of rats around the restaurant and marina. And to think we'd been sitting beneath these creatures for four months. Yuk!

"Look," said Fred. "I can see one of the big ones way up there by that rafter." I wasn't about to look at them—or think about them!

Semana Santa, or Holy Week, in many Latin countries is as much a national holiday as it is a religious one. Many people take vacation for the entire week, tourist spots are overflowing, and, in coastal areas, beach parties are everywhere. A local man organized such a party for the cruisers for the Saturday before Easter. We wanted to experience that local tradition as well as have an Easter observance that was meaningful to us. So, on the morning radio net, I gave an open invitation to an English-speaking Easter sunrise worship service aboard our boat. Only one person responded.

"Shall we go ahead with it?" I asked, aware of my disappointment.

"Sure," said Fred. "We'll enjoy it even if it's just the two of us."

Fifty cruisers joined the beach party and barbeque on Saturday. A few of us brought our guitars and in the evening we sat in the sand around a huge bonfire and sang the old familiar songs of home. The beach was littered with hundreds of similar fires. It appeared that the whole city was somewhere along the beach. A chartered bus brought us all back to Norm's late that night, tired and covered with salt and sand.

"Happy Easter," Fred said early the following morning. We were delighted that six others, from four different boats, joined us in the cockpit for a simple but meaningful celebration of that special day. We shared memories of Easters past, sang some familiar songs, and heard the Easter story once again. It felt good to be with those who shared our faith, and again we experienced the feeling of "family." Afterwards, we served a brunch, enhanced by good food the others had brought to share. We all agreed that it was a memorable day.

The winter winds continued to howl at night, but the locals said the weather was trying to "turn." We hoped that we would soon be able to leave Cartagena and continue sailing north into the Caribbean. Our plan was to go first to Isla Providencia, from there to the Bay Islands of Honduras, and then travel up the Rio Dulce in Guatemala.

There were some long, very busy days ahead as we prepared the boat once again for more blue-water adventure. We found a new way to rig our storm sail and took down awnings to attach it. We pulled out the jib to wash as much of it as we could. We washed curtains and reorganized the bow cabin for storage. We waterproofed all of our canvas awnings after washing them. We repaired windsocks and flags, damaged from the winter winds, *and* we spent countless hours hunting the shops of the city looking for needed parts, or products like boat wax or grosgrain ribbon. Working or walking in the direct sun was *scorching,* and our backs paid a price for all the stooping involved in those projects on the boat. On occasion, I lost patience with it all, and Fred was wise enough to make himself scarce at such times.

As our excitement about moving on grew, it was tempered by the realization that we needed to say goodbye to people whose friendship we had come to value greatly. Staying five months in one place had allowed us some extraordinary experiences and, as always, the relationships and interactions with the people of Columbia and South America were a priceless part of our adventure. Our friendships had included those from diverse economic levels, but we all shared the same concerns: our children and families, the increased costs of living, the desire for the end of violence, and the joy of seeing a home team win a sporting event. Countless times we had been amazed by the overwhelming hospitality and kindness evident in this country's culture. While we were still very proud of our own country and what it represented, we also were aware that there was much we, as a nation, could learn from the people of other countries, such as Columbia.

And then there was our friendship with Saul! Saying goodbye to him would be heart-wrenching. We had asked him to sail with us to Isla Providencia, where we would provide him a return trip to Cartagena by airplane. He was touched by the offer, but questioned if he could obtain the necessary governmental papers, or the time off work. His boss was out of the country, so he never was able to arrange permission to come with us. We were disappointed, knowing that it was not likely we would ever see him again.

We tried to have all of our Columbian friends come to the boat one last time. It was a lot of entertaining, but they had all been so good to us. We also tried to contact family before leaving.

One night we walked to the Telecom office to call Dawn. She was excited: She had been accepted by Delta airlines to train as a flight attendant. It wasn't a long-term career goal, but it was something that should bring her a big change of pace. She would be based in New York after her training.

"Dawn sounded pleased," I said, "but I sure don't like to think of her all the way across the country."

"Got to let those birds fly away from the nest," he grinned. "Maybe it won't be for too long—and besides, think of those free "parent passes" we'll have!"

We were on the final countdown. We had made our goodbyes, gathered all the weather information we could find, and bought the final provisions. Every time I carried supplies home from the grocery store, I found that my arms were a little longer! Two other boats were also going to Isla Providencia, a small island off the Caribbean coast of Nicaragua but owned by Columbia. It would be a four-day sail and we all wanted to travel together. However, when the time came, despite a poor weather forecast, they were anxious to leave and decided to go for it. While patience is not my greatest virtue, it is for Fred, and we reluctantly decided to wait for a better weather window, even though it meant sailing by ourselves.

"Man—are those boats ever getting hammered," I said to Fred after listening to the ham radio contact with our friends a day after they left the anchorage. "I'm so glad we waited."

"Well, the first 24 hours out of Cartagena will probably be tough whenever we go," Fred said, "but hopefully better than what they are experiencing."

It was hard to sit and wait as the anxiety grew. It felt like when I was young and stood atop a high diving board, trying to make myself jump or dive into the pool so far below me. As I looked down at the water, the longer I waited to make the move, the more anxious I became, and the distance to the water seemed to increase with each passing second.

"You know, we've been on this adventure for almost two years.

You'd think we'd feel *less* anxious before a passage after doing it so many times," I said to Fred one evening after listening to the ham weather report. "But it seems like it's actually harder for me now than when we first started."

"I know what you mean," Fred replied. "Maybe it's the old 'Ignorance is Bliss' thing. When we first started, we knew that some nasty things *could* happen, but now we know they really *did* happen—either to us or to our friends.

"I guess you're right—big storms, emergency hospitalization, boats lost on the rocks, boats hit by freighters—even friends killed and lost at sea. That *is* a lot! I guess it's normal to be anxious. Maybe it's even good. It makes us more careful about what we're doing."

"But don't forget—now we have a lot more trust in *Grace* and what she can do, as well as our own abilities."

"That's true. I guess we're in pretty good shape, and *Grace* is truly capable and ready to go," I said, trying to reassure myself.

We walked to a nearby Catholic church just to sit for a while. As we entered, we discovered we were the only ones in the large, beautiful gothic sanctuary. The air felt cooler inside, and sunlight reflected the brilliant colors of the ornately stained glass windows throughout the empty chamber. Candles flickered in small alcoves. Quiet washed over us like a cleansing and refreshing shower. After several minutes, soft music began on the organ, and I felt the return of a welcome calmness—a sense of peace and comfort. With it came a feeling of preparedness and a connection to that amazing Grace of God that had sustained us thus far, and would surely see us home. Fred must have felt the same, for he looked over at me, smiled and squeezed my hand. *Now* we were ready to leave this country that had found a special place in our hearts. And who knew what awesome adventures were yet to come for our beautiful *Amazing Grace* and her grateful crew?

LaVergne, TN USA
08 January 2010
169321LV00003B/7/P

9 781936 107339